NEWSBREAK

A COLLECTION OF MAJOR NEWS EVENTS
IN THE HISTORY OF MAN AS THEY MIGHT
HAVE BEEN REPORTED BY DISTINGUISHED
MEMBERS OF TODAY'S OVERSEAS PRESS CLUB
OF AMERICA

STACKPOLE BOOKS
Harrisburg, Pennsylvania

NEWSBREAK

Will Yolen, N·F·
Editor-in-Chief

Will Oursler,
Consulting Editor

Wendell Sether,
Associate Editor

Library of Congress Cataloging in Publication Data

Yolen, Will H   1908–
  Newsbreak.

  "An Overseas Press Club book."
  SUMMARY: Eighteen important events in history, such as the invention of
the wheel and Resurrection of Christ, are reported by well-known reporters and
newsmen as if they were there.
  1. World history—Juvenile literature. [1. World history] I. Oursler, William
Charles, 1913–   joint author. II. Title.
D24.5.Y64   909   74–13737
ISBN 0–8117–1122–6

Contents

Foreword

By JACK RAYMOND
(*President, Overseas Press Club of America*)

Some years ago, during a staff meeting of the Washington bureau of the *New York Times,* the subject came up of a remark by Arthur Schlesinger, Jr., then a White House aide in the Kennedy administration. Schlesinger said he had not realized, until he got inside the White House, how inaccurate so many newspaper stories were.

Whereupon "Scotty" Reston observed to us at the staff meeting, "In that case I want my money back for all the Schlesinger books I bought."

This is not to argue the point of how dependent historians are on the press, only to call attention to the relationship between history and journalism, positively or negatively.

I happen to believe that even if, as Schlesinger suggested, many individual stories prove inaccurate, Walter Lippman's comment many years ago is more perceptive; that is, the value of journalism is not that each story is a complete and accurate whole, but that the flow of news coverage forces open to public view some semblance of reality not otherwise likely to appear.

At the same time newsmen, who like to say that the journalism of today becomes the history of tomorrow, might also pose this question: Would much of what has passed for "ancient history" have been written at all if the events described first had stood a test comparable to modern journalism, with all its inaccuracies?

Founded in 1939, the Overseas Press Club of America is not only the largest organization of foreign correspondents and former correspondents in the world; in recent years it has been joined by journalists of every background, as well as book and magazine writers, TV and radio broadcast writers and public relations practitioners, many of whom, not surprisingly, are former journalists.

The OPC provides a forum where professionals in mass communications meet to exchange experience and ideas, a forum where decision-makers and/or newsmakers can address the public. Its "professional evenings" and other programs are significant contributions not only to our profession but to the public good.

The OPC's annual Overseas Press Club Awards encourage enterprise, excellence and courage in journalism through public recognition for meritorious work. Its Annual Awards Dinner is a major event.

The Overseas Press Club Bulletin, distributed to members and associates, government leaders and foreign journalists throughout the world, chronicles the day-to-day activities of professionals in public communications. It represents, in tone and content, a force for press freedom throughout the world.

This, the tenth book sponsored by the OPC, is a further example of the professional skill of its members. And we are all proud of it.

Preface

By WILL H. YOLEN
(Editor-in-Chief)

There is a hardy myth among news people that in the heart and mind of every one of them is a great book. This book will be written, goes the myth, when the excitement and grind of daily news work is finished.

This myth is not a myth.

Every year more than fifty members of the Overseas Press Club are published authors—fiction, non-fiction, adult, or children's books.

In fact, it is probably the largest aggregation of published authors in history. These members have brought book journalism to its greatest heights. They have set high standards for OPC books.

Newsbreak is the tenth book published with OPC as the listed author. The club, 2,000 present or former foreign correspondents, is the sole recipient of the royalties. More than 200 members have contributed chapters and other editorial material. The editor of this book has been Chairman of the Publishing Committee for seven of these books and editor of two. The publishing committee listed below is constantly on the alert for publishing opportunities.

E. P. Dutton published the first of the OPC books in 1947 with *Deadline Delayed*. The Introduction was written by the famous war correspondent, W. W. Chaplin, a former president of the club. The publishing committee at that time was headed by Bernard Estes.

This book was followed the next year by *As We See Russia,* with a Preface by the famous correspondent, Bob Considine, also a president of the club. Dutton was publisher again. The publishing committee was headed by Joe E. Phillips. No record seems to be available on a book entitled, *Men Who Make Your World,* which was next in line.

In 1964 OPC members brought in a smashing book, *I Can Tell It Now,* published by Dutton. Richard Bruner, former war correspondent, now a Better Business Bureau executive and David Brown, partner of Richard Zanuck and husband of Helen Gurley Brown, edited this book.

A newcomer to the publishing field, Dwight D. Eisenhower, wrote the Preface. This book was translated into Japanese and more revenue for the club.

In 1967 this was followed by another book in the same genre, *How I Got That Story,* by the same publisher and the same editors, Bruner and Brown. This book also gave some exciting backgrounds into how world famous newsmen got their most important stories despite obstacles by governments, army and other natural and unnatural forces.

The following year Stackpole published one of our most ambitious ventures *Heroes For Our Times,* with Kenneth Seaman Giniger and myself as editors. The distinguished photographer Cornell Capa edited the gallery of "Heroes" which included photos by his late brother, Robert Capa, Phillip Halsman, Margaret Bourke-White, Yousuf Karsh, and other greats.

More books are planned for the future, each better than the last. All inspired by the affection and respect members have for each other and the club.

This book is therefore dedicated by the members to each other.

Although the material herein is myth, legend, biblical, historic and pretty well worked over and over during the years by scholars and historians, new insights and fresh information pop out of these pages.

Ralph Schultz in "The Wheel" suggests, tongue in cheek, that the wheel was nothing more than a square with its corners knocked off. In a chapter on money, Will Sparks, who should know from Pentagon days, confirms that the first money or currency was a sea shell for financing some primitive war effort.

In "The Tower of Babel," the late John McAllister reveals that despite its bad reputation, the Tower was a great engineering feat because it was built high and dry on shifty sand, no stones being available in that part of the country. Morris Ernst, on Moses and early law and order, documents that the life span of men in those days was but a paltry 30 years.

Roland Gammon's thesis on the Buddha reveals that the spiritual leader, a rich prince, gave up his wealth, child, wife and "girl minstrels" to attain Nirvanah. Will Oursler documents the fact that Jesus was buried as a Jew and resurrected as the Messiah for all people.

In "The Children's Crusade," Kurt Lassen shows that 50,000 or more children disappeared into slavery and death by starvation. They were ridiculed and jeered in cities on the road to Jerusalem; no one wanted to feed them. The Church and king could do little to dissuade the children who in many cases were used in opening trade rather than opening the Holy Land to Christians.

Concerning the invention of printing, Dr. Ben Lieberman reveals that the first printing press was believed to be a work of black art and was fought not only by the Church which stood to lose its hold on the written word, but by the king as well. The late Louis Cassels of UP indicates that even before Columbus, the European universities were excited by the notion that the world was round. Furthermore, though Columbus was looking for India when he reached the New World, he thought he could find Japan first.

In the exciting Council of Trent story, Barrett McGurn reveals that "Lucretia Borgia ran the Vatican in July, 1501, when her father, Pope Alexander VI, was out of the country." The Council had set out to cleanse itself and in the process alienated John Calvin, Martin Luther and the Church of England. The Popes' power in those days was so great Pope Alexander VI divided South America between Spain and Portugal, with little resistance from anyone, least of all the South Americans of that time.

Larry Blochman, in his story on blood, points out that Dr. William Harvey was no insignificant blood researcher in an attic laboratory. In fact he was the king's physician and was held in high esteem in the medical science world, unlike an earlier researcher, Servetus, who was considered a heretic and burned at the stake 80 years earlier by John Calvin's orders in 1553. John Wilhelm's story about Peter Zenger and freedom of the press demonstrates that some fine newspaper people were developed even in early colonial days. Zenger had great difficulty with the English language, but had no trouble in proving that truth was the greatest defense against libel even though the judge and prosecutor were determined to send him to jail. The jury saved him.

The Wright brothers' credentials for inventiveness were impeccable, according to Ansel Talbert's story. Talbert sets forth that the brothers' father—a bishop—invented one of the early typewriters, and brother Loren invented a hay press. Furthermore, the brothers had designed and built a printing press on which the Negro poet Paul Laurence Dunbar founded a magazine staffed entirely by Negroes. They also invented a kerosene engine that could deliver power at 15 cents a gallon. Writing about the Russian Revolution, Leon Dennen shows how easy lies the head that wears a crown—the Romanovs stayed on their throne for 300 years of misrule and were still loved by the people whom they abused. Incidentally, the Russian police were called "Pharaohs," but the Czar's troops were Cossacks who hated everyone—Rasputin, Poles, peasants and Jews—in the reverse order. Dennen says that when the revolutionist announced "liberation" the peasants assumed it was liberation from Rasputin.

Adolf Hitler didn't want to be Austrian, says Sigrid Schultz. But he would face any danger as a German, which he became in the latter part of World War I, winning his first Iron Cross under the sponsorship of his Jewish captain. Hitler is credited with inventing "Military-Industrial Complex" which had a role in the overthrow of the Kaiser in 1918. In "Man Walks On Moon," John Noble Wilford reports some new astronaut jargon as follows: "upset":—"went critical"; "drunk":—"something wrong with his inertial guidance system"; "if right":—"nominal"; "if wrong":—"anomaly."

Bill Morris says in his piece on language that Hebrew was seriously considered by the initial American Congress to become the first language of the new country, so much did the colonists hate the British and their language.

In closing these notes, it should be pointed out that though it is a combined club venture, special credit should be given Associate Editor Wendell Sether, a former president of Sigma Delta Chi, and Will Oursler who, in addition to writing a chapter, contributed the name of the book—*Newsbreak*. And special credit, of course, to Clyde Peters, Executive Vice President, The Stackpole Company and fellow club member.

Publishing Committee
-   Will H. Yolen, Chairman
-   Arnold Abramson, President & Publisher, Universal Publishing Co.
-   Simon Michael Bessie, Editor, Atheneum Publishers
    Robert Cousins, Executive Editor, Reader's Digest Books
    William Doerflinger, Editor, E. P. Dutton & Company, Inc.
    Paul Eriksson, Editor & Publisher, Paul S. Eriksson, Inc.
-   Kenneth Seaman Giniger, President, Consolidated Book Publishers
-   Mathew Huttner, President and Publisher, Pyramid Books
    Kenneth McCormick, Editor-in-Chief Emeritus, Doubleday & Co.
    Jerry Mason, President, Ridge Press Inc.
-   Mrs. Eleanor Rawson, Editor, David McKay & Co.
-   Roger W. Straus, Jr., President, Farrar, Straus & Giroux, Inc.
    Victor Weybright, President, Weybright & Talley
    Clyde Peters, Executive Vice President, Stackpole Books

Introduction

By LOWELL THOMAS

(*Past President of the Overseas Press Club**)

The *New York Times* once referred to trench-coated war correspondents as "The Hounds of Gutenberg." Since the founding of our world famed Overseas Press Club we have launched ten books, all involving news gathering and news handling behind and in front of the news. Oh, there were a few lapses from the straight and narrow. One such was Larry Blochman's *Bar Guide* in which the former gourmet editor of the *Paris Herald Tribune* described various lethal potions invented by famous newsmen. Then there was an OPC cookbook, edited by Sigrid Schultz, one time *Chicago Tribune* chronicler of the activities of Adolf Hitler.

As co-editor of the early OPC book, *Cavalcade of Europe,* I somehow now feel some of the old pleasure of working alongside my colleagues, if not in competition with them. This new one of course is mainly the work of a newer generation, correspondents who move at a swifter pace than we did.

Members contributing to this book are turning over all royalties to the OPC in another demonstration of true loyalty. Some original pieces would bring a considerable return to their authors.

A panel of distinguished editors and publishers under the chairmanship of editor Will Yolen helped with this task, among them the late Bennett Cerf, Max Schuster, John Lowell Pratt, Dick Taplinger and Donald Schiffer. Also on this committee were editors Mike Bessie of Atheneum, Victor Weybright, President of Weybright and Talley; William Doerflinger, editor of E. P. Dutton; Eleanor S. Rawson, editor, David McKay; Kenneth Giniger, editor and President of Consolidated Books; Roger W. Straus Jr., President of Farrar, Straus and Giroux, Inc.;

Robert Cousins, editor of Reader's Digest Books; Ted Rinehart, of Holt, Winston Rinehart Co.; Jerry Mason of Rutledge Books; David Dreiman, of Platt and Munk; and, Paul Eriksson, editor of his own company.

* Note: Walter Duranty, legendary *New York Times* Moscow correspondent, once said Lowell Thomas' "discovery" of Lawrence of Arabia and exclusive account of the World War I Near East campaign was the greatest "scoop" of all time. (*Editor*)

World Created

Editor's Note: (W.Y.) The following account is prepared as it would have been handled by a wire service for a.m. or morning newspaper use. For the information of non-newsman readers of *Newsbreak,* when very important news first breaks, the wire service procedure is to interrupt whatever story it is transmitting with a FLASH, giving the news in a word or two. This is followed as soon after as possible with a BULLETIN, containing the barest details. Then, in due course comes a FIRST NIGHT LEAD for morning papers (or FIRST DAY LEAD for evening papers) with the basic story. This is often followed with ADD NIGHT LEAD, then SECOND ADD NIGHT LEAD, etc., with more details as they become available. Sometimes, as a story becomes more clarified, a SECOND NIGHT LEAD is transmitted, telling the news anew from the fresh point of view. In rare instances, the wire editor may send out his own NOTE TO EDITORS alerting the telegraph editors in the various receiving newsrooms to some peculiarity of the story about to be transmitted, or giving important operational information. An "FYI"—meaning "for your information"—is used for lesser items. The modern-language *New English Bible, Old Testament,* 1970 (Dodd et al), has been used as the text for quotations, as befits a modern rendering of the first great newsbreak of all time.

A.M. FILE--DAY 1

FLASH--LIGHT INVENTED

BULLETIN

IN THE VOID, Day 1–God today invented "light"–defined in first reports the opposite of the previous total darkness everywhere. There was no immediate explanation of the purpose or value of this new phenomenon, which defied description.

- 30 -

FIRST NIGHT LEAD--LIGHT

IN THE VOID, Day 1–God today invented "light," a phenomenon which is defying description by eyewitnesses but is declared to be the opposite of the previous total darkness everywhere.

The purpose or value of "light" is likewise a mystery. All that is known is that God created this new phenomenon deliberately by saying, "Let there be light," and that, in the words of the official chronicler of the event, "God saw that the light was good, and he separated light from darkness." The reference to "good" is explained by high authorities as God's assessment of his handiwork, by personal inspection, as meeting his standard of excellence.

God has named the light "day" and has begun calling the darkness "night." Apparently, periods of darkness and light are to take turns in a continuing cycle, with one complete cycle from nightfall to nightfall also being called a "day."

At this point in time, evening--the advent of darkness--has come again, after the "day" of light. By the new form of reckoning, then, there has just been completed the first day that ever was.

- 30 -

A.M. FILE--DAY 2

FLASH--HEAVEN CREATED

BULLETIN

IN THE VOID, Day 2--God today created "heaven" using it to separate the deep, trackless and all-engulfing waters into two. Heaven, described by eyewitnesses as a kind of vault, holds some of the waters above it, the rest remaining below. The usefulness or purpose of the vault and the separation of the waters were not immediately apparent.

- 30 -

FIRST NIGHT LEAD--HEAVEN

IN THE VOID, Day 2--The whole infinity of waters was today separated into two parts by God as he created what he called "heaven" by erecting a vault which is now holding some of the waters above it. The remainder of the waters are below the vault.

As with God's invention of light yesterday, no immediate explanation or purpose for the vault or the separation of waters was forthcoming. The vault itself was called "heaven" by God.

This achievement is expected to go down in history as the greatest engineering feat of all time. To do it, God said "Let there be a vault between the waters, to separate water from water." The reporter on the scene added in awe as the transformation occurred, "and so it was."

In the course of time required to fashion the vault and separate the waters, there was a repetition of the complete cycle of darkness and light which was experienced during the first day. Thus, there has now been a second day.

- 30 -

ADD FIRST NIGHT LEAD--HEAVEN

Highest authorities late tonight hinted that the creations of the first two days are but the early steps in the creation by God of an entire "universe." It was indicated that the vault in particular is the necessary structure around which God will in successive days expand the development of a wondrous creation that cannot even be put into tangible words beforehand.

These sources pointed out that the entire enterprise to date has consisted of precisely the formation of tangibles out of a complete nothingness except for the prior existence of God himself.

- 30 -

NOTE TO EDITORS: While further checking out of the just-sent add is impossible now, we believe the heaven story cleared earlier is much larger than indicated by the first night lead. We are therefore carrying an "interpretive" new night lead for interested editors.

- 30 -

NEW NIGHT LEAD--HEAVEN

IN THE VOID, Day 2--God today took the first tangible step toward creation of a "universe," separating the deep waters into two by means of a "vault" which may turn out to be the structural framework for this universe.

Construction of the vault, considered an engineering marvel for all time, provided a kind of platform holding some of the waters contained above the vault while the rest remains below it. The development took the whole cycle of darkness and light which constituted the second day.

This action followed the invention yesterday of "light" as the opposite of the previous all-pervading total darkness. However, it is not yet clear what the relationship between "light" and the vault is or may become.

Highest authorities hinted that the whole of God's work, apparently planned to stretch out over several days, will constitute a wondrous creation that cannot even be put into tangible words beforehand.

These sources, declining to reveal any of the specifics of the grand design which is now being implemented, pointed out that the entire enterprise consists precisely in forming tangibles out of a complete nothingness except for the prior existence of God himself.

They pointed out, also, that God was not only creating tangibles but also "natural laws" and scientific concepts. "Time," for instance, was the basic invention behind the night-day cycle. "Space" and "laws of gravity" are involved in the vault and the separation of the waters by an intervening "heaven." And the newly-created tangibles themselves represent the formation of "matter," as opposed to "energy," which seems to have been the original creative stuff.

- 30 -

A.M. FILE--DAY 3

FLASH--EARTH FORMED

BULLETIN

IN THE VOID, Day 3--The earth was formed today when God brought the waters under heaven together into a single place so that dry land could appear. Later, he created plant growth on the land. The actions followed yesterday's creation of a vault called heaven, which separated the waters into two entities, above and below the vault.

- 30 -

FIRST NIGHT LEAD--EARTH

IN THE VOID, Day 3--God formed the earth today in his unfolding creation of the universe.

The feat was accomplished when God said, "Let the waters under heaven be gathered into one place, so that dry land may appear." It was reported that God called the dry land "earth" and the gathering of the waters "seas," and that God saw that it was "good," that is, acceptable by his standards, after personal inspection.

Once the dry land had formed, God continued his creation by saying "Let the earth produce fresh growth, let there be on the earth plants bearing seed, fruit-trees bearing fruit each with seed according to its kind.

This then occurred and again, it was reported, God saw that it was good.

The separation of waters into those beneath heaven and those above it had been accomplished yesterday when God built a vault called heaven to hold some of the waters above and some below heaven. The vault thus emerged today as the necessary precondition for bringing together the waters under heaven to allow the dry land to form.

This bore out hints made yesterday by highest authorities that God had a master plan for the creation of an entire universe, and experts today pointed to the formation of the earth as the centerpiece of this creation, at least to date.

There were further hints today that even greater developments were included in God's plans for the universe. However, as before, no specifics were forthcoming.

The process of creating the earth and its verdure occupied the full cycle of darkness and light of the third day.

- 30 -

FYI TO EDITORS

With the formation of dry land, we have established an office on earth, and henceforth our reports covering the Creation will emanate from there.

- 30 -

A.M. FILE–DAY 4

FLASH–SUN, MOON CREATED

BULLETIN

DRY LAND, Day 4–Lights called the sun, moon and stars were put into heaven today by God. Announced purpose of the lights is to mark the days, seasons and years, and specifically to provide light for the earth by day and by night.

- 30 -

FIRST NIGHT LEAD–SUN MOON

DRY LAND, Day 4–God's creation of the world continued through the fourth day with placing of a series of lights in the vault called heaven.

The larger of two great lights, the sun, is to shine by day. The smaller of the two, called the moon, is to shine by night. In addition, at night, the heavens are newly-covered with great numbers of small lights, called stars.

God announced that the function of these lights in the vault of heaven is "to separate day from night" and to "serve as signs both for festivals and for seasons and years." This was taken to mean that some sort of calendar will be set up, based on a recurring pattern of changes in the positioning of these lights. As with the daily cycle of darkness and light, there may be a cycle of heavenly body configurations once a "year."

The need for such a calendar was not immediately apparent, and it was not indicated what kinds of configurations will be involved.

God declared the lights should "also shine in the vault of heaven to give light on earth." The sun is to govern the day and the moon is to govern the night. A spokesman explained that they are also to "separate light from darkness."

After his usual inspection of his new creation, God declared the result "good," that is, of satisfactory quality for use. The event was chronicled in heaven as the fourth day.

In the previous three days, God had invented light, created heaven and separated the waters, and made dry land by gathering the lower waters together.

- 30 -

A.M. FILE–DAY 5

FLASH–LIFE CREATED

BULLETIN

DRY LAND, Day 5–God's act of creation has gone into its fifth day, with living creatures suddenly teeming in the waters and birds flying above the earth. A new unexplained quality, called life, apparently provides the water creatures and the birds with the ability to move about at will.

- 30 -

FIRST NIGHT LEAD–LIFE

DRY LAND, Day 5–God invented a new quality called "life" as his process of creating the projected "universe" went into its fifth day. The result was a sudden teeming of living creatures in the water and birds flying above the earth.

Reports indicate that when God said, "Let the waters teem with countless living creatures, and let birds fly above the earth across the vault of heaven," there appeared "the great sea-monsters and all living creatures that move and swarm in the waters, according to their kind, and every kind of bird."

Following the practice which has become a custom with him since he first invented light four days ago, God inspected his creative work and declared it "good." He then blessed the water creatures and the birds and

said, "Be fruitful and increase, fill the waters of the seas; let the birds
increase on land."

In the official records, the night and day of this activity is shown as the
fifth day. Besides the light invented on the first day, God has also created
the vault of heaven on the second day, the seas and the dry land on the
third day, and the lights in the heavens on the fourth day.

There were indications from high sources that God had still other developments planned for at least the sixth day, just beginning. Although
there were no authoritative hints, observers pointed out that the living
creatures thus far created occupied the waters and the heavens but not
yet the dry land itself. Thus there was speculation that the sixth day
might see living creatures inhabiting that land.

- 30 -

A.M. FILE--DAY 6

FLASH--EARTH CREATURES CREATED

BULLETIN

DRY LAND, Day 6--God's sixth day has brought forth living creatures
from the earth, reportedly cattle, reptiles and wild animals. These had
been widely predicted after yesterday's creation of water creatures and
birds flying the heavens.

- 30 -

FIRST NIGHT LEAD--ANIMALS

DRY LAND, Day 6--God's creation of the universe continued into its
sixth day with the predicted bringing forth from the earth of living creatures, including cattle, reptiles and wild animals, all according to their
BREAK IT BREAK IT

FLASH--MAN CREATED

SECOND BULLETIN

DRY LAND, Day 6--God has just created man, in his own image. This
development followed quickly after an earlier phase of God's handiwork

in the same day, the bringing forth from the earth living creatures including cattle, reptiles and wild animals.

- 30 -

SECOND NIGHT LEAD--ANIMALS

DRY LAND, Day 6--Man was created by God in the sixth day of his making of the universe, just after he had completed the bringing forth from the earth living creatures including cattle, reptiles and wild animals.

First reports indicated only that God had said, "Let us make man in our image and likeness to rule the fish in the sea, the birds of heaven, the cattle, all wild animals on earth, and all reptiles that crawl upon the earth," and that he thus created "male" and "female" in this way. No explanation was forthcoming as to the difference between "male" and "female."

Later reports, however, were to the effect that "the Lord God formed a man from the dust of the ground and breathed into his nostrils the breath of life. Thus the man became a living creature."

The early dispatches said God blessed the male and female, and quoted God as saying, "Be fruitful and increase, fill the earth and subdue it, rule over the fish in the sea, the birds of heaven, and every living thing that moves upon the earth."

The report further quoted God as saying to the male and female, "I give you all plants that bear seed everywhere on earth, and every tree bearing fruit which yields seed; they shall be yours for food. All green plants I give for food to the wild animals, to all the birds of heaven, and to all reptiles on earth, every living creature."

ADD SECOND NIGHT LEAD--ANIMALS

Latest dispatches quote high authorities that God has "planted a garden in Eden away to the east, and there he put the man." These dispatches do not refer to the existence of a female at this time.

The earlier dispatches referred to God's custom, as on all the five previous days of creation, to examine what he had done during the day before certifying it as "good," or acceptable for his purposes. On this sixth day, however, he is reported as declaring the work "very good."

The busy sixth day is seen as a culmination of a sustained period which included the invention of light on the first day, the placement of the vault and the separating of the waters on the second day, the creation of lights in the heavens on the third day, the separation of the earth and the seas on the fourth day, and the bringing to life of sea creatures and flying birds on the fifth day.

What God might do on the seventh day was the subject of considerable speculation as the sixth day ended, but there was no agreement on what possible inventions could follow those already brought forth in the program of creating the universe.

- 30 -

A.M. FILE--DAY 7

FLASH--GOD RESTS

BULLETIN

DRY LAND, Day 7--God began his seventh day of creation of the universe today by blessing the day and making it holy, to mark the cessation of his work. The remainder of the day he spent at "rest."

- 30 -

FIRST NIGHT LEAD--GOD RESTS

DRY LAND, Day 7--God has signaled the completion of his work to create the universe, after six days of continuous invention and development which have seen a whole array of new phenomena from light to heaven and dry land and living creatures including man.

The Creator, as God is now being called, reportedly blessed the seventh day and made it holy, because on this day he has ceased from all the work he had set himself to do. It is understood that he means the seventh day henceforth to be a day of "rest" for all living creatures.

What constitutes "rest" was not immediately made clear.

- 30 -

NOTE TO EDITORS: In keeping with the Creator's request, we are hereby closing the wire until tomorrow for "rest." Good night and thirty.

The Wheel

As reported by RALPH R. SCHULZ

They call it the Wheel, and it should be the greatest thing since man-made fire, if you believe swarthy, intense Sigma Calibrator, research director of Mesopotamian Sled Works.

Described in a new patent application (Mesopotamia 563,217), the wheel is a flat device of wood in the shape of a full moon. One observer likens it to a square with the corners rounded off. "It's so beautifully simple," says Calibrator, "I'm amazed that no one thought of it before."

What got Calibrator thinking in the right direction was a product engineering problem at Mesopotamia Sled. Sled runners, even those fashioned of toughest oak, do not last longer than three or four months in the balmy Mesopotamian climate. That's because the Mesopotamian family sled must do double duty as a work vehicle during the week and a pleasure buggy on inevitably sunny weekends. Unlike the situation in colder northern regions, Mesopotamian roads are clogged every Sunday with long lines of ox-drawn family sleds.

Frequent runner breakdown is not only an irksome inconvenience for the driver who must wrestle with his spare runner, but a definite liability to the sled manufacturer. Mesopotamian Sled's attempt to promote sleds of higher ox power failed, for example, because runners could not stand up for long at the higher speeds—approaching nine miles per hour for the big, four-ox model. And the company's campaign to penetrate the upper-middle-class youth market with its aggressive "Get Runners" ad program was only a middling success for the same reason.

It was with these disappointments gnawing at his mind that Z. Z. Omega, flinty-eyed president and chief executive officer of Mesopotamian Sled threw the problem at his research department. "Give me a better pair of shoes," vowed Omega to research man Calibrator, "and I'll put the sled industry into high gear."

"We'll give it a whirl, sir," replied the future inventor of the wheel.

Last week, two years after he got the assignment, Calibrator showed off his invention at a news conference jammed with reporters, television cameramen and science editors at the Mesopotamia Hilton. "This device," he said, "developed after years of intensive research, will obsolete present-day sleds. Everything will be moving on wheels."

The wheel shown at the news conference consisted of three shaped planks clamped together with copper clasps to form a thick disc. A hub was drilled at the true center of the disc and an axle was inserted in the hub. Jubilant Calibrator spun the device by hand and let it rotate freely. The disc turned freely around the axle for several minutes without further manual effort.

"What makes the wheel turn freely," Calibrator said, "is the centrifugal force caused by its rotary motion. Actually, it is a form of lever, which has been used for many years here and abroad."

The center, common to both the wheel and the axle, corresponds to the fulcrum—the support on which the lever rests, or turns. The radius of the two parts corresponds to the lever's arm. The effort to overcome resistance acting upon the axle is relatively small. The mechanical advantage conferred by the device is determined by the radius of the wheel versus the radius of its axle, the inventor explained.

Taking the floor, Mr. Omega told reporters that the device marks only the beginning of what he termed "a technological revolution," which would make life easier and industry more efficient.

"Farmers will be able to carry their produce to faraway places with a minimum of human effort and exchange their goods for items not available in their own communities. In addition, people will be able to travel farther, meeting citizens of other countries and learning about their lives, ideas and ways of doing things," he said.

Calibrator told the news conference that he sees "thousands of uses" for his invention and exhibited a prototype model of a new machine registered under the patent name of Wheel Vehicle. "This," he said proudly, "will make present-day sleds obsolete in a short period of time."

The vehicle exhibited by the company consisted of two pairs of wheels firmly connected to their axles, which, in turn, were loosely attached to covering wooden planks by means of copper half-rings. Heavy rocks were placed on the planks, whereupon Calibrator gave the device a slight push. It rolled freely for several meters.

"This revolutionary machine," Calibrator said, "can be loaded with heavy material and pushed to remote places with a minimum of muscular effort. We have even developed a special device, called the harness, which would completely eliminate human effort. Your ox will be able to pull the vehicle hundreds of kilometers away from home. If you get tired, you may ride on the vehicle yourself."

Omega admits that the invention of the wheel was the result of "pressure" on the company. At the company's last annual meeting, stockholders expressed dissatisfaction about the company's poor earnings and the adverse publicity resulting from sled breakdowns. It was learned that two years ago the company's board of directors considered replacing Omega.

Omega says research and development of the company's new line of products would require additional capital, "which has been made available to us." He declines to identify the company's financial backers before the filing of a preliminary prospectus with the Mesopotamian Securities and Exchange Commission. Informed sources, however, said that shipping interests as well as several investment bankers both in Mesopotamia and abroad have pledged considerable financial support to the venture.

Calibrator admits that the company still faces minor technical problems but expresses confidence that they would soon be solved.

As an example, he cites the problem of friction. Ground friction as well as hub friction affect the rotation of the wheel by slowing down the vehicle and increasing the human or animal effort to pull the device. In addition, he says, wooden wheels wear easily or break on bumpy surfaces.

"We have been able to increase the strength of our wheels and reduce ground friction by means of iron rings (tentatively called 'tires') firmly nailed around the discs," he explained. "This new development will also eliminate the need for copper clasps to hold the wood together. Axle friction will be considerably reduced by another new device, called a roller bearing, developed in our research laboratories. It's another first by our company," Calibrator declared. He declined to give a technical description of the roller bearing, pending filing of a patent application.

Calibrator also revealed that his company is planning to cover or replace the iron rings with a new type of gum, known as rubber. Object: to make the ride smoother and reduce strain on the wheels. Harnesses for ox-drawn or mule-drawn vehicles, similar to those used to pull today's sleds, have also been developed by the company.

"We have now on our drawing boards a more sophisticated type of wheel," Calibrator declared. "Instead of being solid and heavy, it would be spoked, with the rim made of a single piece of wood bent in a full circle by heat and covered with rubber. This new type of wheel would be more expensive, but it would be much lighter and more attractive to the eye than the solid wheel. Thus, we are planning to use our spoked wheels only for passenger vehicles and continue using the solid types for cargo vehicles."

The research executive, son of the well-known Mesopotamian potter, Alfa Calibrator, said the idea of the wheel first came to him while observing his father pressing, molding and coiling the clay, but the actual development of the device was the result of an accident.

It occurred, he said, when his eighteen-year-old son, Delta, was building a marblestone patio on his back yard. "It was a hot summer afternoon and I felt sorry watching the boy lifting up large, heavy squares of marblestone and putting them in place. I thought there must be some easier way to do the job," he said.

The breakthrough occurred when Delta accidentally dropped a square on the already finished section of the patio. Somehow, all four corners of the plaque were cut off, making it almost a perfect circle. Instead of lifting it up, the young man put it in vertical position and rolled it away with virtually no effort.

After observing the incident, Calibrator could envision many potential uses for circular objects. To test his theories, he constructed wooden wheels by clamping together three planks and fashioning them into a perfect circle by means of a string and nail, and saw.

Calibrator's first wheeled device was the potter's wheel, which he made by enlarging the hole left by the nail in the middle of the disc and inserting an iron rod of slightly smaller diameter than the hub. The loose end of the rod was firmly hammered into the ground.

When he spun the disc with his hand, it kept rotating freely for several seconds without further human effort.

Calibrator wasn't sure how his horizontal wheel could be used, but he showed the device to his father. The older man placed a lump of wet clay at the dead center of the disc, gave it a spin and then used his hands to shape a vase. In a matter of minutes, the vase was ready—and more evenly round than any piece of pottery the older man had ever produced.

The potter's wheel is now being manufactured by the Big Wheel

Corporation, a wholly owned subsidiary of the Mesopotamian Sled Works.

Now available throughout Mesopotamia and several foreign countries, the potter's wheel sells for two sheep for a twelve-inch machine and three sheep for an eighteen-inch wheel. Calibrator said a more sophisticated type of potter's wheel involving two discs and enabling the potter to rotate the machine with his foot, thus leaving his hands completely free, will soon be available for five sheep and a goat. Do-it-yourself kits are available from the company's mail order department at lower prices.

By using the wheel, states Calibrator, a modern potter can boost production three-fold and amortize the equipment in less than a year. He added that barter-short producers may obtain the machine in exchange for fine pottery, which would be marketed worldwide through affiliated companies.

"Our machine has sparked a revolution in the pottery business," Calibrator avers. "It saves time and energy by employing centrifugal force to form the clay placed on the center of the disc. A well-centered lump, when spinning fast, needs only light guiding pressure from the potter's hands to assume any desired circular form."

The elder Calibrator was on hand to demonstrate the potter's wheel at the press conference. In less than ten minutes he produced three finely-shaped vases by using the foot-operated machine.

Omega told the news conference that his company's original wheeled products are only the beginning of what he terms "a technological revolution." He cites the following products now under development at Mesopotamian Sled's laboratories:

Spinning wheel: This device consists of a wheel permanently attached to its axle and revolving vertically with the rotary motion supplied by the operator's foot. This machine, it is claimed, would increase the production of yarns, thread and rope tenfold by providing uninterrupted spinning action and leaving the worker's hands free. The garment industry, in turn, would be able to increase its own production on the basis of a relatively modest capital investment. He declines to give technical description of the company's spinning wheel pending patent application, but says that it will be marketed next winter.

Grinding wheel: This machine, also to be marketed next winter, would sharpen knives and tools in a matter of seconds. "At this point," says Omega, "we spend hours and much muscular effort rubbing the sharp or pointed edges of our tools against flat rocks in order to make them cut or drill more efficiently.

"Our company will soon be making available its Grinding Wheel—a perfectly shaped wheel made of high quality stone and rotating vertically with power supplied by foot. All you'll have to do is apply gently your tool or knife against the revolving wheel and we can guarantee it will be razor sharp in a matter of seconds," says Omega.

Pulley and winch: Landlubbers will not be the only people to take advantage of the invention, Omega states. The company is developing a new device, called Pulley, which would enable seamen to raise and lower their sails with far less tugging and hauling.

Another company product, consisting of a wheel and a handle, is called the Winch. It would also enable sailors to trim their sails and raise and lower their anchors with considerably less muscular effort. "These devices could make seamanship safer and save many lives each year," Omega declares.

Relaxing over cocktails following the formal press conference, Omega and Calibrator talked of other products in the works.

"We have a winged wheel, which, when raised high above the ground, turns with the force of the wind. It's a fascinating machine that could eventually be made to raise water from the ground for irrigation," Calibrator said, adding that a prototype has been produced and successfully tested.

"Another intriguing wheel could be rotated by water motion," Calibrator continued. "It's specially designed so that its axle spans a stream. As long as the stream flows, the wheel turns." He revealed that the company's prototype of a "Water Wheel" had been continuously revolving for more than six months until its axle failed because of friction. "That's why we badly need that device—the roller bearing—I told you about at the press conference," he said.

With the exception of the potter's wheel, Omega declines to estimate prices for the company's other wheel. A lot will depend on contract negotiations with the firm's forty-two-man labor force.

Assuming no union problems, Mesopotamian could be producing a full line of wheels within twelve months. No restraining antitrust action is anticipated from the Mesopotamian Department of Justice.

Capital to finance construction of a new plant and equipment will be sought from a secondary stock offering. One of Mesopotamia's major underwriters is involved and Omega feels confident that the issue will be oversubscribed at premium prices.

Calibrator believes that possibilities for his invention in transportation, agriculture, pottery making and labor-saving devices are limitless. "Wheels will be everywhere," he enthusiastically predicted. "There will be wheels within wheels. Someday, it's going to be a round world."

Ralph Schulz didn't witness the invention of the wheel. But he did make his professional debut in the relatively primitive days of business journalism. That was back in 1950, before the advent of strident consumerism and environmentalism. Multinational corporations hadn't been invented, inflation was a chapter in the economic textbooks, and energy was something you were short of when the alarm clock rang in the morning. Business was a lot simpler and the business writer had a lot fewer angles to worry about when he went out to cover a story.

Today, after two decades of chronicling the fascinating and frenetic international business scene, he counsels other business journalists in his capacity of Director of McGraw-Hill World News. Before joining this international wire service serving McGraw-Hill publications and other news media, he was editor of the influential *Chemical Week* magazine. His background includes a stint with McClean-Hunter Ltd. which includes McClean's magazine and a number of business publications in its stable. A one-time contributor of articles on business and finance to publications here and abroad, he has also lectured on his specialty at journalism schools.

Ralph Schulz was born in New York, graduated in chemistry from the College of the City of New York. He served in the Navy, is a member of the board of governors of the Overseas Press Club of America.

The Invention of Money

As reported by WILL SPARKS

This small North African town, most prosperous of what the Phoenicians insist is a separate and independent continent which they were the first to circumnavigate, is currently in the midst of an unprecedented economic turmoil. There are ominous indications of possible government intervention in the local economy to stem the tide of what most local officials consider to be a fiscal insanity approaching flood-like proportions.

Cause of the commotion is a tall burnoosed young man who calls himself Salem al Sebah who arrived here recently with a bag of esoteric sea shells. Some of them have stripes, some of them have spots, some of them are plain white but good to the touch. He is even rumored to have some block-buster sizes which, when held to the ear, will actually replicate the sound of the sea itself. The latter, however, have not been seen, or heard, by this reporter.

In itself, this might seem of no importance. But what is significant is that Salem—as he calls himself—is trading these shells for everything in sight—cows, oxen, bows and arrows, even houses. He has convinced most of the population of this very sophisticated country that shells are the wave of the future.

Enthusiastic followers of Salem's innovation, which, incidentally, he calls "money" or sometimes "currency," are convinced that what we are witnessing here is a great breakthrough in the field of economics.

As one leading trader told this correspondent: "Salem has it figured out. Look, we here in Phoenicia have understood for generations that one bow and arrow does not make a house. We were constantly getting into situations where Nazim the bow maker was giving 2000 bows to Gabrin the roofer for a roof on his house. But what the hell was Gabrin going to do with 2000 bows?

"Now, we solved that problem a long time ago by converting it into cows. Nazim didn't have to give him all those bows and arrows: he just gave him some cows. You know how it works: one cow is worth ten bows, ten cows are worth one roof—and so on.

"But, as it turned out, that wasn't really the final solution. A cow is a very big animal. How do you buy half-a-cow worth of roofing? Now along comes Salem who shows you how to do it with sea shells. Do you realize how much smaller a sea shell is than a cow?"

The above is certainly representative of the popular opinion around here at this point in time. But it is by no means unanimous. For example, a prominent local merchant was asked this question: "What basis do we have for believing that these shells are really worth anything? Why would anybody trade a healthy cow for a bag of sea shells?"

His reply: "Well, of course, everybody wants to believe it because— you have to admit—it's a lot more convenient. But you've got a point. All we really have is Salem—we like him and trust him, but I suppose he won't always be with us. Who's going to guarantee the value of the shells when he leaves?"

This reporter is able to report that in response to this interview the merchant in question met with the local monarch and suggested the creation of an official to be known as the "Minister of Finance."

It can be reliably reported that the king's initial reaction was: "You mean to tell me that these people will trade cows for sea shells? Well, that certainly opens up possibilities. You can have your Minister for Finance. We'll appoint my brother-in-law; he spends most of his time building sand-castles—he ought to be able to learn something about sea shells."

That decision has not been met with unanimous approval. Student groups, in particular, have organized protests against what they condemn as ultimate control of daily life by the ruling powers.

In response to these objections, the new Finance Minister (Salem al Salem, which means Salem's brother-in-law) states: "The fact that we start with sea shells or clam shells or whatever doesn't mean we have to stay with them. Plans are already underway to convert eventually to hard metals. Iron is a definite possibility. And there is research underway to explore the possibilities of finding metals which do not corrode. We have seen small samples of such minerals, which we have provisionally named 'gold' and 'silver.' They are buried deep in the ground, so that digging them out should have a very positive effect on employment."

At the end of a tumultuous press conference, the newly created "Minister of Finance" was asked by a reporter: "Even if we go from shells to iron and from iron to silver or gold, or whatever you're talking about, how do we know that you won't suddenly change the rules about what anything is worth?"

"Trust us," said the Minister.

"Wait and see what happens," said one financial analyst after the conference, "when they invent paper."

Will Sparks was born in Detroit, Michigan, and educated at Knox College and the Georgetown University School of Foreign Service. He received a degree from the University of Chicago and a certificate in narcotics investigation from the New York Police Academy. He served as Assistant to the Secretary of Defense from 1964 to 1965 and as Assistant to the President of the United States from 1965 to 1968. He has been a frequent contributor to *The New Leader* and *Commonweal*. Mr. Sparks lives in New York City.

The Tower of Babel
—A Breakdown in Communications

As reported by JOHN McALLISTER

Watch for the development of an important community on the plain of the land of Shinar when a large group of wanderers from the east finally arrive in this fertile section of the Tigris-Euphrates Valley. According to advance scouts of the large caravan, the travelers are mainly grandsons, great-grandsons, and other descendants of the late patriarch Noah, along with their families and retainers. Noah was famed as the builder of an ark that brought him and his family, along with much livestock, through the Great Flood of distant unhappy memory. Leaders of the migration include a noted hunter and warrior, Nimrod, his father, Cush, and other tribal chiefs among them, Gomer and Asshur. The travelers are reported to be eyeing the easy-to-irrigate territory between the rivers, about where they run twenty miles apart.

The apprentice brickmaker Haran already was on his way to the kiln as the first rays of the morning sun lit up the fast growing new community on the plain of Shinar by the east bank of the Euphrates River. The day's work begins early in Babel, this settlement established several moons ago by the descendants of Noah after long wanderings in the northeast.

Soon Haran was joined by other workers converging on the kiln where the fires already were being started by the boss brickmaker, Tarshish. Young and old, men and women, all the Babel residents were up early and eagerly going about their jobs—in the marshes cutting reeds, in the fields, in the shops making pottery and tools. There was much to do, for the people of Babel have big plans and high hopes for their town. This is reflected in its carefully selected name. Babel means "gate of God."

The town is growing rapidly. Brick dwellings and buildings for tradesmen and artisans are spreading over a large area. On the outskirts, farmers and herdsmen are putting up more modest structures, generally made of the abundant reeds, dried and bundled to use instead of the scarce timber. All activities are proceeding at a fast pace from dawn to dusk. The settlers have quickly caught on to and made good use of some of the inventions of the Sumerian natives, such as the potter's wheel, the wagon, and the sailboat. The latter has sparked the growth of a fishermen's colony along the river banks.

But the leaders of Babel have a more grand design than merely to establish a mighty city. As Nimrod, the chief of the city government puts it, "We aim to build us a tower whose top may reach unto heaven!"

While some of the Babel citizens, including a few in the administration, feel that this is a wildly extravagant, if not impious, statement of the true aims of the Tower Project, a majority go along with the comment of one master builder that "the sky might as well be the limit."

The Babel leadership is well aware of the serious engineering problems facing them, however high the Tower may rise. The flat alluvial plain of Shinar is not an ideal spot for the erection of a soaring tower. Building project director Salah, who like Nimrod is a grandson of Noah, explained the principal difficulties to this reporter:

"No stone. You know, these plains are great for crops and grazing and all that, but there are few rocks like there were up in the northeast. There's no lime around here either so we can't make mortar. We've got to build with bricks and stick them together with slime."

The slime Salah referred to is known to scholars as bitumen, a substance taken from pits and containing natural mineral elements. It is prevalent just north of the area. However, the local resources are excellent for making bricks. Many bricks are now drying in the sun ready for construction to begin at the Tower. And kilns are working at top speed to fire special bricks for the outside of the structure.

Why do the citizens of Babel want to erect such a high tower? The general feeling is that it will give the community a sense of pride and togetherness in accomplishment. As Nimrod states it: "We want to make a name for ourselves. We want a good reason to stay here and not be scattered all around the earth."

For the people of Babel, the next new moon promised to usher in a period of wild celebration. By then the city's spectacular tower was to be completed as far up as the eighth story.

Just what will happen next is not clear. But spurred on by tremendous public support for the project, the Babel administration now intends to continue building upward toward the heavens as far as possible.

As it stands now the tower is a most impressive sight. It is in the style of Sumerian ziggurat, a roughly pyramidical structure built in progressively smaller, steplike stages, with outside staircases and usually a shrine on the top. The Tower of Babel has a huge base about 300 feet by 300 feet containing rooms to house the temple. The setback on each floor is spacious. Ceremonies could be held on some of the lower ones. The eighth story level now under completion is about 325 feet above the ground.

"It's the greatest thing ever built by man," says the burly city boss, Nimrod. "All our people now are united in a common pride and loyalty that will make this state endure forever."

The same point of view was echoed by project chief Salah, who over a luncheon of mutton and lettuce, washed down with quantities of beer, told this reporter about the glories and difficulties in his triumphal mission.

"I've never seen such motivation among ordinary working men," he exclaimed. "First it was making bricks practically day and night, then slapping them in place with each crew racing the other to see who could finish a section first. And the higher we got, of course, the tougher it was to lug more bricks up to the building site. The women and children did a great job here—and so did our few slaves."

Asked for the basis of the motivation, Salah reflected for a moment, chewing on a fig, then said, "Well, we're the best and we all live here together and will never have to go anywhere. We don't need anything from the gods or from any man. This Tower shows how great we are. It may please God, or the gods, or it may be frightening. Who cares?"

The question was asked whether fear of another deluge had spurred the activity of the people to build a high place of refuge.

"Maybe at first," said Salah. "Everyone has some old folks in the family who've heard the stories about Noah's troubles. But, hades, we could build arks if we had to. Besides, our weather-watchers tell us that a flood that bad isn't likely to happen again in our lifetime. Let the next administration worry about that. Meantime, we've got a place to go if the water does rise a bit."

What is planned when the eighth story is finished?

"After the celebration at the new moon we'll decide on that. Probably some sort of shrine or small temple, if we top out at eight, but of course we may go much higher still," said Salah. "We've had some careful deliberation and hot debates over this."

This reporter asked if he could see the tablets recording the minutes of these deliberations so that the public could be informed about what was being planned.

"Sorry, can't do," Salah said emphatically. "That would violate executive privilege. We can't let the public in on all our secret talks. They might misunderstand what was being said or it might give wrong ideas to some of the native Sumerians. It's a matter of city security. Everything will be made perfectly clear in due time."

Actually, nearly everyone in Babel seems to have complete confidence in their leaders and to take immense pride in the tower. Although there has been some opposition to the Nimrod leadership—notably on his program to try to hold down the exchange value of cattle—there has been no important dissension over the Tower. In fact, the tribal leader at first most actively opposed to the Nimrod regime, the portly brickmaker Tarshish, is an enthusiastic booster for the project.

"The Tower is great for my business," he declares, "and what's good for bricks is good for Babel."

The general man-in-the-street view was summed up by Dedan, a pottery-maker located on a corner near the Tower: "Everything is humming, and we sure are the greatest. Nothing can stop Babel if we all just stick together." Pointing skyward, he added, "Those up there must be jealous of us."

Miriam, a lithe dancing girl, was interviewed on her way to practice with other fair maidens for a production number to be staged on the Tower's first floor on opening night of the celebration.

"It's going to be a ball," she said laughingly. With a swish of her thin flaxen skirt she bounded up the steps of the Tower where the rehearsal group was waiting and called back over a generously bare shoulder, "Nobody has more fun than us Babylonians."

All over the city, private parties and lavish home entertaining was going on in anticipation of the celebration. Beer and wine flowed freely in even the most humble huts. A leading vintner, Ludim, said that his storage wine was nearly used up and that he and his family were exhausted from tramping out grapes.

The entire city seemed to be trembling with anticipation, awaiting the new moon.

On the night of the new moon Babel was the scene of joyous celebration and unrestrained revelry. Official ceremonies and private festivities were marking the completion of eight stories on the city's fabulous tower.

The next morning the entire community was overwhelmed with chaos and despair almost impossible to describe.

The incredible fact: As the day dawned, no one could understand what any one else was saying. All speech was confused, all language confounded.

Within a few days, families and groups of people bound together by common habits or by instinct were streaming out of the city to disappear in different directions. They went on foot, clutching their possessions, or on mule back, or sometimes driving heavily ladened ox carts. Sheep, cattle, and goats were driven along with them, although some sharp disputes broke out over which animals were going with which group—disputes settled either by force or by resignation, since none of the disputants could understand the other's arguments.

By week's end there was almost no one left in Babel except a few stragglers and some native Sumerians, stunned by what they had seen and heard.

As best I can reconstruct the stupefying events to which I have been an eyewitness, the trouble began about the first watch on the night of the new moon, just as the ceremonies and shows on the Tower were breaking up.

A violent thunderstorm struck the city with vivid lightning, crashing booms, and torrential rains. The crowds scattered to seek shelter in the nearest buildings and huts. Some huddled against the Tower, and the performers and celebrants on the first and upper floors took refuge under overhanging cornices. Then the Tower's top was struck savagely by lightning several times and everyone streamed down the stairs and off the Tower, joining those at the base in fleeing in panic every which way. Soon the mighty monument stood deserted in the center of the terrified city—as though the inhabitants somehow sensed that the Tower was the cause of their troubles.

The worst trouble was soon evident when the rains stopped and the first rays of sunrise spread over the stricken city. People emerged into the street to console each other about the storm and the breakup of the celebration. But conversation stopped abruptly as no one seemed to make sense.

At first many attributed the confusion of tongues to drunkenness, and many sharp glances were cast back and forth. Or terror caused by the storm might have seemed an excuse. Soon, however, it was apparent that nearly every person was speaking in a different language.

True, close family members seemed to understand what each other was saying, although there was considerable difficulty in one generation talking to another. But good friends living in the same neighborhood could not understand each other.

I located a few acquaintances with my native Sumerian background and was able to converse with them despite the appearance of new speech patterns and idioms. My countrymen all confirmed what I had learned. It was impossible to talk with the settlers although we had all become proficient in the language they spoke when they first arrived.

At the municipal building in the center of the city, near the Tower, the scene was one of utter panic, which increased as the day went on. All the city leaders were in the courtyard, pacing back and forth, waving their arms, shouting at each other but with no apparent mutual comprehension. The massive figure of Nimrod loomed over them all, his face black with rage.

Apparently, the Tower was the main object of their concern as each man kept pointing to it. Some would make gestures as though piling brick on brick, while others would wave their arms contemptuously at them and shake their heads. My impression was that some of the leaders wished to continue with the building, while others did not want to, and still others seemed to not know what to do next.

Finally, project-chief, Salah, stepped into an inner office to emerge shortly with a large clay tablet which I recognized (from having had a glimpse at an interview weeks earlier) as the master plan of the Tower. Salah handed it to Nimrod, who stared at it blankly, shrugged his shoulders, and handed it back to him. Examining it closely with a look of disbelief, Salah suddenly in a fit of passion hurled the tablet to the ground, smashing it into a dozen pieces. My impression was that neither man could comprehend what was written on the plan. At any rate, whatever the leaders had planned as the future of the Tower was now effectively reduced to hearsay. But no one could hear because no one could say.

In the following days some communication was established by simple sign language and the repetition of meaningful gestures. But on the whole the residents of Babel became increasingly suspicious of each other, impatient, and hostile.

I met Miriam, the dancer, on the street one evening and greeted her in a cheery fashion in her own tongue. She looked at me vacantly and passed on. Just then a man emerged from a nearby courtyard, put his arm around her, and led her off into the shadows, she smiling up at him. Apparently Miriam had been more successful than most others in re-establishing communication with her neighbors.

Trade and barter gradually petered out. The herdsmen spent their time with their stock but did not bring them to town. Faithful workmen arrived at the Tower each day and argued furiously and uncomprehendingly with each other, but there was no one to tell them what to do and they soon would drift away.

In the Temple, which had been located in the base of the Tower pending a decision as to what would go on top, the priests seemed helpless to give comfort to those who thronged the corridors. Neither could they discuss with each other what was going on. This applied both to those who supported the patriarch Noah's belief in one mighty God and to the newer priests who were leaning toward worship of the local Sumerian deities such as Ea, Anu, Enlil. Kindly gestures did not seem to comfort the people and they sadly drifted out of the Temple, while the priests paced back and forth, occasionally looking up into the skies as though searching for some sign.

Parents took their children to the schools, mostly to keep them busy, but the teachers, who reported there out of habit, soon wearied of shouting incomprehensible instructions at uncomprehending youngsters. A few imaginative schoolmen managed to keep their pupils busy with mechanical tasks, such as making marks with the stylus on small wet clay tablets, but since the marks meant little to anyone this activity soon became a bore. School attendance shortly dropped off to nothing.

A serious civic breakdown occurred in the management of the irrigation canals and dikes. The Babel engineers had devised an elaborate system of dams and controls so that the life-giving water from the Euphrates could flow wherever needed into fields, grazing lands, or residential areas. It was a triumph of civic cooperation. But when the farmers, grazers, and residents were unable to explain their needs and the engineers could not instruct their helpers, the whole operation fell apart, leading to much dissension and hardship.

The first family to leave Babel departed quietly during the second watch. I happened to see them go, a sorrowful caravan moving generally in a northeasterly direction from which the whole community had come originally. The next morning no one seemed surprised that they had gone.

The departure of Nimrod made quite a stir. Holding his favorite bow and spear in one hand and carrying a giant axe in the other he strode out of the city toward the north, leading a parade of intimate family members with their goods and animals. He never cast a backward glance at the city of which he had been chief.

After that departures were rapid and soon almost became a rout. The caravans took off in all directions. The slave colony, perhaps the only immediate beneficiaries of the disaster, simply took off with what they could carry, and no one seemed to question their right to go.

The fishermen boarded their precious sailboats and proceeded upstream. Some colonists were seen on the banks of the Euphrates preparing rafts of palm-tree logs with evident intent of crossing the river and heading westward as soon as possible.

Soon nearly all the settlers had gone. The streets and huts were deserted and the Tower of Babel stood stark and alone thrusting itself upward toward the heavens.

As a death-like silence descended on the still unfinished city of Babel, I sought out an old friend, a wise white-bearded Sumerian philosopher, who had lived in a solitary hut in the Babel area before the settlers arrived, and now had seen them go. Despite the events of recent days, we still spoke essentially the same language, although curiously we could not remember each other's name—nor indeed our own names. This is my interview with him:

Q. What do you think happened, old friend?
A. I don't know, really, but I think some great light, some true insight came to those people.
Q. What kind of insight?
A. Well, they had all been so proud and prosperous and smug about being one tight little group, better than everybody else and not needing anything from anybody. Well, something blew. Maybe it was the gods. Maybe it was seeing that crazy Tower all lit up by lightning and standing there so useless when they needed so much down on the ground. Something rattled their minds and confused their speech. Anyhow, they seem to have been shocked into going off to do their own thing, even if it meant talking differently. From being closely knit arrogant zombies they suddenly became ordinary human beings.

Q. But where will they go?

A. Anywhere and everywhere. This whole area north and curving westward is said to be great country. You might almost call it a Fertile Crescent. I'd especially keep an eye on those that settle up northward. Nomads tell me there's a Great Sea up there, and maybe there's other people beyond it. The sea might be in the middle of a lot of land—they'll think of a good name for it. The crowd going north will be the energetic ones and now that they've lost the idea they are perfect maybe they'll do something really important, like founding some new religions, discovering other people, getting ideas from them and influencing them too. Might be a good thing. Could be good for your business too.

Q. How so?

A. Instead of putting out your weekly tablets by yourself, or with a few local friends, you could have contacts, correspondents all over the place sending you in stuff occasionally by caravan or whatever. Then we'd know what is going on outside this valley. You could have translators—we now see there's going to be a lot of languages —and researchers working with you to put it all together in a big, broad report—sort of a group effort, I mean you could call it group journalism.

Q. Maybe so. I hope people would pay for it. Anyhow, Babel sure is dead.

A. Oh, somebody will come along and complete or rebuild it, I expect. But those settlers sure did make a name for themselves here. I bet that Babel will stand for confusion for a long time to come. Maybe the name of the city will have to be changed—something like Babylon, after the Babylonians as they used to call themselves.

Q. Then you don't think the Tower happening was entirely a disaster?

A. Not necessarily. People have to learn not to be smug and arrogant. They have to be themselves and learn to get along with others, who may be different but also are being themselves. I'm hopeful, young fellow, very hopeful.

John McAllister, born in Cohasset, Massachusetts, has been with *Newsweek* since 1937, serving at various times as a Business writer, Press Editor, News Editor, General Editor, and Public Affairs Manager. His journalistic experience covers a wide range—from the founding and publishing of his own weekly newspaper in Westchester County to a faculty post in the Department of Journalism of Long Island University.

He was graduated *cum laude* from Amherst College in 1931 and attended the Harvard Graduate School of Business Administration. After a brief term with *The Reader's Digest* as an Assistant Editor, he began publishing a weekly newspaper, *The Townsman,* in Pleasantville, N.Y., in 1943. After joining *Newsweek* in 1937, he continued publishing and writing editorials for *The Townsman* until it was sold in 1956. The citizens of Pleasantville honored him at that time for his many years of service to the community.

John McAllister began at *Newsweek* as a researcher in the Business section and was shortly promoted to writer in the department. In 1942 he began a three-and-a-half year hitch in the Army Air Corps as a weather forecaster. Rejoining the magazine, he soon moved to the Periscope section. In 1953 he became editor of the Press section. He was advanced to News Editor in 1955, to General Editor in 1964, and was named Public Affairs Manager in 1971.

As General Editor he was involved in the editorial development of new projects for the magazine, especially in the field of education. In 1964 he recreated and restyled the *Newsweek* house organ, and he has been involved in collecting and preparing material for a history of the magazine.

Teaching and free-lance writing are among his major outside activities. He has been a faculty member of the New School for Social Research in New York City and an Adjunct Assistant Professor in the Department of Journalism at Long Island University.

J.T.M. and family reside in the Village section of Manhattan. He is a member of the Cohasset Yacht Club, The Harvard Business School Club of New York, the Overseas Press Club of America and its Overseas Yacht Club, the National Press Club, and the Deadline Chapter of Sigma Delta Chi.

Moses and Law and Order

As reported by MORRIS L. ERNST

When I located Moses for an interview he was footsore and tired. Because the memory of his slavery under Pharaoh was acute, he was not inclined to talk about those early years of misery. This interested me particularly because man's memory of recent events in one's old age decreases whereas memory of childhood days usually increases.

The flight of Moses to Midian should some time be amplified in greater detail, and maybe a travel agency could now organize tours to retrace the entire Exodus journey. The "call" of Moses at that time to establish "one nation" and then "conduct" it to what he always termed The Promised Land was clear in his mind.

The long journey of Moses, as best I could trace it, with his help, went over what man centuries later called the Suez Canal Zone, where he fortunately caught a low tide for the passage. He gave me long descriptions of the Wilderness—a word he used for what others on the journey called the "Great Forest."

When he encamped the competitive tribes at Sinai his first job as a man of law and order was to reduce the competitive jealousies of the so-called lost tribes. He often said that competition of lost souls is never as rational as among secure people. To build up solidarity among the competitive tribes it was natural for each tribe to deem itself superior to every other one although there existed no valid standards for judging superiority. Certainly literacy was too scant to be used as a basis for conceit. Likewise—physical stamina was not the sole trait needed for leadership. The only basic trait to induce a following, as I gathered from Moses in my interview, lay in the art of creating and perpetuating tribal or folk heroes—but as with all heroes—each and every saga soon becomes apocryphal and is changed to suit the yearnings and dreams of each new generation.

Although Moses claimed no special skill as an architect or builder, he was proud of his design for the Tabernacle, which he thought was the first movable community shrine in history. As to the Hebrew Code which he deemed his greatest creation, it seemed to him to derive from the Law of Hammurabi.

Moses spoke with some regret that not all the tribesmen dared the passing over and that so many stayed behind. He seemed to regret most the loss of a part of the tribe he called the Levites—who remained to live in Palestine after the Exodus.

(As a footnote I should record for my readers that four centuries passed before the fuller life of Moses was put into final form. For those who enjoy significant and comparative dates of historical import, it will be recalled that the Exodus took place in what was an undateable age but what we now call the fourteenth century B.C., and then, not until 399 B.C. do we find a record of another Leader.)

Socrates operated in a somewhat similar polytheistic culture which, though literate, was without systematized doctrine. Although I could not locate Socrates, the newspaper accounts of his era show that the so-called corruption of youth for which he was condemned to die was directly related to Mosaic "impiety," which was an offense against the community as well as against the gods. Socrates relied on mythology. This was not equivalent to the Bible or the Ten Commandments, or even the Golden Rule. Ritual and myth always increase basic confusions and we can thank Moses for creating man's first desire to reduce the power of mythology—other than as a gay tool for fiction writers, novelists, and scenarists of operas.

When I first came across Moses, he was with his brother Aaron who never did believe that any God could bring water from those solid rocks at Meribeh. I was assigned to interview Moses because after the flight from Egypt he was the lone symbol of law and order, and certainly was the most controversial man of the district. Everyone from mouth to ear was talking about the "old geezer" who claimed he had the final answers for the Tribes, directly and in stone from Yahweh.

Before I approached Moses I had done my homework and had a brief history of his relation with his mother Jochebed, his sister Miriam and his wife Zipporah. Maybe the great excess of females over males at that time through all the tribes made the dames unnewsworthy. In brief I could find no sex theme in what was called the discovery of law and order on the mountain by Moses. No female had prodded him into his leadership and he did not first show his discovery to any woman.

I caught up with him half way up one of those rough hills—called Sinai by the people of the vicinage. Then and there I asked the old man: "Moses, can I look at your find?" There it was, a rough stone tablet, carved with numbers from one to ten with a few lines after each number. I could not read the words or even decipher the letters, although I had seen a sample of what my editor once told me was called "writing."

Moses was easy to interview as soon as he had shown me the Tablet. Here is my report in detail.

"I see number one says in brief, 'you shall Have no other God.' "

"Yes," Moses said, "there are so many gods that people are fickle and indecisive and hence this command points to 'law and order' in the sense that there is to be only final God, Word, or Supreme Court."

He then continued: "Command number two—as you will see on the stone—says the same thing and for emphasis, uses negative terms—in brief—'I am a jealous God and I don't like competition, for competition in any authority can be confusing to illiterate people, and confusion is anti-law and anti-order.' "

Then number two also, as Moses translated it for me, pointed to a penalty if people had competing gods. The penalty although not precise would endure to the "third and fourth generations"; it ended, rationally, for as Moses said, "If you have punishments you also should have rewards." Here the reward was "Steadfast Love." Not bad, I thought, as a basis of law as a deterrent in any culture. On the same accented theme Moses explained how there should be no doubt or jesting about the *single* God referred to on the tablet. No catchy slogans such as—"God Damn It" or any other taking the name of God and hence any other leader "in vain." That breaks down the respect for authority which is law and order. But, I asked, after these three items created the law of authority what the other lines meant.

Moses smiled and said: "Mankind some time may come to the thirty hour or four-day work week but now in this poor soil we worked seven days." But the Tablet said: "Six days is enough for you to do all your work and on the seventh day just loaf and don't even make your servants work on what will be called the 'Sabbath.' " Moses had no explanation as to why the week was to be seven instead of six or eight days, although months were lunar. He did suggest I not confuse Sabbath and Shabuoth

—the date for the commemoration of the discovery of the Ten Instructions for law and order.

I interjected, "Why did the tablet refer to the fact that its author in six days made heaven, and sea, and earth and then took a day off?"

Moses, after a moment's hesitation, gave me a snappy reply: "You see, if the creator of all that we live on and with took one day off out of seven certainly all lowly folk would be complimented to be thought able to follow his habits—or, as we call it—law—since law comes always out of the juices and habits of life or history."

Moses then transferred the symbol of law and order, or "work and rest" to father and mother, who laid down the law; and so it could be said that if all children honored Mom and Pop, the family law givers, the kids would be rewarded by a long life. At that time life expectancy was less than thirty years.

Then I said—"Here you now shift to more definite symbols of law and order." "Oh, yes," said Moses, "no more killing." I did not have the nerve to ask: "Even in self-defense?" I also slipped up as a reporter, I imagine, because I did not ask about "An Eye for an Eye."

As to number seven, I was troubled: "What's wrong with adultery?," I asked, while Moses frowned and quietly said without a sexy smirk: "You see, where there is adultery there will be few offspring and because we have many enemies at our borders, and we need a big population explosion because our infant mortality rate in babyhood is shockingly high. Even though we have a life expectancy of only about thirty years, our women live so much longer than men, we have a great widow problem even though widows are instructed to marry again in their husband's family. In fact, we need more people and in marriage our crude methods of birth control are not much used while adulterers try to prevent the obligations of parenthood. Because our people are nomadic immigrants, they must take their babies with them even though many are purposely left in the fields to die. But these are mostly females who are worthless as workers in the fields and vineyards."

Law number eight seemed to raise few problems. There was so little to steal and even if stolen it was difficult to hide any loot while always on the march.

Number nine arose only when the dictator, known as the judge, called a member of the tribe to account. I thought of the places still on the planet where there was no law—or advocacy—or matching of wits to look for "truth." Who would ever try to lie to a Dictator?

Number nine seemed to me to be really a part of eight—except that here the lying was only condemned if the false witness was against a neighbor. I noted that it was lawful to "bear false witness" against a stranger. Thus we have the origin of two rules of law—one for "us folk" and one for the newcomers, strangers, or immigrants.

And then number ten confused me no end. Thou shalt not covet anything that your neighbor owns. Of course, neighbors owned very little other than a wife or servant or ox.

I did not want to offend so I shied away from pointing to the great values of "coveting"—that is, wanting what someone else, perhaps a bit better off, owned. Moses cut me short when I tried to make an argument for coveting even though he knew that advertising to increase coveting might some day go to extremes and make people jealous of those who were tyrannized by owning too many homes and things and jewels. But Moses did realize the difficulty of drawing a line as to where envy and jealousy and coveting should end, for surely Law and Order are easier to preserve in a society of unambitious or unwanting people.

"Covet is attached," he said, "to gossip, and gossip undercuts law and order." I then recalled that in Nehemiah 8 in what we now call 45 B.C., gossip took place at the water gate and made trouble by false rumor particularly inducive to the breakdown of authority and law among illiterate people.

I would have enjoyed a more extensive interview but Moses was still on the march. He did ask me to come back some time for another talk. When I asked him where it would be convenient for him he merely said: "If you enjoy milk and honey, meet me in the Promised Land."

Morris L. Ernst was born in Uniontown, Alabama (1888), and educated at Williams College (A.B.) and New York School of Law where he received his L.L.B in 1912. A member of the law firm Greenbaum, Wolff & Ernst, New York, since 1915, he has held many official appointments and performed nearly a score of special missions for various organizations and officials, including mayors, governors and U.S. presidents.

He served as personal representative for President Roosevelt to the Virgin Islands (1935); during World War II he was sent on various missions for the President to England. He represented President Truman on a mission to Germany (1946), and was appointed a member of President

Truman's Civil Rights Commission, also to membership on the Post Office Department's Advisory Board.

A prolific writer, he is the joint author of over twenty-five books and a frequent contributor to various magazines, encyclopedias and newspapers.

Morris Ernst was honored by the Bar Association, City of New York (1960). He was elected Honorary Member, Phi Beta Kappa, Williams College (1961). He has Honorary Doctorate Degrees—in Jurisprudence, Nasson College (1963), and in Humane Letters, Lincoln University, Lincoln, Illinois (1964). He was awarded Honorary Membership in the National Honor Fraternity, Alpha Kappa Delta, Gamma Chapter, New York University. In 1969 he became a member of the Chancellor's Council, University of Texas. Place of residence—New York City.

The Lord Buddha Creates New Life System

As reported by ROLAND GAMMON

Siddhartha Guatama, the handsome young price who was to become the Buddha, sat entranced in contemplation. His mind purified, his heart fixed, he had remained in yoga lotus-posture throughout the night. Now, lighting the forest gloom, a first flush of rose pierced the cathedral dome of Bo trees to shine on his motionless, brown head. No bird sang; no breeze stirred the rainbow lotus at his feet. The silence of Eternity filled all time and space even as it sounded in his heart. Steadily, strangely, a light never seen on land or sea—that light which the sages said equaled the splendor of 1000 suns—flooded the jungle darkness and the prince's moon-sweet face. Surrounded only by his first disciples and those few adoring animals drawn—who knows how?—to the scene, a Son of God was reborn on earth.

For the silent sovereign, who six years before had abandoned his queen, baby son, and all the pomp and ceremony of royal power, the moment of divinity had come. Now his foot-weary wanderings across India had ended; his pain-wracked pilgrimage to find the truth at the heart of life, with all its bodily anguish, self-mortification, endless fasting, penance and prayer, at last was over. As the morning stars sang together and a host of witnesses hovered near, the Light divine illuminated Siddhartha's soul. The imprisoned splendor burst from his inmost self, a love-lighted power transformed his consciousness, an immense and immortal bliss thrilled his very being. In that one incarnating experience, known to the seers as *satori* or illumination and vouchsafed by the *avatars* or God-men of all the ages, this chosen son of heaven became the Enlightened One. At age thirty-five, in a deer park at Uruvela, India, high-born Siddhartha Guatama became the Buddha.

The Buddha, of course, went on to found one of the world's great living religions. Setting forth from that obscure deer park near Benares and destined to preach his new gospel of peace and compassion for nearly half a century, the Buddha proclaimed one of the noblest systems of rational thought and supernatural insight ever created by the human spirit. Today, 2500 years have passed since that holy transformation under the bodhi tree, and more than 500 million people worship the Buddha's name. Today, this kingly contemporary of Confucius and Lao-Tse, Jeremiah, and Zoroaster, still shines as Asia's light of the world. Today, too, the Buddha's *Dharma* or doctrine seems surprisingly modern with its ethical purity and psychological emphasis appealing strongly to young seekers everywhere and its Zen stress on meditation setting millions on the upward path to liberation. But who that mystic morning could have foretold all this? Who among his first five followers could have sensed the awesome significance of that hour? Fortunately, I was there as the disciple Ananda in a previous incarnation, and only knew that the Blessed One awakened from his long *samadhi* smiling with some divine secret.

Serene and silent, his great renunciation and painful quest behind him, still the Buddha sat in breathless adoration. Although we disciples seated in lotus-posture did not know it, our destined master had attained to that highest state of consciousness or mystical oneness with Creation which he was later to name *Nirvana*. Although only a lambent smile lighting his round face hinted at the eternal enlightenment which he experienced, we faithful at his feet had just witnessed an epochal turning point in human history. A new Buddha had been born on earth; a new romance of the human spirit had begun. Climaxing a million years of man's evolution toward the Light and completing his own pursuit of perfection in one final incarnation, this saintly teacher destined to give suffering humanity a new Middle Way of Wisdom had just resisted a final temptation to remain in heavenly Nirvana and resolved to return to earth to teach all men his Eightfold Path to Buddhahood. Now, at last, as the rising sun splendored the sheltering Bo tree for the forty-ninth day, the new God-man opened his eyes and spoke: "Many births have I traversed seeking the Builder. In vain; weary is the round of rebirths. But now art thou seen, O Builder! Never more shalt thou build the house. All thy beams are broken; cast down is thy cornerstone. My mind is set upon Nirvana; it has accomplished the extinction of all desire." (From that day onward, as we disciples noted, wherever Buddha went, people felt more peaceful.)

A light seldom seen on earth played about his person, and his rich voice stilled the singing birds above us. Some strange morning glory fell from the air, as he spoke those first inspired words to the world: "Home have I left, for I have left my world! Child have I left, and all my cherished herds! Lust have I left, and ill-will, too, is gone; and ignorance have I put far from me. With craving and the roots of craving overpowered, cool and composed am I now, knowing the peace of Nirvana . . . Faith is the seed I now sow and good works are the rain that fertilizes it; wisdom and modesty are the parts of the plough, diligence my draught ox, and my mind is the guiding rein. The harvest that it yields is the ambrosia fruit of Nirvana, and by this ploughing all sorrow ends."

The disciple Mahamati spoke: "Tell us, master, what is this Nirvana?"

The Buddha replied: "Nirvana is the supreme bliss. All earthly glory and heavenly joy, and the gain of Nirvana, can be attained only by this treasure of charity, piety, and self-control. Just as all rivers lose themselves in the great ocean, and all the waters of the air pour into it, yet the great ocean knows neither increase nor dimunition. So when many *Arahats* or worthy ones become extinguished in the pure realm of Nirvana, the Nirvana realm knows neither increase nor diminution. There water, fire, earth, and air are not. There no candle gives light, no sun beams, no moon shines, no darkness is. And when the enlightened has attained in stillness to insight, then is he free from form and formless, from pleasure and from pain . . . then, composed, upright, firm, free from desire, free from harshness, free from doubt, he attains deliverance."

So it was that Siddhartha Guatama in 528 B.C. became the Buddha. Now thirty-five years of age, fully awakened, selfless and yet self-realized, filled with love, joy, and that redeeming grace heaven reserves for its God-men, Buddha believed he knew how to end human suffering and resolved to proclaim his doctrine to the world. Accordingly, he arose and, rapt with his divine mission, made his way on foot to the holy city of Benares where, in Isipatana Park outside the city, he preached his first sermon on the meaning of life, outlined the Four Noble Truths of Salvation and announced he had come to "beat the drum of ambrosia and to reveal the light of Nirvana in the darkness of the world."

Who among the faithful five then present—to whom the Blessed One said, "I shall preach the Law to you first because you attended me during the time of my ascetic discipline"—will forget that sacred hour and the Sermon at Benares in this or any successive incarnation? In the cool of the evening, the new prophet or *Tathagatha* (the "Thus come" teacher who fulfills the law) stood before us at last, commanding in presence, radiant in light, more majestic in his word and wisdom than any of us had ever seen. Then, the Buddha lifted up his voice and addressed us: "Brethren, there are two extremes which he who has given up the world ought to avoid. What are these two extremes? A life given to pleasures, devoted to pleasures and lusts—this is degrading, sensual, vulgar, ignoble, and profitless. And a life given to mortifications—this is painful, ignoble, and profitless. By avoiding these two extremes, brethren, I have gained the knowledge of the Middle Path which leads to insight, which leads to wisdom, which conduces to calm, to knowledge and to supreme Enlightenment. . . . It is the right views, right intent, right speech, right conduct, right means of livelihood, right endeavor, right mindfulness, right meditation.

"This, brethren, is the Noble Truth of Suffering: birth is suffering; decay is suffering; illness is suffering; death is suffering; presence of objects we hate is suffering; separation from objects we love is suffering; not to obtain what we desire is suffering. In brief, the five aggregates which spring from grasping are painful.

"This, brethren, is the Noble Truth concerning the Origin of Suffering: verily, it originates in that craving which causes the renewal of becomings, is accompanied by sensual delight, and seeks satisfaction now here, now there; that is to say, craving for pleasures, craving for becoming, craving for not becoming.

"This, brethren, is the Noble Truth concerning the Cessation of Suffering: verily, it is passionlessness, cessation without remainder of this very craving; the laying aside of, the giving up, the being free from, the harboring no longer of, this craving.

"This, brethren, is the Noble Truth concerning the Path which leads to the Cessation of Suffering: verily, it is this Noble Eightfold Path, that is to say, right views, right intent, right speech, right conduct, right means of livelihood, right endeavor, right mindfulness and right meditation. . . .

"As long, brethren, as I did not possess with perfect purity this true knowledge and insight into these Four Noble Truths . . . I knew that I had not yet obtained the highest absolute Enlightenment . . . in Brahma's world. . . . Then I knew, brethren, that I had obtained the highest, universal Enlightenment in the world of men and gods. . . . And this knowledge and insight arose in my mind: the emancipation of my mind cannot be shaken; this is my last birth; now shall I not be born again."

Thus, the Blessed One spoke—bringing to mankind a higher light, peace and wisdom than the world had ever known—and we disciples rejoiced in his message: A new Doctrine of Deliverance had been proclaimed; a new Reign of the Law had begun for suffering men and women everywhere; a new system of moral and intellectual training for the eradication of hatred, lust, and ignorance had been given for all generations to come. Of this new life-style of personal serenity, compassion, and indifference to the things that perish and bind men to the cycle of birth and death, a brother disciple later wrote: "As the Blessed One has set going the Wheel of the Law, the earth-inhabiting gods shouted, 'Truly the Buddha has set going at Benares the Wheel of the Law which may not be opposed by any being in the world. . . . Thus, in that moment, in that instant, in that second the great shout reached the Brahma world; and this whole system of 10,000 worlds quaked, was shaken and trembled; and an infinite, mighty light was seen throughout the world.' "

Into that world stirred and shaken by his cosmic presence, the Buddha now sent us out to preach the doctrine which was to become known as the *Dharma,* the "Good Law" or "Right Religion." Announcing that he himself was going first to the General's Village in Uruvela, the Buddha now began forty-five years of constant preaching, teaching, and counseling along the highways and byways of northern India—returning to Benares yearly during the rainy season when the rest of us recollected around him. Stressing the relationship between meditation and wisdom and stressing the sacred Eightfold Path or Middle Way as the sublime truth of the ending of suffering, the Buddha bade us farewell: "Go ye now, O monks, for the welfare of the many, for the benefit of mankind, out of compassion for the world. Preach the doctrine, which is glorious in the beginning, glorious in the middle, glorious in the end, in the spirit as well as in the letter. Proclaim the pure and perfect life. There are beings whose eyes are scarcely covered with dust, but if the doctrine is not preached to them they cannot attain salvation. Proclaim to them a life of holiness. They will understand the doctrine and accept it."

Recalling all this through a self-hypnosis, age-regression technique which enables me to relive the events of a previous incarnation, I am happy to report these dramatic beginnings of Buddha's mission for the first time. Recording on twentieth-century, 1⅞ two-speed Sony tape the historic happenings and inspired words of that first Reformation, I am privileged not only to pay overdue tribute to one of the noblest edifices of human thought, but also to show how its creative influence affects man's arts and sciences even today. Preaching and practicing a new religion which stressed human rationality, renunciation and compassionate service rather than ritualistic idol-worship and a preoccupation with paradises to come, the Lord Buddha brought to men and women long before Christ a sense of their individual worth and eventual salvation. Long before Christ too, this towering Oriental teacher—this prince turned pauper turned God-man—developed his religion of faith, austerity and good works as a Middle Way of personal perfection. "Be ye lamps unto yourselves," he told his followers, "work out your own salvation with diligence."

Venerated in his own time, worshipped throughout the ages, followed today by 500 million believers, the Buddha began life auspiciously as the son of a Hindu king in what is now the Nepalese town of Lumbini. The obscure place was a tiny kingdom in the High Himalayas. The year was 563 B.C.—a mysterious time when also appeared on earth such other titans as Confucius and Lao-Tse in China, Plato and Heraclitus in Greece and Jeremiah and Isaiah in Israel. By birth a member of the warrior caste and brought up in princely luxury in not one, but three, palaces, the young Guatama lived a life of sports and sensuous pleasures, of music and flowers, wine and dancing girls. Hear this playboy prince of Old Asia as he speaks to us: "I was tenderly cared for, brethren. At my father's home lotus pools were made for me . . . in one place for blue lotus flowers, in one place for white lotus flowers and in one place for red lotus flowers—all blossoming for my sake. Day and night a white umbrella was held over me, so that I might not be troubled by cold, heat, dust, chaff or dew. . . . As a youth, I had three palaces, one for the cold season, one for the hot season and one for the season of rains. Through the four rainy months, in the palace of the rainy season, entertained by female minstrels, I did not come down from the palace. . . ."

Like other aristocratic lads of ancient India, Guatama excelled in sports, especially riding and archery. Despite the objections of his rajah father who strove mightily to shield him from the world, he often mounted his chariot and galloped beyond the palace gates into the picturesque countryside. He also took part frequently in royal archery tournaments, and it was in an archery contest at age nineteen that he won the affections of his beautiful cousin, Yasodhara, who became his bride. During the next decade Guatama and his comely queen had a son, traveled to neighboring kingdoms, lived in regal splendor and domestic bliss. But to the mystical-minded heir to the Sakiya throne, something was missing—*true happiness*. More and more, too, as he related to us disciples after his conversion, the misery of man troubled him. For example, on one of his chariot drives to a favorite pleasure-park he was shocked by the sight of an old man tottering along the roadside, on another occasion by the sight of a man crippled by disease, on still another trip by a sight of a corpse decomposing in a ditch; months later he saw a Hindu *sadhu* or holy man walking in a calm detached manner and, asking who he was, was told by his charioteer, Channa, the career and character of India's mendicant wanderers and ascetic teachers who play such an integral part in the sub-continent's social life. Sickness, old age, death —what a trinity to plague the life of man!—so mused the future savior in his palace gardens.

Thus introduced to the sad frailties and inevitable suffering of the human condition, the young *rajput* began an agonizing self-appraisal comparable to the retreat of Jesus in the desert when the Christ was tempted by the Prince of Darkness. In the light of the torment suffered by millions of his fellowmen, Guatama thought, what avails the crown and the pomp of power? What permanent good can even a benevolent king bring to his subjects? What avails either victories in war or peace when both victor and vanquished soon follow the same pathway to the grave? On the other hand, there must be some undiscovered way of salvation, some unchartered pattern of life which might free men from their grievous burdens of pain and frustration, sickness and death. Finally, in one of humanity's most momentous decisions—in line with a seer's prediction to his father, King Suddhodana, that his son would become a savior of the world—Prince Siddhartha made his irrevocable choice: to give up all that he loved most, his wife, child, father, crown, wealth and love of his future subjects to become a homeless monk and penniless wanderer. In the spirit of Hindu renunciation, he resolved to solve the mighty riddle of life and vowed to dedicate his life to the liberation of mankind.

So began the *Sutra* of the Great Renunciation. In the time-honored narrative of the Buddha's life, we now come upon this dramatic scene: the young prince, aged twenty-nine, is stealing in the night toward his young wife's bedchamber. She and his infant son are lying asleep there, and he tiptoes to the bed to take a last look at them. He dares not touch either for fear of waking them. That might interfere with his purpose which is now fixed and decided. He would go forth into the world, to what holy men and ascetics in his country called the homeless life, to try to solve the problem of human misery.

Is there any way to escape from the human scourges of sickness, old age, and death? The answer to that is what he must set himself to seek. He leaped upon his horse Kanthaka, accompanied only by his charioteer, Channa, rode out of the palace gates and left his native city, Kapilavastu, behind him. After traveling a certain distance, he changed his garments, donned the yellow robe of the ascetic, and lost himself in the immemorial roads and bypaths of India.

For the next six years, his head shaved, begging bowl in hand, the saffron *dhoti* of a monk about him, the future Buddha sought life's supreme answers walking the plains, fording the rivers, visiting the deerparks of India. He sat at the feet of famed gurus; he lived the life of a simple student studying the sacred texts of Hinduism; he practiced the severest penance and self-torture until, emaciated and near starvation, he gained his first five disciples and his fame as an ascetic filled the countryside, (in the words of a contemporary chronicler) "like the sound of a great bell hung in the canopy of the skies." But neither the teaching of the sages nor mortification of the flesh provided the key to liberation and Guatama came to see that it profitted the Creator nothing when, as he put it, "the bones of my spine, when bent and straightened, were like a row of spindles because of little food. . . . If one could attain perfection and liberation from the bonds which tie man to earth only through the renunciation of food and normal human conditions, then a horse or a cow would have reached it long since." Alone, agonizing, abandoned by his friends, he seated himself at last under the sacred bodhi tree and vowed he would not move until death or the secret of enlightenment came to him. In still another parallel to the temptation of Jesus in the wilderness, one final ordeal awaited him: in a meditative vision, the armies of the world's evil tempter, Mara, attacked him with a fiery rain of rocks, spears, and blazing weapons. The devil himself offered him the wealth of the world if he would quit his high quest. But, resisting the satanic temptations and pointing to the earth beneath him as a symbol of his steadfastness, Siddhartha sat unmoved; at last, the armies of Mara fled.

The teaching of *Dharma* or "right religion," with its moral training, mind control, meditation techniques and constant admonitions to overcome selfishness, anger, avarice, deceit, ill-temper, treachery, and low desire, became the Wheel of the Law, from the beginning. "People are in bondage," the Buddha often told us, "because they have not yet overcome the idea of 'I'." The noble Eightfold Path is central to Buddhism because in its practice lies one's liberation from egotism, craving, cruelty, selfishness, jealousy, spite, illusion, and all attachment to what Hindus of his time called *Maya,* the world of everyday appearances or sensory shadows around us. Right Knowledge, Right Mindfulness, and Right Meditation are emphasized just as fully in the Eightfold Path as Right Intention, Right Conduct, and Right Livelihood because it is these severe mental disciplines and mystical practices which free men from body-bound bondage and lead to a life of good works and inner peace. Ultimately, for the good Buddhist of 2000 years ago *and* of the twentieth century who follows the Middle Way between asceticism and self-indulgence, there shines the crest and crown of the spiritual way—the experience of Nirvana, the blissful discovery of the supreme Self, that egoless, wordless illumination which dispels all ensnaring sensuous perceptions and which lifts the purified consciousness into union with the Divine. For the earnest seeker of every age, this direct experience of Reality must form the very center of the Eightfold Path, and every earnest seeker can be encouraged in his quest because Buddha himself attained to this all-liberating, love-lighted bliss. In his own timeless language he calls to us today: "Let us live happily, then, free from hatred among men who hate. Let us live happily, then, free from care among the busy-busy. Let us live happily, then, free from ailments among the ailing. Let us live happily, then, free from craving among men who are anxious. Let us live happily, then, though we call nothing our own. Let us live like the bright gods feeding on happiness!"

In order to help men and women to practice meditation and the virtues necessary to illumination, Buddha encouraged the formation of communities for the study of the Good Law and the preparation of their minds for what he called in his first sermon "almsgiving, morality, heaven." Monastic life—and the exemplary conduct of the monks in inspiring laymen to stricter and saintlier living—became an outstanding feature of Buddhism as happened again in the medieval stages of Christianity. Thus, the three most eminent and enduring aspects of the Buddhist religion are: (1) the promethean personality of the Buddha who brought to all men the light of salvation; (2) *Dharma,* the Good Law and noble Eightfold Path pointing the way to self-realization; (3) the *Shangha* or brotherhood of the monks who have guarded the truths and traditions of the faith to this day. Thus, too, there endures the famous Buddhist profession of faith, which corresponds to the Christian credo and which has been repeated daily by billions of human beings for nearly twenty-five centuries: "I take my refuge in the Buddha. I take my refuge in the Law. I take my refuge in the Brotherhood."

But, perhaps Buddhism's most profound and perplexing doctrine is its mystical essence of Nirvana. For the teachings of the blessed Tathagatha are no mere dustbin of petty prescriptions and joyless laws of conduct. Rather, to the spiritual freeholder and adventurous devotee, they become the living waters of the Spirit and an exciting call to the nobler virtues of love, joy, and ecstatic meditation. If Buddhism can be summarized as a philosophy of salvation which warns its followers of excessive addiction to "the things of this world" and which provides a practical science for freeing men from this deluding shadow-show, it is also one of mankind's most beautiful expressions of the mystical way leading to personal enlightenment and "the fulness of the Void." Here, the disciplined practice by both Buddhist monks and laymen of Right Effort, Right Mindfulness, and Right Concentration—what the Christian mystic, Brother Lawrence, 2000 years later was to describe as "the practice of the presence of God"—lifts the disciple eventually to a direct "seeing into his own nature and the attainment of Buddhahood." Not by books, bans, preachings, prohibitions, disputations, or theories is the heavenly kingdom gained; rather it is gained by those flashes of intuition and peak experiences of transcendental Reality which the seers of all faiths know. This personal attainment of Nirvana or cosmic consciousness was undoubtedly what Buddha referred to when he said: "Mindfulness is the way of immortality; heedlessness is the way of death."

Indeed, Zen itself—the most mystical and austere of Buddhist doctrines—inspires its followers to seek the truth in meditation, service and intuitive revelation. Zen devotees strive for self-realization through simplified living and silent contemplation; its spiritual training, centered in the master's awareness of a timeless Self slumbering within our everyday selves, aims for that spontaneous awakening or Buddha-knowledge which reveals the divine Ground of existence; dying to petty ego and living to eternal Spirit, the mystic sooner or later develops a cosmic sense and comes at last to "behold but One in all things." So, in a lovely legend preserved in the sacred *Sutras*, the Buddha is approached one day by a disciple who gives him a golden flower and asks that he explain its secret to the world. Instead of a sermon or metaphysical speculation, the Buddha held the flower gently in his hands and gazed at it in silence, indicating to all who had the wit to understand that the secret lay not in words but in contemplation of the flower itself. So, the "teacher of gods and men" himself said: "Without knowledge there is no meditation, without meditation there is no knowledge; he who has knowledge *and* meditation is near unto Nirvana."

Herewith, in my view, rests Buddhism's ever-growing appeal in our own time. For, it is a fact that twentieth-century Buddhism has flowered anew, renewing itself in its roots, sending forth its modern message to peoples everywhere, becoming again the fastest growing religion in the world. In fact, the Lord Buddha who became the light of Asia shines more brightly today for more millions of human beings than ever before in history. Whereas Buddhism is a pure ethical and psychological religion —without priestly intermediaries and encumbering theological baggage —it attracts the world's new wave of youth who, often rejecting doctrinaire Christian churches as part of the Western Establishment, seek to follow their own spiritual way and find in Zen Buddhism a faith that fulfills. Whereas Buddhism postulates an evolving universe of non-mechanical forces, ever-higher harmonies and what the *Sutra Scriptures* call the pervading "Store Consciousness," it also attracts the world's pace-setting scientific community which in this century has constructed a boundaryless, space-time continuum surprisingly akin to Zen's "splendid Void." Buddha himself, although profoundly subtle in his references to deity and deliberately negative to all requests for a detailed description of the divine, nonetheless refers repeatedly to the infinite in the finite as Universal Mind or the Buddha-womb. Stressing the oneness of the Atman inner Self and the Brahman universal Self, Buddha affirms in the Third Patriarch of Zen:

> When the deep mystery of divine Suchness is fathomed,
> All of a sudden we forget the external entanglements;
> When the ten thousand things are viewed in their oneness,
> We return to the origin and remain where we have always been. . . .
> One in all, All in one—
> If only this is realized, no more worry about not being perfect!

Our seeking young people—the restless flower-children, unchurched believers, far-ranging heralds of the Aquarian Age—especially identify with a master Teacher who views the "ten thousand things in their oneness," cherishes all life in a conscious spirit of reverence and lovingly leads them on the Eightfold Path to a unitive knowledge of God. When the young followers of Zen practice Buddha's contemplative disciplines and compassionate life-style, they often develop that liberation from things and insight into their own Buddha-nature which they seek. When they perfect the *Dhyana's* one-pointed contemplation and come to that conscious discrimination between the petty ego and the divine Self, they often experience that radical "change of mind" which enables them to see the One in all things and attain personal peace. At the very least, under Zen's demanding authority, they walk the razor's edge of spirituality even while living a sacramental life in the world; at the very peak where individual illumination and God's grace coincide, they become *Bodhisattvas* (beings destined for enlightenment) who master the supraphysical in its fulness and, pure in heart and humble in spirit, realizes what Buddha calls the Divine Suchness.

> In the root divine Wisdom is all-Brahman;
> In the stem she is all-Illusion;
> In the flower she is all-World;
> And in the fruit, all-Liberation.

Complementing world youth's devotion to modern Buddhism is the scientific community's admiration of Buddhist thought. The basic reason for this surprising admiration is that modern science now constructs a universal cosmology vividly similar to Buddha's undifferentiated Divine Suchness. For example, when nuclear physics posits a world of non-causal, non-mechanical energy fields, exact science reflects the ultimate reality which Buddha described as the "Light of the Void." For example, when parapsychology today speaks of mind-in-action as the first and final law of the universe, philosophers are only confirming the Buddha's earlier intuition that "the visible world is nothing but a manifestation of Universal Mind." In sum, what the Einsteins, Plancks, Paulis, Millikans, Jeans, Bohrs, DeBroglies, Heinsenbergs, and Rutherfords of our century discovered to be an integral order of nature brimming with mental essences and conscious energies, Buddha experienced as timeless Reality or Nirvana—the Bliss, Knowledge, Existence Absolute—behind the phenomenal world around us. As Aldous Huxley has pointed out, "The Buddhism of the Far East, more systematically perhaps than any other religion, teaches the way to spiritual knowledge in its fulness as well as in its heights—and that knowledge embraces the visions of art and the constructs of science."

Thus, in the Twentieth Century, the renowned Danish physicist-philosopher Hans Oersted, who first demonstrated the essential relationship between electricity and magnetism, could write: "The universe is a manifestation of infinite reason, and the laws of nature are the thoughts of God." And yet 2500 years before him, the enlightened Indian prophet, Tathagatha, who encouraged believers to reach "highs" of consciousness far beyond ordinary awareness could affirm: "If the Mind retains its absoluteness, the ten thousand things are known to be one substance. . . . There is an unborn, an unoriginated, an uncompounded; were there not, O monks, there would be no escape from the world of the born, the originated, the made and the compounded."

Where the eminent British scientist, Sir Arthur Eddington boldly proclaimed in the 1940's, "The final stuff of the universe is mind's stuff," the Buddha declared in the sixth century B.C.: "These ignorant ones cling to a notion of Nirvana that is outside what is seen of the senses. They are not aware that Universal Mind and Nirvana are one, that this life-and-death world we are now in and Nirvana are not to be separated." Obviously, there is here a striking identity of vision and rare similarity in philosophy between an ancient religion that expounds a spiritual supra-cosmic reality and a modern science which has not only demolished the last remnants of nineteenth century materialism but today recognizes the real as a unified harmonious force field where Mind is paramount.

Similarly, Buddha, who in his teaching of love, compassion, selflessness and the mystical way, preached much the same doctrine as Jesus, became 500 years before him a "Brother of the Radiant Summit." Where Jesus spoke of the true light, Buddha spoke of the true path. What Christ called the Kingdom of Heaven, Buddha identified as Nirvana, or "the highest happiness." The power St. Paul ascribed to Christ when he was "caught up into paradise," heard "unspeakable words" and beheld "heavenly visions," Buddha recognized when he declared his Noble Truths were not doctrines handed down, but that "there arose within him the eye to perceive them, the knowledge of their nature, the understanding of their cause, the wisdom that lights the true path, the light that expels the darkness." Jesus, who became the Christ, and Guatama, who became the Buddha, both began their preaching missions at the age of thirty, both experienced supernatural insight or cosmic consciousness, both attained to what Christ treasured as the "peace that passes understanding" and Buddha as "emancipation of heart and emancipation of mind." Of this moving Spirit and its powers, Buddha said it "will cause a man to become beloved, popular, respected among his fellows, victorious over discontent and lust, spiritual danger and dismay; will bestow upon him the ecstasy of contemplation; will cause him to become an inheritor of the highest heavens; will endow him with a clear and heavenly ear . . . and a pure and heavenly vision surpassing that of other men."

In a word, Buddha believed in God. Although the master teacher discouraged metaphysical speculation and wisely resisted attempts to elicit his definition of deity, he revealed in word and deed his awareness of an infinite spiritual reality. Far from denying the existence of God as alleged a century ago by self-serving rationalists, materialistic scientists and even sincere students who misread the difficult Palli texts, Buddha constantly alludes to a transcendent and immanent divine Power—that Hindu-held Brahman who not only rules over the created universe of forms but also becomes the formless essence present in all separate beings. Indeed, for Buddha, it was the Cosmic Self within the individual self that made Nirvana possible; indeed, for Buddha, the ambrosial fruits of Nirvana, inherited by a man made perfect through the study and practice of the Good Law, meant the extinction of the ordinary, unenlightened sinful state of mind and heart and its replacement by a blissful holy state, here and now, characterized by perfect peace, wisdom, and love.

Acquiring this Buddhist *summum bonum* in this lifetime, a human being thereafter, "walks in the knowledge of the Good Law." Entering a new life of joy, freedom, and exalted intelligence while still on earth, a man or woman thereafter knows that "all things are equal" . . . that "every living creature is holy" . . . that "what is most needed is a loving heart!" Above all, Buddha said, "There is no real Nirvana without all knowingness (cosmic consciousness); ever try to reach this." His last admonition to his followers, "Live ye as those who have the Atman as lamp and Atman as refuge" did not mean that man was to attain liberation through the dedicated use of only his personal powers, but rather by following the Law in a complete surrender to spiritual truth or God. Thus, the Good News of Buddhism is simply this: there is a state of consciousness so happy, so glorious, so blessed that it is the pearl of great price for which a wise man willingly sells all he has; that Buddhahood or kingdom of God can be achieved in this lifetime. ("One's Buddha is oneself.")

In contrast to Christ's death on the Cross at thirty-three, it was not until the age eighty that the Buddha's long creative life and unique pilgrimage on earth came to an end. We had been on a summer preaching mission in the Ganges Valley and, after his midday meal and a short rest, the Blessed One decreed we should journey on to the town of Kusinara. But, he had not walked far when he was obliged to rest near the banks of the Kukushta River; he bathed for the last time and, lying down under several Sal trees with his face toward the south, he asked for a drink of water and then began to talk earnestly to me about his burial, his philosophy and the direction of the brotherhood after his death. Toward the end of the conversation, which I recall under hypnosis today as vividly as if it were yesterday, I suddenly felt that my beloved teacher was dying and began to weep. But, with loving eyes he comforted me with the promise of Nirvana and repeated what he had often said about the impermanence of all things: "O Ananda! Do not weep; do not let yourself be troubled. You know what I have said; sooner or later, we must part from all we hold most dear. This body of ours contains within itself the power which renews its strength for a time, but also the causes which lead to its destruction. Is there anything on earth which shall also not dissolve? But you too, Ananda, shall be free from this delusion, this world of sense, this law of change.

"Beloved," he continued speaking to the rest of the disciples, "there is only one way to the true wisdom, the way that is laid down in my Eightfold Path. Many have already followed it and, conquering the lust, pride, and anger of their own hearts, have become free from ignorance and doubt and wrong belief, have entered the calm state of universal kindliness and have reached Nirvana even in this lifetime. O brethren, I do not speak to you of things I have not experienced. Since I was twenty-nine years old until now, I have striven after pure and perfect wisdom and, following that good path, I have found Nirvana. . . ."

Toward morning the Buddha spoke again, urging us to reverence one another and asking whether anyone harbored any doubts about the Buddha, the Law and the Society. When no one answered, he laid stress on the final perserverance of the saints and said that even the least among the disciples, who had entered on the first path and still had his heart fixed on the ways to perfection would become a *Bodhisattva* or being on his way to Enlightenment. After another pause, he said: "Brethren, this is my exhortation to you. When I have passed away and am no longer with you, do not think that the Buddha has left you. I am still in your midst. You have my words, my explanations of the deep things of truth, the laws that I have laid down for the Society. Let them be your guide; the Buddha has not left you."

Just before the end when he closed his eyes and slipped into unconsciousness, I asked one final question. "Master, if you had to summarize your message to mankind in one word, what would that one word be?"

The Buddha remained silent for a long time, but at last he spoke in a surprisingly strong, sweet voice: "That word is *Now*."

Roland Gammon, religion author, lecturer and communications specialist, who has been a writer-editor on *Life Magazine* and other national periodicals since 1946, is author of the Harper book on the world's great living religions, *Truth Is One*, and the E. P. Dutton bestseller on American leaders, *Faith Is A Star*. President of Editorial Communications, an international public relations firm, he also serves as religion editor of the North American Newspaper Alliance which reaches 200 newspapers.

Mr. Gammon's most recent book, *All Believers Are Brothers*, was published in 1971 by Doubleday and Company. It is a study of the world's great living leaders in government, culture, religion, and the arts with special emphasis on their philosophy of life. *A God for Modern Man*, another of Gammon's inspirational volumes, was published in September 1968 by the Sayre Ross Company and distributed nationally by Random House, Inc. Praised by critics as a brilliant study of the growing unity between science and religion, the book has especially impressed young people groping for a meaningful philosophy of life.

Mr. Gammon, who has led various interfaith tours of Europe and Asia, today is a writer of religious articles for *The Reader's Digest, Redbook, This Week, Good Housekeeping, Parade, Pageant, McCall's, Unity, Unitarian Universalist World, Christian Century, Variety,* etc. A graduate of Colby College and Oxford University, he is a member of Phi Beta Kappa, Kappa Delta Rho, The Overseas Press Club, Society of Magazine Writers, Religious Newswriters Association, American Veterans Committee, the World Congress of Faiths and The Temple of Understanding, Washington, D.C. He served with the U.S. Army Air Forces in the Middle East and Asia during World War II. President of the National Association of Unitarian Universalist Men from 1958 to 1962, he today is dean of the Universalist Unitarian Church of New York City.

The Resurrection of Christ

As reported by WILL OURSLER

—Riots have broken out in Jerusalem today following reliable reports that a convicted heretic, crucified last Friday, has been seen this morning on the city streets, apparently alive and well.

Known as Jesus of Nazareth, the heretic is said to have had unusual "gifts" of healing and even to restore dead people to life. Over the last several years, he has attracted many followers, mostly ill-kempt, unemployed, and without funds.

Accounts of the "resurrection" have aroused widespread anger. Some local citizen groups are already said to be hunting down supporters of the new cult. Reliable sources now claim that many followers of this Jesus have gone into hiding.

Search of the homes of persons known to be associated with the radical movement is in progress and a round-up of many, of the so-called "Christians" is underway.

Some of the "disciples" who were intimate associates of this Jesus are said to have found refuge in the homes of local "believers" who refer to Jesus as the "son of God."

This reporter talked at length today with one of the most important disciples, a rough, blunt man who formerly went by the name of Simon but who now calls himself Peter.

As I began asking him about Jesus of Nazareth and the extraordinary events of the past three days, the Christian became agitated and cried out angrily, "I tell you I don't know this Jesus. Never even met him. Don't know who he is."

The towering man then rushed past me and lost himself in the crowds and pack animals thronging Jerusalem streets.

One report heard in the city, however, claims that this same Peter alias

Simon declared to Jesus at a supper with other disciples, the night before the execution, "I will lay down my life for your sake."

Jesus is said to have replied with his now familiar candor, "The cock will not crow till you have denied me three times."

By coincidence, it is reported that this disciple Peter did deny knowing Jesus on three occasions earlier today as authorities were trying to round up other supporters of this radical sect.

Perhaps the most extraordinary episode to date occurred at the site of the tomb itself where the body of Jesus was interred and a stone placed before the entrance.

The body, according to witnesses, was wound in linen cloth with spices, the proper manner in which a Jew is buried.

This was a new sepulchre in which no body had ever been placed previously, situated in a garden, close to where Jesus was put to death by crucifixion. Two other felons were crucified alongside of Jesus on charges of thievery.

Early this morning, a woman known as Mary Magdalene, said to have been a common prostitute until converted to the teachings of Jesus, went to the tomb and discovered that the stone had been rolled away and the body of the crucified man was gone.

The woman ran to notify Simon Peter and the other disciples of what had happened. Peter came at once to the tomb. All he reported finding were the linens—strewn on the ground—in which Jesus had been wrapped.

The body of Jesus was gone. The woman Mary Magdalene was reported to have been standing outside the tomb, sobbing. She then stepped down, still weeping, and looked into the sepulchre. It was at this point that the first alleged "miracle" reportedly occurred. Piecing together the basic information, the chronology follows:

Most of the disciples went away from the tomb—apparently aware of the personal danger they were all facing as a result of these occurrences.

The woman Mary Magdalene remained. According to her statement, as she peered into the sepulchre where the body of Jesus had been placed, she saw two white figures, one at the head, the other at the feet.

One of these figures—described by her as "angels"—is said to have asked her why she was crying. She answered that they had taken away "my Lord" and she had no idea "where they have placed him."

It was then, the woman claimed, that she saw standing in front of her the figure of Jesus himself.

Assertedly, believing him to be the gardener and, still searching for the body of Jesus she is said to have asked this man: "Sir, if you have taken him from here, please tell me where you have taken him. I wish to claim his body."

The resurrected figure of Jesus is then reported to have said to her one single word: "Mary."

Mary recognized the man as Jesus and cried out to him, "Rabboni! (This is a title of highest respect, equivalent to the term, "Master.")

Jesus then gave the former prostitute certain specific instructions, including an order not to touch him "for I am not yet ascended to my Father." He further instructed her, "Go to my brethren, and say unto them, I ascend unto my Father, and your Father, and to my God, and your God."

Mary Magdalene transmitted the information to the disciples in compliance with these orders.

Despite efforts of authorities to break up any meetings of the Christians, an assembly of the group was held in a secret place in the city. All the doors were shut by the disciples for fear of trouble from local police or outraged citizenry who insist that Jesus is preaching an entirely new religion.

Another episode regarding this cult concerns the disciple Thomas, know also by the name Didymus. Use of double names is a common practice with many of these men.

Thomas is considered one of the few if not the only disciple who expressed doubt that Jesus actually had risen from the dead.

A serious rift among these followers themselves very nearly occurred over the doubts of Thomas—despite their dedication to "brotherly love" and their claim they had "seen" the risen Jesus alive after his supposed execution.

All except Thomas accepted the post-crucifixion events as valid. Their spokesmen put in what was virtually a defiant challenge to the entire religious leadership of the city: "We have seen the Lord."

The controversial "Messiah" named Jesus, who claims to have risen from the dead, is now reported to have been present at a meeting held here yesterday behind closed doors.

His disciple known as Thomas, however, who was not with the group when Jesus first appeared, refused to believe the others and informed them bluntly, "Unless I see in his hands the prints of the nails, and put my finger into the prints of the nails, and thrust my hands into his side, I will not believe."

References to his side refers to a severe wound Jesus sustained from the spear of one of the Roman guards on duty at the execution site.

Despite the doubts of Thomas, it is stated on good authority that at the meeting, with all the disciples including Thomas present, Jesus himself did appear.

After giving them the Shalom greeting, "Peace be unto you," Jesus is said to have turned to Thomas and said, "Reach hither thy finger, and behold my hands; and reach hither thy hand and thrust it into my side: and be not faithless, but believing."

The "doubting" Thomas did as Jesus directed. At the completion of his inspection, apparently in shock at his own doubts, Thomas declared, with obvious deep emotion, "My Lord and my God."

Jesus, considered by some the greatest teacher of the new religion, replied to the words of the doubting disciple, "Thomas, because you have seen me, you have believed; blessed are they that have not seen, and yet have believed."

It is also asserted by some that other disciples had doubts about the resurrection, and particularly of seeing and touching the "risen Christ." It is reported that the "risen Jesus" later appeared before the eleven while they were eating and sternly chastised them for what he called "their disbelief and hardness of heart."

Despite this, he did not reject them but rather urged them on with even greater effort "to go into all the world and preach the gospel to every creature."

Religious leaders and scholars doubt that the "Jesus movement" will go very far. "Where do they think they are going with this business of turning the other cheek, giving up your money and following one more deluded preacher to an empty tomb?" one high official demanded.

It appears, however, that thousands, even tens of thousands, are already beginning to accept this teacher as the long-awaited Messiah and these followers say they are ready to give up all their worldly goods and even their lives, families and home, to pursue the teachings of Jesus.

Despite the radicalism of his concepts, the ideas are taking hold, not only among the young but also among older people and some in high office. Some believe there is a strength that might be overwhelming in the simple teachings of this simple man who died on a cross for a creed of love and brotherhood.

He could indeed become the greatest religious leader of all history— without even a church of his own in which to pray.

Well-informed religious authorities, however, consider such a possibility something that couldn't happen "in two thousand years."

Will Oursler was born in Baltimore, Maryland, raised in New York City, decided to become an artist but gave it up for the greener fields of authorship. He is the author of more than thirty books ranging from crime and murder to religion, ESP and social-action religion.

A *cum laude* graduate of Harvard (B.A.) he began his journalistic career as a reporter on the Hearst papers in Boston, Massachusetts. His articles have appeared widely in popular magazines including *Parade, Reader's Digest, Cosmopolitan* and many others. He is also the author of a number of novels. He is in addition a lecturer and is frequently heard on radio. He is married to the former Adelaide Burr of Brookline, Massachusetts. The Ourslers have one son, William Fulton Oursler, (Bill), also a journalist specializing in action and high speed photography for magazines and news media.

Oursler is also a former President of the Overseas Press Club of America.

The Children's Crusade

As reported by KURT LASSEN

The enigma faced in a contemporary reportage of the Children's Crusade is the paucity of information and the disparities found in the meager sources of research. This is partly explained by the fact that literacy, by and large, existed only in the church and, more rarely in the courts of royalty. It is understandable, therefore, that the exploits of kings and lords was well documented for history. Such details as the number of men, types of weapons, lengths of marches, casualties inflicted and received and even the speeches of the leaders to the warriors were dutifully recorded. Often the record was carefully kept by the retinue of men of the Church who accompanied these crusades.

Not so the details of the Children's Crusades, the two largest of which formed in Germany and France. The disappearance of almost 50,000 young people, fired by an almost fanatical religious zeal, became but a footnote in history. The formation of these Crusades understandably caused great dissension in thousands of families and hundreds of communities. The Church was often embarrassed by the existence of hordes of children walking through towns and villages on their way to the Holy Land to rescue Christendom from the Saracens.

At times they were cheered and praised for their dedication and determination as well as their faith. More often, however, they were ridiculed and victimized while their suffering was viewed with utter disinterest. So it is that today huge, two-volume tomes on the Crusades devote at most only a chapter to these disastrous events. Most scholarly reference works provide but a paragraph. Scores of romantic children's tales have been written on the subject making fictional heroes of the pitiful young people who found death or enslavement on foreign soil.

The fascinating parallel, however, between these medieval events and

those of contemporary times make reconstruction of the scene both possible and plausible. Alienation from parents and the establishment combined with the emergence of young hero figures and the search for an
alternative, whatever that alternative might be, create a mood which
serves to stimulate a reporter to take the known facts and transport himself back seven centuries in time.

To the extent that one can evaluate the meager material available
this is a report as one might have written it were the tragic events to
have occurred today. Inherent in this reportage are Haight-Ashbury,
Newport, The Beatles, flower children, Jesus freaks, Watkins Glen, the
drug culture, the coffins from Vietnam and a society caught up in these
events. A society which is seemingly powerless to stop them or is more
attuned to the hectic complexities of modern life than it is to the weary
shuffling of young feet towards death or enslavement.

Stephen of Cloyes did attract some 30,000 followers and march to
Marseilles. Nicholas gathered some 20,000 young people at Cologne and
only a mere 2,000 managed to struggle back through the Alps from Italy.
A Friar Anthony did return 18 years after his enslavement to give his
account of the sad, debasing betrayal of the children and their Crusade.

This reporter traveled back seven centuries in time to accompany
Stephen on the March to Marseilles, to huddle with the dispirited young
people in the cold mountains and to interview Friar Anthony on his
return from Cairo.

INTERVIEW OF THE WEEK: STEPHEN OF CLOYES

The heavily perspiring, tired horses plod slowly along the hot, dusty
road. In the carriage beneath the canopy to shield him from the merciless
summer heat Stephen of Cloyes gazes out on the multitude of young
people, most no more than twelve years old, who crowd close to the
vehicle to see their hero, to touch the carriage and, perhaps, even to
reach up and touch his garment or his person. Pieces of his garment
have been torn away and are jealously guarded by those who have had
the good fortune to be so blessed.

Eventually the intense, almost hypnotic brown eyes turn their attention back into the carriage. "Hear that! Hear that! They're singing 'The
Seas Will Open' . . . and open they will! What the kings and knights
have failed to do in the name of power we shall do in the name of faith.

It is a mandate from Christ. How can the Saracens fail to fall before such devotion? Do you know that since we left Vendome we have grown to 30,000 strong?"

Stephen speaks not as to an interviewer, but as if he is addressing the multitudes gathered together to march to the port of Marseilles. At fourteen there is a mystic, power-filled quality to this shepherd boy from Cloyes. If it were not for the thirsty, hungry, shabby line of young people, many even now dropping by the wayside, one could expect that perhaps a miracle inspired by his magnetic mysticism might come to pass.

"The king," Stephen almost spat the word. "The king. I traveled to St. Denis but King Philip had left for Paris. I walked to Paris and they couldn't refuse me an audience. When I told him I had a mandate from Christ he smiled a smile that was almost a laugh and told me, 'Go home, little boy, go home.' If he could only see me, see us now!"

Stephen's missive from Christ, it is reported, came to him by way of a bedraggled, dusty, barefoot Franciscan monk who had stopped along the road in Cloyes for a drink of water. He talked to Stephen while the boy was tending sheep. "The rich and the mighty," he said, "were desecrating the Church in the name of the cross in Jerusalem. Only the innocent and the pure in heart could save it. Only the young are innocent and pure in heart."

The words kindled a fire in the heart of Stephen. Strongly, almost fanatically religious, he took the message from the monk to be a message from Christ himself. Children armed only with the cross would rescue the Holy Land from the Saracens. The very seas would part, or, like Christ, the children would walk upon the water to accomplish their mission. The monk told Stephen that for those who joined in the quest for the true Cross there would be a place in heaven and a place for their parents and for their parents before them. It was these promises which had convinced Stephen's religiously zealous parents. He was, they were sure, indeed the chosen one.

"Our meeting place was the Cathedral at Vendome," Stephen told us. "We gathered by the thousands. We sewed a cross on the front of our clothing and when we return victorious we shall place it on our backs as a sign of victory. At first we gathered only the poor, but as we made our way from Vendome we gathered many of the rich. The parents even came out to cheer us as we began our trip to Marseilles.

"Those whose parents are not for Christ tried to hold back their children, but there was no holding them and our numbers grew; boys and girls and even some older people who walk along the edges just to be a part of this new resurrection."

Why a carriage for Stephen while thousands of his disciples walked? "My mission is a high one," he explains. "One of our number is the son of a Count who gave me the carriage. For me as the leader there will be much for me to do. I sit here to search my soul for the strength and dedication Christ has asked me to give to our Crusade."

A girl of no more than 14 manages to break through the close barrier Stephen's supporters have built with their bodies around the carriage. "Stephen, Stephen, blessed Stephen," she cries, "let me but be blessed by thee, let me but touch your sleeve to give me the strength I shall need."

Stephen turns, waves his guards away. Deliberately he makes the sign of the cross, extends his arm out the carriage window. Exultantly the girl kisses his hand. "The seas will open," she screams as she runs back into the multitude of children to report her good fortune.

SPECIAL FEATURE:

Disillusioned Young Germans Return from Abortive Crusade

They huddle near the fire to find some measure of comfort from the cold, night, Alpine air. On their faces the flames highlight their defeat and despair. This handful of young Germans is fighting hunger, the bitterness of defeat and the derision of the multitudes who gathered in towns and villages to taunt and stone those they had so heartily cheered only a short time ago.

These pathetic young people are part of approximately 20,000 who first gathered at Cologne to rescue the Holy Land. They and other small, straggling groups add up to some 2000, representing the only survivors to return to their homeland.

"What faith we had," says an 18-year-old boy. "When Nicholas gathered us at Cologne he told us, 'When the Saracens see us, thousands of pius children, they will become Christians at once.' What hope, what faith we had then! We were the lucky ones, I guess, we never managed to find a ship to the Holy Land."

Reluctantly a 16-year-old girl tells her story. "There was this family in Italy that took me in. I thought they were being very kind. I woke up in the night and the man was in my room . . ." she trailed off, then resumed. "I want to go home again but I don't know what my parents will do to me. When I left home I was 14 and innocent. My parents were sure I would die on this Crusade. I told them that they had always told me how to live but that they couldn't tell me how to die. Perhaps," she said with aged bitterness, "it would be better if I had died."

"It was beautiful," says a 17-year-old boy. "There was fire! Nobody thought we would make it, but we did. At Genoa some of those who survived the trip over the Alps got on ships. I continued on to Rome with Nicholas. We finally realized the truth, that we couldn't rescue the cross. But, we became a symbol, we breathed new life into the Crusades. We kept the dream of the Cross alive and the grownups and the Pope began to talk of another attempt to defeat the Saracens."

An obviously educated young man adds, "Yes, remember what the Pope (Pope Innocent III) said? 'These children put us to shame. They rush to recover the Holy Land while we sleep.' I heard from one of the gray friars that the Church is more interested in opening trade than in opening the Holy Land to Christians. There's something wrong in this world . . . ," his voice drifts off on the chill mountain wind that flares the fire.

"Where have all the children gone?" The words occurred to the reporter as he talked to the young people. "What madness, whose madness is sweeping the world? When will they ever change?"

The chill wind stiffens sharply. There are no blankets. Few of the young people have shoes. Most are lightly clad. It is a travel-weary, saddened, disillusioned band that gradually huddles closer and closer to the fire and closer to each other. Wearily in each other's arms they fall into the sleep of an enormous fatigue, dreaming lost dreams.

The heightening wind brings a cold, dry snow swirling from the skies.

INTERVIEW OF THE WEEK: FRIAR ANTHONY

Friar Anthony sits droop-shouldered, dejectedly on a coil of rope on the dock where he has just disembarked from a ship out of Cairo. Eighteen years have passed since he debarked in 1212 with seven shiploads of children on their way to wrest the Holy Land from the Saracens. As he talks his weary, saddened eyes gaze into some distant future or some departed past. He speaks in a passionless, drained monotone.

"When we arrived at Marseilles," he tells us, "we were many, many less than the 30,000 who gathered between Vendome and the seaport. Stephen of Cloyes had not lost his devotion and those who were left had the faith of saints. The waters didn't part and it defied walking upon to that distant shore we all sought.

"Then, there was hope. Two merchants, Hugh the Iron and William the Pig, offered us seven ships to carry us to the fulfillment of our mission. The ships couldn't hold all of us so we left many tearful young Christians weeping on the shore. We prayed for them for they had traveled so many hot, dusty, hungry miles and were left to bless us on our way.

"What joy we felt. What hopes for the completion of God's work! We were small in number, but our strength and faith were a thousand times our number," Friar Anthony continues. "We grieved when two of our ships sank off an island in the Mediterranean. But, those who were lost were with God and had earned the opening of the gates for their families. It was God's will. We continued on."

His shoulders sag further, his eyes search his own distant shores. His tattered garments bear no cross either on the front or on the back. "What then?" he was asked. He gazes off to the rolling sea, crosses himself slowly. "What then?"

"What then?" he repeats, pauses, crosses himself again. "In the middle of the sea we were met by foreign ships, Saracen ships, and we were transferred to them as the merchant ships from Marseilles turned back. We had been sold but we didn't lose faith. We felt this was part of God's design. Christianity would once again possess the cross.

"We finally landed in Algeria still bearing peace in our hands and faith in our hearts." Then, dispassionately, "We were brought to the slave market, sold like cattle. The beautiful young girls, those delightful, free souls were bought first. Then, the strongest of the boys. I was sold to a slave trader and when he found I could read and write he sold me to a man who took me to Egypt and sold me to the Governor. I have served as his secretary until now. He gave me my freedom to be a slave to my memories."

"What of the children?"

"What of the children?" he echoed. "Those who survived were about

12 then, they are now thirty. They were scattered to the winds of the
Near East and down into Africa. Many of the girls as concubine slaves
have changed the colors of the skin and eyes and the features of children
in the courts of the Caliphs. Most of the boys worked till they dropped
from fatigue. Only a very, very few still survive. In Baghdad 18 were
beheaded for refusing to become Moslems. It is said that when they
died they sang 'The seas will open' while making the sign of the cross."

"And Stephen of Cloyes?"

"I saw him taken away from the slave market by a huge eunuch.
I have heard nothing about him to this day. That was 18 years ago. As
he was taken away he turned and looked at me. That look burned my
soul. Then, the Shepherd from Cloyes was gone."

"Where," he was asked, "shall you go now?"

"Where have all the children gone?" he asked.

Kurt Lassen has been editor/writer for "Under Twenty," a syndicated package for Columbia Features for the last 15 years. The columns, primarily for young people, are syndicated in approximately 100
newspapers in the United States and Canada. Writing an "Interview of
the Week" on celebrities on the youth scene he wrote the first syndicated
column on The Beatles in the United States and specializes on the contemporary scene which has kept him in close touch with such phenomena
as the 60's rock scene, the drug culture, drop-outs, career guidance and
the so-called "generation gap."

As a vice-president of Columbia Features, Inc. he concentrates his
efforts in the development of new syndication properties and the syndication of books to dailies.

Born in Denmark he began work for the Gannett Syndicate in 1938
upon graduation from high school, at the same time continuing his education at Rutgers University. Prior to the war he spent almost two years
in Newfoundland as a free-lance stringer.

During the war he served as an intelligence officer in the ETO and
was awarded the Silver Star, Bronze Star, Purple Heart and three
campaign ribbons. Following hostilities he published newspapers and
magazines for the Information Control Division in Munich, Germany.

After the war he spent five years working for *Newsweek* magazine in
their International Editions, traveling around the world. Subsequently

he worked for *McCalls* and *Seventeen* magazines, the latter stimulating his interest and eventual creation of a youth package for newspapers.

He has for the past fifteen years been active in the writing and production of documentary films. He produced the award winning "Step by Step" and wrote and produced the award winning ". . . not by bread alone," a documentary on Puerto Rican culture and heritage. For NASA he wrote and directed "Above the Weather," the story of the early TIROS weather satellite. He wrote and produced a career guidance film for the United Brotherhood of Carpenters, a documentary series with CBS and, under the Kennedy administration, wrote "Light from a Black Box," dealing with the education and training of secondary school-age retardates.

He has lectured widely to youth groups in high schools and colleges.

(The author gratefully acknowledges the research assistance on this chapter by Ms. Beatrice Shnaider.)

The Invention of Printing

As reported by J. BEN LIEBERMAN

Mankind began a new age today, June 24, 1453, when a secret mechanical writing process called letterpress printing was revealed.

Johann Gutenberg of this city is credited by knowledgeable insiders as the inventor, although this has not been officially confirmed. Gutenberg himself has evaded the most persistent efforts of reporters to get any direct quotation from him, not only today but through the years.

Within the book trade and among students of social change, there was sharply divided opinion here about the value and consequences of the invention, ranging from ecstatic praise to fear of it as a "black art." There were even threats of laws to suppress it.

But for the general public, the advent of mechanical writing was unnoticed, because the first known book "off the printing press"—a Donatus Latin grammar, closely resembling the best handiwork of commercial copiers or scribes—is just now being bound into volumes. According to one source, its existence, and thus the existence of printing itself, became known only because a usually discreet book binder was overheard to remark how many sets of lettered sheets he had been given, and how uniform they all looked.

Observers of the spreading Renaissance and the growing general interest in books, ideas and new ways of life saw in the invention a two-fold import:

First, books and other messages can now be produced quickly, inexpensively and accurately. Instead of a book costing the equivalent of a fine city house, it may come down in price to a day's wage. This means the "printed word" inevitably will spread out to educate, inform and influence people everywhere, and provide a voice for the common man in public affairs. This would make it a direct challenge to the power of

Church and kings, and would certainly change the course of history. The consequences in political, economic, social and cultural terms are virtually incalculable.

Second, printing inaugurates a whole new manufacturing principle, "mass production," applicable not only to books but to other products as well, made by machine in identical copies in any quantity. Furthermore, they can be made cheaper, faster and perhaps even better than by hand-crafting. This can mean more material goods and a better life for the common man as well as the nobility and the rich. "Mass production" may change the world's economy beyond recognition.

However, these prospects were not greeted with unanimous enthusiasm today. On the contrary, some cultural leaders foresaw a demeaning of human dignity in the use of "inferior imitations" such as printed books and other mass-produced goods, and a great loss to the culture if the present handcrafted economy succumbed to the competition of technology. "Letting personal greed force shoddy goods onto the public must be resisted," a major producer of manuscript books declared, "even if it takes some new kind of law to cope with this peril of the Devil."

Because the printed Donatus looked so much like a handwritten copy, some scribes even charged that Gutenberg deliberately intended to pass off his "meager substitute as the real thing." The inventor's defenders replied that he was simply using the lettering of the time, and that the quality appearance of the printing really proved his point.

The craft guilds, and especially the scribes' guild, deplored the loss of jobs that could result from the incursions of new technology in the book-making field and the threat of extending the mass-production philosophy to other present craft industries. Just what action they might take was not made public.

Among scholars generally, the importance of printing has been immediately connected with the unsettling news reports which are now reaching here from Constantinople after the fall of the Byzantine Empire and the death of Emperor Constantine XI Dragases in combat on May 29. Reliable dispatches state that while intellectual activities in that city are disrupted and the great libraries destroyed, many hundreds of Greek scholars are fleeing with their most important manuscripts.

The availability of printing, so Mainz scholars said today, means that these manuscripts can now be reproduced in quantity and given wide distribution, a development that should help spur the current humanistic revival of ancient learning. And the success of printing should guarantee that the manuscript losses at Constantinople, while not as great a blow to the Western cultural heritage as the destruction of the library at Alexandria in classical times, will be the last time civilization will be so hurt, because copies of great works will be so scattered as to defy all efforts to destroy them.

In fact, the more enthusiastic scholars here believe that libraries will in due course proliferate beyond any prior dreams, so that some day even small cities will have printed resources dwarfing the greatest manuscript collections of today.

Johann Gutenberg shields his invention and business in as much secrecy as possible, presumably to protect himself from imitators and potential competitors in the absence of patent laws as yet. Characteristically, he was unavailable today for comment. His office said he was away, "celebrating his birthday," and he could not be located by would-be interviewers.

Apparently, he is destined to go down in history as an elusive genius. A most diligent search of all available records reveals no statement he has ever made. However, enough can be pieced together about Gutenberg's personal history to indicate that he was in effect born to be the inventor of printing and has worked hard to bring to fruition a major step forward for mankind.

This is the opinion of experts who know his background. They say, for instance, that probably no one could have put together the letterpress printing process—at this point in time—who did not have first-hand knowledge of metalworking and coin-making; who did not have an aristocrat's interest and taste in manuscript books and art; who did not have an independent income to enable him to invest both his time and money in the laborious, painstaking and painfully slow experimentation involved, and who did not come along in a period when the market for books was expanding beyond the capacity of scribes to produce and when the logical printing medium, paper, was for the first time available in quantity in Europe.

Gutenberg fits all these requirements. No one else is known who does.

The inventor, whose full name is Johann Gensfleisch zur Laden zum Gutenberg, is a member of the once-powerful Gensfleisch family of Mainz, patricians owning choice real estate throughout the city. He shortened his name in the custom of the times, "Gutenberg Hof" being the particular family mansion in which he was reared. ("Gutenberg" translates as "Good Mountain," of course, and "Gensfleisch" means "gooseflesh.") The founder of the family, Friele Gensfleisch, was a leader of the conservative party of Mainz during the fourteenth century. Pictured as self-willed, pugnacious and physically strong, Friele was once involved in a disturbance over how the rule of the Free City of Mainz should be divided between the aristocratic guilds and the fast-growing tradesmen's associations. Johann Gutenberg is reputed by some to have the founder's characteristics, although others say he is elegant, gracious and good-willed—even idealistic in his belief in the human value of printing.

An uncle of Johann's, Rudolf zum Gensfleisch, was master of the archbishopric mint here for some years, until the patrician families were exiled in 1428. While Johann's name never appeared on the list of "fellow companions of the mint," the privileged group to whom the archbishop entrusted the operation of the mint then, he almost certainly observed the techniques used, including the steel punches that struck off the letters on the dies from which the coins were stamped.

Because Mainz is a center of gold and jewelry crafting, young Gutenberg also had other continuing opportunities to learn about engraving, punching and stamping, alloying and casting, the making of small molds and other skills involved in metal crafts. As a patrician, he could do this without having to serve as an apprentice or journeyman.

It is considered possible, therefore, that Gutenberg first got the basic idea for his printing process as a youth watching operations in the mint and the metal crafts; certainly the elements necessary to the central part of his invention were there.

When the democratic members of the Mainz city council—the tradesmen—gained enough power in the late 1420's to levy stringent taxes against the landed proprietors and to curtail the privileges of the old aristocratic families, Gutenberg was exiled or left voluntarily in protest, and settled in a suburb of Strasbourg, near the Convent of St. Arbogast. At that time, he was in his early thirties, having been born some time in the last years of the fourteenth century.

He was among those invited to return to Mainz in 1430 "upon condition of good behavior," but chose to remain in Strasbourg until the mid-1440's. Annuities from his inherited property holdings in Mainz let him live in appropriate patrician style and still spend considerable amounts on the materials needed for experimentation on the process revealed today.

During most of his exile and since his return, he has apparently concentrated his efforts on his invention and its perfection.

Gutenberg seems never to have married. There is a court record in Strasbourg showing that in 1437 he was sued for breach of promise on behalf of a maiden, Anne of the Iron Door. The details are not public knowledge, but he won the case. However, he used rather abusive language about a shoemaker who was a witness against him in the trial, and for that he was fined fifteen guilders.

Although he is not a recluse—his social activities being appropriate to his station—no known likeness of Gutenberg exists. "Portraits" have been offered showing him with a beard of various kinds, but these obviously were not made by artists who knew him, since as a member of a patrician family he almost certainly is clean-shaven.

In principle, Gutenberg's invention is quite simple, combining a new concept of "interchangeable parts" with the age-old technique of making an impression, as with a monogram seal or even a fingerprint.

Printing as such, in fact, is most easily explained by the fingerprint. The human fingertip has various patterns of tiny ridges standing out "in relief" from the otherwise smooth skin. If these ridges are soiled in some way and the finger pressed down on a clean surface, the image of a pattern is impressed or "printed" on that clean surface. In the same way, a seal with raised or "relief" monogram—carved by cutting away other parts of the surface—is pressed into softened wax, and this leaves an indented monogram impression.

Using the same principle, printing starts with raised or "relief" surfaces. These are covered with ink, and then they are pressed against paper or vellum, so that the ink will transfer to the paper and leave the desired image. Since in Gutenberg's case these are primarily letters which are pressed against the paper, his process is being called "letterpress" printing.

The "interchangeable parts" concept is little more than its name implies. If a monogram seal which reads ABC is carved out of one piece of stone, a gem-cutter would have to start over with a new stone to make a monogram reading CBA. However, if the letters A, B, and C were cut out of separate little stones and fastened together to make the monogram seal, the ABC monogram could be changed easily to one reading CBA simply by moving or interchanging the C and A. Or a letter D could be substituted for the A, B or C if it was "standardized" as to height, size, etc.

Thus, Gutenberg's invention consists of creating in metal a quantity of each letter of the alphabet, in capitals and small letters, perhaps including the new so-called Arabic numerals, plus a supply of different punctuation marks, abbreviations, etc., all called "type," which can be "moved" about or put together as ABC blocks are put side by side, to form words and messages. These are then inked and pressed against paper, and a printed sheet results. "Movable type" is thus considered the crux of the process.

While critics immediately charged that the mechanical printing is an aesthetic and humanistic debasement, other experts pointed to new standards of legibility, readability and accuracy made possible by printing. Not only can the design of a given letter copy the best form of the scribe, but it will reproduce it precisely the same way, in its best form, each time. By contrast, the scribe will—out of haste or boredom or an imperfection of the writing surface—often write letters that are of lesser beauty and sometimes even illegible. Especially, scribes tend to crowd together or stretch out the letters at the end of a line, whereas in printing the letters retain a uniform width. And, of course, the inaccuracy of manuscript copies is legendary, because of all the lapses involved when one reader dictates a manuscript to a whole group of copiers, each hearing in a different (or indifferent) way.

It may in fact have been Gutenberg's study of this difficulty with hand-lettered texts—their lack of uniform quality, legibility, and accuracy—that led him to his invention.

Hand-cutting of letters for woodblocks has the same problem of non-uniformity and illegibility as hand copying. The only answer, therefore, was to make all the same letters from just one raised surface. Gutenberg knew about such a surface from his youth: the steel letter punch used by goldsmiths and bookbinders. And so it might have come to him that the punch could make a die from which many duplicate punches (in effect) could be cast in metal to make printing type.

With this type, a "proof" can be printed and read for errors in spelling, etc. These are simple to correct, and after that the printing process itself guarantees that all copies that are produced will be identically accurate.

However, there is a great deal of difference between inventing a process and perfecting it, and between the simplicity of a concept and the sometimes highly technical means needed to make the concept work. In the case of Gutenberg and letterpress printing, some twenty to twenty-five years seem to have been required to achieve a satisfactory production process and publish the first results.

From scholarly circles, there has come evidence that Gutenberg was not the first to use movable type for printing, although the scholars are certain there is no way Gutenberg could have known of these earlier usages.

The first such use was in China about five hundred years ago, when separate characters were cut from wood and cast in porcelain. Whether independently from the Chinese tradition or not, the Koreans also are reputed to have cast separate characters in bronze, about fifty years ago, and to have printed from them.

However, the difference between the Chinese and Korean calligraphic character system and the present Latin alphabet of twenty-four letters made a crucial difference. The Chinese and Koreans needed literally thousands of different characters, versus the need to produce only about two hundred different characters for the Latin alphabet (including both capital and small letters, punctuation marks, and abbreviations). The cost involved in making all these types, in many duplicates, plus the storage problem of keeping all those thousands of different characters immediately available for setting into place in a text, defeated the advantage of having them available for reuse in other texts. So, the Chinese and the Koreans dropped the movable type concept, and continued their basic process of printing from carved-surface woodblocks.

Perhaps more importantly, from a modern point of view, the Oriental printing was committed to a gummy water-soluble ink much like pen-writing ink. This was ideal for use on woodblocks, to which it adhered and from which it could easily be transferred to porous Oriental papers by rubbing the paper against the blocks to soak up the ink. However, such ink does not adhere to metal or ceramics.

Also, the thin ink soaks not only into the paper but through it, so that the other side cannot be printed on. With the cost of paper and the bulk of books, this is basically uneconomic; true printing must be able to use both sides of a sheet of paper.

What makes all this pertinent today is that Gutenberg did know about this basic Chinese technique of woodblock printing. The block-printing books introduced into Europe about a generation ago are a continuation of that principle, probably carried from the Orient to Europe with the mania for playing cards which were invented in China and printed the same way. These block books are mostly illustrations, with the lettering less than perfectly carved because of the variations of the wood grain.

It was this level of printing, as well as handwriting, that Gutenberg worked to surpass. Letters cut into wood could not be clear and sharp and exact enough to meet the scribes' competition. And like the scribes, the woodcarver was using a hand operation that could not produce what was needed fast enough. Even if he could produce individual letters on small pieces of wood, printing a book like the Bible would require perhaps 120,000 different pieces of type, and the woodcutter would need a lifetime to handcut so many.

As one expert put it, "True printing had to wait 500 years after the invention of movable type in China until a genius could come along to take advantage of the genius of the alphabet itself—which can use twenty-four letters so flexibly as to encompass all thoughts for all time."

Not only among critics poor-mouthing Gutenberg's invention, the question was being asked today, "If Gutenberg did not invent the idea of movable type, or of relief printing, then what *did* he invent?"

Technical experts were answering this in terms of Gutenberg's technological developments as such, primarily an adjustable mold which makes possible the casting of type with all the characteristics needed to print letters that equal or better the letters handcrafted by the best scribes.

That is, the device must insure that each piece of type cast is of the same height and thickness, and yet be of appropriately different width for such letters as i, k and m. The device must also cast and eject a piece of type quickly, and be ready for another casting quickly, to be economical in the cost of labor; it must be simple to operate, not involving great skill (skill being a scarce item, as always); it must be able to withstand an alloy at molten temperature. The resultant type must be absolutely rectangular without shrinking, since otherwise the separate pieces could not be held together snugly, and it must have the image of each letter on an exact "alignment" with all other letters, else the printed line would be wavy and distracting.

Working this out apparently took Gutenberg at least fifteen and more likely twenty years. But without it, his concept of movable type was useless.

However, non-technical observers insist that even so it was Gutenberg's basic conception of a printing *system* that constituted the invention. In their terms, the invention was all the various technical parts in relation to one another in a way that would make each part work completely, to provide the highest quality of lettering quickly, inexpensively, and accurately.

It is the nature of a technological process, they explain, that the machine or system is not usable unless *all* the parts work well, and work together. Therefore, Gutenberg had to bring up all the elements to the same level of performance. If a change must be made in the way one part functions, that change then requires changes in some or perhaps all of the other parts. Thus, for example, the change to metal type required a change to a previously unknown oil-based ink which would stick to the type surface; without such an ink, the whole concept failed. But this ink in turn required a whole new conception as to what kind of pressure must be applied to do the actual printing—because oil ink does not transfer to paper in the same way as thin water-based inks. So a new kind of press had to be adapted from some other use, or invented.

The result is a kind of "mechanical writing" so clearly beyond the combined quality and economic factors of any previous lettering craft, and so flexible for different kinds of use, that it is considered by some experts on communication to be the greatest advance since the invention of the alphabet itself.

Gutenberg is not on record as revealing when and how the concept came to him. However, friends credit him with an orderly mind that draws upon a broad range of craft experience that is unusual in a patrician. Indeed, in a time of specialization when each craft is jealously guarded by its guild from incursions by other crafts, it is considered remarkable that anyone might have such a range of technical knowledge.

Perhaps, one observer suggested today, the secret of the whole enterprise lies in Gutenberg's seeming lack of commitment to any one specialty or craft against another. His economic status was such that he was not bound to the success of one particular craft. He could afford to be interested only in a broader application and result than any one craft could provide. So he used what he could of all the different experiences he had among a variety of specialized crafts. This is reputedly a new "renaissance" quality, although there is no evidence that Gutenberg developed along these lines by any cause except his own inclination. At any rate, Gutenberg has used this new "generalist" approach to invent a whole new principle of manufacture—mechanization—and to perfect the first process under this new principle, true letterpress printing.

Despite today's newsbreak with the revealing of the Donatus, historians may have some trouble unraveling the exact date when the new era of the printed word actually began. In fact, even today's event was the revelation that printing has been accomplished, rather than the actual issue of the book, which could have been weeks or months earlier. This historic confusion results from the mystery surrounding Gutenberg's business dealings.

Johann Gutenberg apparently has not used his press to record any of the vital information about the history of the invention, even though the preservation of knowledge is being hailed as a major function for the new process. Presumably this is to protect his interests against imitators. But ironically, because of the secrecy there is every likelihood that other printers will in due course claim to have beaten Gutenberg to the invention itself.

Even within Gutenberg's recent operations, the record is not clear.

While the Latin grammar—a reprinting of the work by Aelius Donatus that has been a basic school text since the fourth century—is the first full book known to be produced by printing, it probably was not the first book to be undertaken using the new process. Gutenberg may have begun his full-scale production in about 1450 by starting on an edition of the Bible, using the so-called Vulgate text in Latin as established by St. Jerome. Sources close to Gutenberg say it may be 1455 or later before the printing of this work is completed. This is the book which Gutenberg believes will be his true symbol and memorial, they add.

Some sources maintain that the Donatus was not even the first printing issued by Gutenberg. They say a fourteenth-century German poem, *Sibyllenbuch*, of 1,040 lines, famous now for a section on the judgment of the world, was produced in a seventy-four-page booklet with twenty-eight type lines to the page, the work being completed either in 1451 or last year.

Apparently, Gutenberg has already cut and cast two different typefaces to use in his printing, in addition to various initial letters and decorations. The Bible is said to have two columns to the page, each column having 42 lines; hence the type for this work is called the forty-two-line type, involving 290 different characters including initial letters and abbreviations. Another Bible is contemplated to be printed later, in larger type making 36 lines to the column; hence this is called the thirty-six-line type, with something over 200 characters.

The *Sibyllenbuch* was printed in what is considered an early version of the thirty-six-line type and the Donatus in the forty-two-line type.

For the historical record and from what information is available, the following seems to be the sequence of development of letterpress printing to this point:

Gutenberg began making models and testing materials and processes some time during the 1430's—probably by 1435—while he was exiled in Strasbourg. Having been familiar with the related crafts and the need for books since he was a youth, he may have conceived the basic idea for a true printing process long before the 1430's.

Experiments on the metal alloy apparently were in full swing by 1436, when Gutenberg bought about 100 guilders worth of metal from the goldsmith Hans Dünne in Strasbourg. The sum then was the equivalent of a city dwelling or a good-sized farm. Only master members of the guild could buy the raw materials, and the goldsmith must also have fused the alloys for Gutenberg according to the different formulas he provided. The product would be bars or sticks of the alloy which Gutenberg could then remelt in small quantities as needed for making trial pieces of type in his mold.

Gutenberg's final alloy is lead with additions of tin and antimony. This adroitly takes advantage of one of the cheaper and more available metals while meeting some highly technical requirements of low melting point, fast casting, durability in use, and absolutely no shrinkage. However, finding the optimal formula may have taken hundreds of trials.

Ink also must have taken much experimentation, to get it to stick to both type and paper, to print cleanly, to leave no trace of excess oil or soak through the sheet of paper, and to stay the same despite temperature changes. Any one problem means that no printing can be done. Even putting the ink evenly across a page of type needed the invention of a new device, the "ink ball."

The original idea for an oily ink undoubtedly came to Gutenberg from the oil paint which happened to be popularized by the Flemish artist, Jan Van Eyck, at the turn of the century. Gutenberg is believed to use nut oil varnish with lampblack (soot) as the pigment, plus driers and other additives, including turpentine.

By 1439, Gutenberg had worked out most of the details of the printing press itself. It seems likely that some of his ideas here came from acquaintanceship with the Reverend Father Anthony Heilmann, whose brother Nicholas owned a papermill near Strasbourg. Gutenberg must certainly have become deeply familiar with its operations in a way not generally available to non-guild members. First-hand knowledge about the characteristics of the magical new material, paper, undoubtedly helped solve many problems. And it may have been one of the inventor's lesser problems to adapt the paper press (used to squeeze water out of newly formed sheets) into a printing press.

In fact, it would seem from legal documents in Strasbourg that he had worked out the entire process in detail and tested it by 1439. Printing, therefore, is said to have been invented in that year. However, the results were not fully satisfactory in quality; that is, the printed letters on the sheet were not comparable to the scribe's handiwork. Obviously, more development work was required "to achieve printing that equalled formal handwriting of the finest sort," as his goal has been put.

The next period covered some ten years, until 1450, although it is not certain that Gutenberg worked at his problem the whole time. For a time around 1444 or 1445, at least, his workshop was inoperative as he finally moved it to Mainz. Possibly he did not want to disturb his work on the invention by moving earlier. But by the mid-1440's, having to start afresh on his experimentation, and perhaps having exhausted sources of financial support in Strasbourg, he saw the opportunity to break away with little harm to his life-long project.

By 1450, it is believed, Gutenberg finally had worked out the bugs in his process, and he began the flawless printing of the Bible. Thus, it can be said that whereas printing was invented in 1439 in Strasbourg, it was perfected in 1450 in Mainz. It will take until 1455 or perhaps even 1456 to produce the monumental work, a lectern-size book in 1,282 pages of two-columns each, with forty-two lines to the column.

Bookbinding today is a separate guild craft, and Gutenberg does not seem interested in assuming the function, since today's Donatus was delivered in sheets to bookbinders. The number of sheets in the Bible indicates it probably will be bound in two volumes.

There is no doubt among observers of the book trade that Gutenberg has correctly foreseen an enormous market for books, once they can be made cheaply and quickly in quantity. However, because mass production involves considerable expense and "tooling up" time before finished products can return a profit, and also because of the inventor's inability under law to protect his process, the chances are that Gutenberg will die poor and obscure, rather than wealthy and famous.

More specifically, Gutenberg is said to have been forced to turn to money-lenders recently for the large capital investment needed to produce the Bible on which he is working. Cynics are predicting the money-lenders will end up—quite legally—taking his whole physical plant away from him, as well as full knowledge of his technology.

The economics of the printing enterprise are highly tempting to money men, for all that others may wonder how the expense of creating and operating a complex printing plant with heavy machinery can possibly be less costly than a scribe sitting at a desk listening to dictation and copying down the text.

The new technologists, however, insist that a distinction must be made between the initial cost—capital investment of money or human energy—and the subsequent operation of that capital equipment. Admittedly, the initial step of providing the means of production is far more costly than the old, simple hand process. But once it is available, the *unit* cost drops fantastically.

If, for instance, a scribe can turn out a two hundred-page manuscript in three months, it would take seventy-five scribes to turn out three hundred copies of that manuscript in a year. Yet once a printing shop is in operation, six men will be able to produce perhaps two or three books of 200 pages in 300-copy editions in one year.

Furthermore, they will be better copies, because they will be corrected and freed of the errors that scribes make, they will be uniform, and they will be of high quality. This is because the division of labor now exemplified by the specialized guilds is combined and brought to bear in a systematic way on one product, so that separate skills are brought to very high levels of performance. Thus, while workmen at one press can print 1,000 or more sheets in a ten-hour day, other workmen can be setting up the type forms in advance for the next pages; and others can be dampening the paper, or mixing the ink, proofreading and making corrections, etc.

There is little question in the minds of the experts, therefore, that the new mass production by equipment can outdistance hand skills, as they say, hands down.

As the machine creates new skills, paradoxically, it makes obsolete the traditional skills. It is this threatened displacement of so many highly-skilled workers by the new technology that is creating consternation in both official circles and in the craft guilds which control jobs and protect each one. What will happen to the estimated hundreds of employed scribes in Mainz, for instance, if Gutenberg can replace them with a few printers?

The fear is not only for the scribes. If mechanization can be applied to printing, can it not in time be applied to other crafts, with equal loss of jobs?

Students of social change concede the short-run validity of the fears of job losses and aesthetic decline in the early stages of a new technological level. Nevertheless, they insist that the long-range gains of not only printing but of the invention of mass production will increase jobs manyfold and need not necessarily result in aesthetic harm.

In any case, the fear would seem to have no immediate justification.

The social change specialists do not expect Gutenberg's invention to have much immediate impact. In fact, they predict the first decade or so of the age of printing will be required to get over the idea that it is simply an inferior substitute for the "real thing," scribe-written books—or worse, that it is but a counterfeiting device to cheat unwary bookcollectors.

At some point, however, perhaps by the end of a decade, printing can be expected to spread to neighboring cities, if only because Gutenberg's workers, once they learn the secrets, will strike out on their own. Also, they may go, too, to the Italian peninsula, where the humanistic Renaissance already offers a large market for books in quantity, and where new technologies are welcomed as a force for change instead of an evil to be repulsed by the defenders of the status quo.

Then, the specialists believe, some time around 1470 awareness of the business potentials of printing will become clear to the growing class of European entrepreneurs, and the new process will spread throughout the continent. The increase in the number of books produced is likely to be almost beyond comprehension to a generation which knows only the pace of hand copiers. One estimate, in fact, puts the total number of different titles produced by the year 1500 at 40,000 with perhaps a total of 20,000,000 books printed within the fifty-year "incunabula" or "cradle" period of the new art and technology.

According to some computations, this would be more books than have thus far been produced in the history of the world, no doubt including the lost continent of Atlantis.

As to Gutenberg's threatened financial position, for the most part, he is said to have used only his own resources on the development. However, on two occasions, when there was a special demand for working capital, he brought in partners.

The first time was in Strasbourg, in 1439, when he made a five-year agreement with three partners who not only put in five hundred florins each but also participated in the actual development work under Gutenberg's direction. At that time in Strasbourg, 500 florins could buy two fine houses with gardens and extensive fields.

After the five years, with the invention not yet perfected, the partnership apparently was allowed to die.

The second partnership is a new one, understood to have been begun around 1450, with the loan of eight hundred guilders to Gutenberg by Johann Fust, the prominent Mainz money-lender, to finance the production of Gutenberg's Bible. Recently, instead of simply lending a second 800 guilders, Fust bought a partnership with Gutenberg. Fust, it is also understood, is beginning to take an active interest in the work of Gutenberg's plant. A young apprentice, Peter Schoeffer, has caught on so fast and proved so dependable that he has been moved up to foreman in the expanded plant operation for production of the Bible.

Gutenberg seems to be counting on the sale of the Bible to pay back his indebtedness to Fust. However, in the money markets there is speculation that once the project is far enough along to convince Fust that it can be completed without the inventor, Fust will pull the rug out from under him by demanding his first 800 guilders or the plant and inventory, and Gutenberg will lose all.

The cynics also suggest that young Schoeffer will be available to carry on Gutenberg's technical supervision. Furthermore, so rumor has it, Fust has a quite marriageable young daughter who seems already to have caught Schoeffer's eye. So Fust may even contrive to keep his new acquisition entirely in the family.

The estimates of the book market by the end of the century assume a tremendous leap in literacy and a demand for books far beyond anything that has been known in history. But experts insist the trends have already begun and Gutenberg's new process is really just a response to the market.

For instance, they point to a bookseller in Florence who is even now keeping 50 scribes busy on "light reading" books. And they say the demand is for all kinds of reading, from liturgical material to technical manuals to scholarly tracts to educational textbooks from primary levels upward. Literacy is already on the rise among the trading classes, instead of being the virtual monopoly of the Church and the skilled professions such as medicine and law.

Printing, therefore, may even expand beyond books to new forms and uses which cannot yet be imagined.

There is, of course, always the possibility that conservative forces will move to stop any great expansion of reading and reading matter. Some critics are already calling printing "the black art" and the work of the Devil because of its mystery and the power that they fear can stem from the millions upon millions of black printed words that will come from the presses. "If God had meant for people to print," one theologian thundered, "he would have provided for it in the Garden of Eden."

However, the Church has been quite receptive to Gutenberg and his ideas to this point, and is considered likely to remain so at least through the beginning period—because printing, with its quantity and low cost, offers a chance for promulgation of the faith widely and with great impact.

One early use predicted for printing is its adoption by the newsletter services which have been sent since Roman times from European capitals to businessmen and politicians in other centers. There could even be a revival of a news medium something like the Roman posted bulletins, such as Daily Events (*Acta Diurna*). And, of course, the publication of news pamphlets or news books seems a strong likelihood.

If literacy and other education are encouraged to the point where whole populations can read, "news" can be expected to be in more demand than books. Ultimately, so some observers are convinced, there will be broadsides printed on both sides of the sheet, perhaps in folded sets of several sheets each, constituting what might be known as "news papers" that will report occurrences on a monthly or—so some "blue-sky thinkers" assert—even perhaps weekly, printed very cheaply in great quantities so that even the masses will have the "news" to read.

But, they say, news would not be the only commodity. There would be opinion, meaning differences of opinion. The so-called Renaissance which is rising out of Rome these days is creating a new humanism that may end up challenging the Church—and printing presses would be readily available to heretics to publish their heresies. Worse, the general population would just as readily have them to read. Similarly, kings and other noble rulers may expect their enemies to produce treasonable tracts to stir up their subjects against them.

Such can become the power of the presses in due time that the printers and publishers, perhaps including also the writers, may become a "fourth estate," in the terminology of the old French States-General, sharing power with the clergy, the nobility, and the commoners.

Scholars are reported to be generally viewing printing as a potential great educational force, making literacy and texts available to all who would learn. They see their own work given circulation and attention far beyond what could ever be expected in a publishing economy limited to scribal production. (In addition, they are pleased at the ability to "edit" their writing and "proofread them" when set in type but not yet printed.)

Scholars believe, too, that one effect of printing will be to standardize the spelling and meanings of words in the language of a given nation, and thus help unify the people and spread the growing nationalism of our time. One way it will do this is by reducing oral traditions to print, thus discouraging the variations that make for local ethnic differences.

Another possible application of printing being forecast is for utilitarian uses—what might be called "job printing"—custom-designed materials produced to order to fit specific commercial, official or ecclesiastical needs.

Thus, high Church officials today were discussing the use of printing for their voluminous instructions to the far-reaching hierarchy including the local priests. Specifically, also, they were considering the possibility of having ready-printed Indulgences which could be available upon urgent need to raise funds for pressing cause—the growing danger from an invasion by the Turks being taken by some as a case in point.

Manufacturers of various products for the market also saw good use for printing. Most intriguing to some of them was the possibility of producing "handbills" which could be circulated to the buying public to inform all concerned of the availability of the merchandise, and perhaps even contain some content about the superiority of the particular manufacturer's wares over his competitors. Other manufacturers, however, noting that this would involve a great amount of paper (a relatively costly item) derided the thought as uneconomical.

This latter view brought some cheer to the town criers' group, who at first began fearing that printed materials—of news as well as the calling of wares—might put them out of business. "However," said one spokesman, "it just doesn't stand to reason, when you really think about it, that people paid to distribute pieces of paper which cost money as paper and cost still more money to print and deliver to the public, can do all this cheaper and faster than we town criers can walk the streets ourselves. Besides, we're *telling* the people, so they can hear with their own ears. They'll believe this a lot more than what they read from the Devil's own work. If they can even read at all. After all, don't forget, it does take skill to be a town crier. We have to know how to read ourselves, or else have a very good memory for what we're told to cry out."

Gutenberg supporters say that large-scale printing production will inevitably lead to cheaper paper costs and to vastly increased literacy. As for job printing itself, they see it as ultimately a very important area, not only for such items as calendars, notices, business forms, tickets, etc., but more especially for "advertising" which will be needed to promote the sale of the large quantities of the new mass-produced products. Printing will not only create mass production, they say, but will sustain and stimulate it.

Thus, the proponents of printing insist, there will almost certainly be many more jobs created in the community than the loss of scribes and related craft workers can possibly represent.

The opposite of job printing is also suggested as a possibility: printing for pleasure or personal purposes—private presses, as it were, owned by individuals who would print small editions of books or ephemera for themselves and their friends, outside any commercial considerations, being captivated rather by the magic of printing itself, by the joys of creativity, self-expression and free opinion, by the love of letter forms.

And from there it will be but a step to a rebirth of regard for the scribe and the wondrous beauty of his loving handiwork.

As one student of social change summed it up, "If Gutenberg has this day supplanted the written word with the printed word, he has only thereby ennobled the human race with all its aspirations and accomplishments, and helped it to further glory."

Dr. J. Ben Lieberman started newspapering on the *Evansville* (Indiana) *Courier,* where he became Sunday editor at 22. In 1938–39, he was a free-lance correspondent traveling Europe, North Africa and the Near East. In World War II, he was Director of Informational Services, U.S. Navy, Washington, and editor of *All Hands* magazine, with the rank of Commander. Afterwards, he came up the editorial side of the *San Francisco Chronicle,* rising to Assistant to the General Manager, and then was an economist at the Stanford Research Institute and a communication consultant to the Ford Foundation and international development agencies, including the U.N. and OECD in Paris.

Since 1967 he has been a Hill and Knowlton, Inc., vice president, as a social scientist (Ph.D., Stanford, in political science) on the cutting edge of social concerns. Printing is his hobby; he is proprietor of the world-famous private Herity Press; is the author of books on printing; holds patents on three simple printing presses and a softwall typecase he invented. And he is President of the American Printing History Association.

Columbus Discovers America
—Seeks New Route to Indies

As reported by LOUIS CASSELS

—We arrived safely today, October 12, 1492, in the Indies, completing a voyage never before matched and until now generally thought to be impossible.

After sailing westward for more than 3000 miles across an unknown ocean never before traversed by man—and pressing on far beyond the point at which our mutinous crewmen feared we might fall off the earth—our little fleet of three Spanish ships has reached a new land.

We anchored early today at a small island populated by strange but friendly red-skinned savages whom our commander, Admiral Cristoforo Colombo, calls "Indians" because, he explained, they are natives of the fabled Indies he set forth to find. Startlingly, they are unclothed.

The long-awaited cry of "land in sight" went up from a lookout at 2 A.M., while the anxious admiral paced the deck of his moonlit ship. Landfall came only twenty-four hours before the time he had promised fearful crew members we would turn back toward Spain, whence we departed ten weeks ago.

We still have not reached our destination—Japan and China. But Admiral Colombo, a courageous man who succeeded by sheer force of character in facing down open mutiny among his ninety crewmen, told me late today he is "absolutely confident" Japan lies only a day or two's journey further west.

He said we will remain here a few days and then proceed westward to Japan and other principal lands of the Indies, of which this small island clearly is an outpost.

As the only news correspondent accompanying the fleet, I must confess I was afflicted by the same apprehension as the crew—an apprehension that seemed to grip everyone except our steel-nerved admiral—during the past two weeks of our epic voyage.

Our fleet, commissioned by their Catholic Majesties, King Ferdinand and Queen Isabella of Spain, sailed from the port of Palos de la Frontera August 3. After refitting in the Canary Islands, we sailed steadily westward across an uncharted ocean never before explored by any human being.

We were out of sight of land for thirty-six days.

The magnitude of Admiral Colombo's achievement can hardly be overstated.

The successful voyage was scientifically significant for three reasons:

(1) It vindicated by practical demonstration the theory long taught in European universities that the earth is not a flat plane, but a spherical ball on whose curved surface one may reach the East by sailing westward.

(2) It quieted the fears of many mariners that a ship might drop off the earth if it dared to sail onto its underside.

(3) It will alter all existing maps and all previous concepts of geography to a degree which we cannot now fully envision.

The economic and political consequences of the voyage are more difficult to appraise at this point, but they also could be enormous. Indeed, they were and continue to be the prime concern of Admiral Colombo.

He hopes to bring home from the Indies—principally from the lands of Japan and China previously reached only in an overland journey by Marco Polo—many exotic types of spices, as well as large quantities of gold which is reputed to abound here.

Confirmation of the presence of gold was received shortly after our ships—the *Santa Maria, Nina,* and *Pinta*—dropped anchor inside a coral reef of this island and sent boats ashore.

The landing party encountered a tribe of the friendly natives, many of whom wore gold trinkets as nosepieces. They were glad to give us these valuable golden objects in exchange for some of the small red hats and brightly colored glass beads which we brought along as cheap trade goods.

The Indians are an amiable and hospitable folk but totally lacking in civilized arts such as weaponry. Admiral Colombo is preparing a report to their Spanish Majesties expressing confidence these primitive peoples can easily be subjugated by relatively small forces of Spanish troops, and their rich lands brought under Spanish rule. In fact, he already has claimed this island for Spain, planting the flag of Ferdinand and Isabella and proclaiming himself Viceroy of all the Indies.

The island is at latitude 24 degrees North and longitude 24 degrees and 20 minutes, very near the point at which Admiral Colombo had predicted we would find Japan.

It is a small island, about thirteen miles long and six miles wide, without mountains, but lushly grown with trees. The natives call it "Guanahani," but Admiral Colombo renamed it in honor of Our Savior (San Salvador in Spanish).

The admiral's first act upon reaching shore, on a long curved sand beach, was to kneel and give thanks to God for a safe voyage. He then planted the flag and formally took possession of the island for the Spanish sovereigns who underwrote his voyage of exploration and discovery.

In a brief interview with this reporter, Admiral Colombo said he was pleased to find the native Indians to be "a gentle and peaceful people of great simplicity." He expressed some concern that they go about stark naked, even young maidens being entirely unclad with no apparent sense of their immodesty. He has a fear—(Ed.'s Note: Which later events proved to be well-founded)—that the presence of these nubile, unclothed girls would prove an irresistible incitement to sailors who have been so long at sea. By a late hour today, despite the admiral's efforts, fraternization between our sailors and the native girls had become quite advanced.

"The male Indians are of good stature, strong and handsome folk," Admiral Colombo noted. "Their hair is not kinky nor their skin black, as is the case with the natives I encountered in my previous voyages along the coast of Africa. These natives have long, loose, coarse hair, and the skin is reddish in color, rather like that of Canary Islanders who spend much time in the sun."

The admiral said we would remain on this island for two or three days, taking on water and provisions, and then sail on to the west until we reach Japan, which cannot, by his reckoning, be far away.

Reaching Japan is important to the admiral, whose primary objective from the start has been to pioneer a new sea route over which trade may be conducted with the Indies.

Cristoforo Colombo (known in Spain as Cristobal Colon) is a forty-one-year-old native of Genoa, who has spent most of his life at sea. After acquiring a vast store of navigational experience as master of Portuguese vessels sailing northward to Iceland and southward along the coast of Africa, he approached King Joao II of Portugal with a proposal for a voyage due westward across the Great Ocean—a direction no sailor had hitherto dared to go.

Despite glowing assurances from Colombo that the westward voyage would open up the vast wealth of the Indies to Portugal, the king referred the enterprise to a commission of scholars, who recommended it be rejected as unfeasible.

Colombo then moved to Spain, where he spent the past six years in an often-frustrating but ultimately successful attempt to secure backing for the voyage from King Ferdinand and Queen Isabella. Ferdinand remained unenthusiastic about the project until the day we sailed, but capitulated to his queen, who took a great liking to the affable and handsome Colombo. The queen declared her readiness to pawn her crown jewels if necessary to finance the voyage, but she did not actually have to resort to this expedient, as adequate funds were provided by her Keeper of the Privy Purse, Don Luis de Santangel.

Colombo asked for and received three ships, manned by ninety officers and men and provisioned for a voyage of one year. He also requested and was granted a royal commission in the Spanish Navy as "Admiral of the Ocean Sea," a title never before conferred on any mariner.

The flagship of the fleet, under the admiral's personal command, is the 100-ton caravel *Santa Maria.* The other two ships are the *Pinta* and the *Nina,* each vessels of about sixty tons. They are under command of the famed seagoing Pinzon brothers of Palos de la Frontera. Captain Martin Alonso Pinzon commands the *Pinta,* and Captain Vincente Pinzon the *Nina.*

All three vessels proved extremely seaworthy on the long voyage. But their small size—about seventy feet long, with a single deck—made our living accommodations somewhat cramped, to put it mildly.

The *Santa Maria,* aboard which I am travelling, has no sleeping facilities above deck for anyone except the admiral himself, who occupies a small cabin (which sailors call "the dog house") on the poop deck.

The rest of us have slept on the open deck, wherever we've found room to lie down. In rougher weather, we have had to go into the smelly, rat-infested and terribly overcrowded forecastle or even into the steerage to find sleeping space.

All cooking is done over an open fire box on deck. Although *haute cuisine* is hardly to be expected from such a "kitchen," we have fared surprisingly well, thanks to the admiral's foresight in laying in very large stores of food, wine, and water.

We sailed from Palos de la Frontera about 4:45 A.M.—a half hour before dawn—on August 3, after the admiral had attended a special mass at the Church of St. George at which he prayed for the success of our voyage.

It was a grey, calm day, with the sea like a mirror. Spectacular cloud masses appeared on the horizon at dawn, and the rising sun made them look like huge pillars of flame, beckoning us onward. Colombo considered this a good omen. He reminded us that the children of Israel were led out of Egypt by a pillar of flame.

Outside port, our square-rigged sails finally picked up a fair breeze, and the admiral set course for our initial destination, the Canary Islands. With good winds, we reached the islands and anchored in the roadstead of San Sebastian on August 12.

During our sojourn in the Canaries repairs were made to the minor damages which came to light in our shakedown cruise from Spain. Then at dawn September 6, we weighed anchor and set sail due west across the vast unexplored ocean.

Fortune—or the Divine Providence—protected us throughout the long voyage. We encountered no storms, no heavy seas or foul winds, and only a few days of calms. Most of the time, the brisk trade winds carried us along at a good speed. On many days, we averaged more than seven knots.

But sailors are always able to find something to grumble about, and even the fair winds which we enjoyed finally became an object of concern to them. They argued that if the wind always blew this strongly toward the west, we would never be able to beat our way back eastward to home. Colombo disabused them of this notion by giving all hands a lecture on navigation, including the art of tacking. But on September 23, the crew found a new occasion for panic. We awoke to find our ships sailing through what looked like a great meadow of green and yellow plants. Again, the admiral, by drawing up specimens, was able to calm fears by pointing out that this was simply *sargassum*, or sea weed, of a type reported in accounts of previous explorers in other areas. He also noted that it was only about half an inch thick, and hence provided no deterrent to our progress.

On September 25, Captain Martin Alonso Pinzon raised our hopes prematurely by sending up a shout of "Tierra, Tierra"—the agreed signal for the first sighting of land. Colombo promptly fell to his knees on deck to give thanks to God. But it proved to be a false landfall—the kind of mirage which sailors too long at sea often construct in their minds from cloud formations on the distant horizon.

Vexed by the effect of this episode on the increasingly restless crew, the admiral issued orders that anyone who cried "land" prematurely in the future would be disqualified from the reward he had offered for the first sighting.

During the first week of October, the grumbling of the crew passed into a more ominous stage of incipient mutiny. Walking about the deck of the *Santa Maria,* I overheard sailors making such remarks as:

"This foreigner from Genoa will kill all of us in his mad pursuit of personal glory."

"If we keep going, we surely will drop off the earth and perish."

"Why don't we throw him overboard and tell the king and queen he drowned by accident?"

I felt compelled to report the latter remark to the admiral, for his own safety. Instead of flying into wrath, he received the news calmly.

"These are good men," he told me. "But they have had about as much as they can take. I shall talk with them."

He called together all of our crew, and later visited the other two boats to talk to their crews as well. In each talk, he stressed the point that mutiny was pointless. "You can kill me any time you wish—I have no defense against it," he said. "But if you do kill me and turn back to Spain, you can rest assured their majesties will see you hanged the moment you land."

Morale rose suddenly at sunset on October 7, when great flocks of birds were seen overhead, flying in a direction slightly south of west. Colombo, convinced that the birds were heading toward land, altered our course a small amount to follow the birds.

"Those birds know their business," he told Captain Martin Alonso Pinzon, in my hearing.

The trade winds continued brisk, and we logged a fine run of 171 miles on October 10. But we were still going west into the unknown, and we still had not sighted land. That evening, open mutiny flared in the *Santa Maria.*

The admiral quelled it with soft words and the example of his own serene confidence.

"Give me three more days," he asked the crew. "Unless we make land by the end of that time, I promise you we shall turn back."

Mollified by this promise, the crew returned to their stations.

Colombo now put on all possible sail to make the most of his remaining time, and we fairly scudded over the sea. Signs of land were now becoming more and more plentiful. A sailor on the *Nina* picked out of the water a green branch with a little flower on it. More and more land birds could be seen. By sunset on October 11, every man in the fleet was straining his eyes, trying to win the 10,000 maravedi reward for being the first to sight land.

Although navigators usually consider it prudent to lower sail at night when approaching land, in order to avoid going aground in the dark, Colombo was keenly conscious that his three days of grace were running out. He ordered the fleet to proceed under full sail throughout the night.

As it turned out, we didn't have to sail all night. At 2 A.M., under a full moon that turned our sails into silver sheets, a sailor named Rodrigo de Triona, on lookout duty aboard the *Pinta,* gave the glad shout: "Tierra! Tierra!"

This time it was no false landfall. Ahead on the horizon we all could see the gloriously welcome outline of an island.

At the admiral's orders, all ships lowered sail until daylight. Then we carefully made our way through a narrow opening in the dangerous coral reefs surrounding the island, and cast anchor in five fathoms of water, a few score yards from the sandy beach.

A spirit of great excitement and rejoicing prevailed on all three boats. We knew we had successfully completed a hazardous and unprecedented adventure. We had done what no one had done before—sailed westward and reached the Indies.

Reaction to Admiral Cristoforo Colombo's discovery of a western sea route to the Indies ranged today from open skepticism to exultant celebration.

Queen Isabella, informed that Colombo had landed on a hitherto undiscovered island and claimed it for Spain, replied: "Who needs another island? Did he find any gold?"

The queen's confessor, Fray Hernando de Talavera, Prior of del Prado monastery near Valladolid, was one of the skeptics.

Although he does not share the superstition, now current only among the uneducated, that the earth is flat, Talavera had opposed Colombo's voyage because his own calculations indicated Colombo had vastly underestimated the size of the earth—and therefore the distance that would have to be traversed in sailing westward in order to reach the Indies.

"I'm still not convinced he has reached the Indies," said the Prior today.

"He has found an island, but who knows whether that island is actually part of, or immediately offshore of, the Indies, as Colombo thinks? He sailed just over 3000 miles westward. I calculate he would have to go more than 10,000 miles in that direction to reach Japan or China."

But another famous scholar, the Florentine physician and mathematician, Paolo dal Pozzo Toscanelli, hailed the Colombo voyage as justification for his own long-standing belief that a relatively short sea route to the Indies could be found by sailing due westward from the Canary Islands.

Dr. Toscanelli had tried in vain to get the Portuguese monarchy to subsidize Colombo's voyage as early as 1474, writing to King Joao that a study of maps and globes, based on Marco Polo's overland voyage to the East, had convinced him there is "a shorter way by going by sea to the lands of spices than that which Portuguese navigators are now attempting by way of Africa."

Unable to comprehend the continuing quarreling of scholars over the significance of the expedition, sailors at Spanish ports voiced amazement at the hardiness of Colombo and his men for sailing so long over an unknown sea.

"Man, that's a long time to be out of sight of land," said Alfonso Bachiler, first mate of a coasting caravel.

In Cordoba, a merchant who asked that his name be withheld told UPI he was principally interested in the possibility that the Colombo expedition would result in discovery of much gold.

"If the king and queen can get gold from the Indies, maybe they won't tax us so heavily," he said.

Portuguese authorities greeted with obvious consternation today reports that a Spanish fleet under command of Admiral Cristoforo Colombo had discovered a western sea route to the Indies.

It was recalled here that Colombo approached King D. Joao II of Portugual in 1484, and urged him to sponsor such a voyage. King Joao consulted a commission of experts who said the idea was impractical. On their advice, the Portuguese monarch rejected Colombo's proposal.

Portugal has been trying for years to open sea trade with the spice-rich Indies. Most of the exploration by Portuguese ships has followed a route down the coast of Africa. In 1487, Captain Bartholomew Dias set out for India with two caravels and a storeship. He felt his way along the coast of Africa and finally rounded the tip of that continent, which he named "The Cape of Good Hope."

Dias then turned northward and in early 1488, reached the mouth of a river which abounded in great fish. At this point, his seamen refused to go further, and Dias was forced to return to Portugal.

Don Manuel, the Duke of Bejar and heir to the Portuguese throne, has confided to friends at court that he still believes the best sea route to the Indies lies around the southern tip of Africa.

He is reported to have summoned the great Portuguese navigator Vasco da Gama to the court as soon as word reached here of Admiral Colombo's landing, and to have commissioned da Gama to outfit a fleet for a long voyage that would go beyond Dias' "River of Great Fish" in the hope of finding the Indies.

The late Louis Cassels was a Senior Editor of United Press International. Based in Washington, D.C., for nearly a quarter of a century, he covered the whole gamut of national affairs news, including White House news conferences, presidential election campaigns, national political conventions, Congressional legislative actions, the U.S. economy and the era of rapid social change which featured the black man's drive for equality and the rise of a youth counterculture. His coverage of the urban ghetto riots of 1967 won him a Front Page award for the best national reporting of the year. He received many other journalism awards over the years.

He was born Jan. 14, 1922 in Aiken County, South Carolina. He graduated Phi Beta Kappa from Duke University, and served in the U.S. Army Air Corps in World War II. He worked for UPI since leaving military service in 1945. He married the former Charlotte Norling of Oberlin, Ohio, in 1943. Mrs. Cassels was one of the unpaid volunteers who worked for years to make the John F. Kennedy Center for the Performing Arts a reality.

Council of Trent Ends;
Europe's Unity Unrestored

As reported by BARRETT McGURN

Christendom's nineteenth ecumenical council ended here amid indications that the Europe of the past half millennium never again will be the same.

The council failed in one of its main stated purposes: the reunion of Christianity. Instead of meeting the demands of northern European protesters that the faith return to the simpler forms and formulas of fifteen centuries ago, and that broad freedoms be granted to individuals, the council has spelled out doctrines and rituals in greater detail and rigor that the Church has known. A negative reaction from the followers of the German Martin Luther, Geneva's John Calvin and the newly independent Church of England is considered certain.

On another score the council ironically has conceded the main point of the Rev. Mr. Luther's revolt of 45 years ago—that corruption and illiteracy radiating from the papal court down to priests in their parishes has been making a mockery of religion and is in crying need of reform. A series of drastic decrees calling for "nurseries" or "seminaries" in which to train churchmen, and new regulations to guarantee that bishops and popes will be chosen in the future for moral and spiritual qualities, provide impressive assurances that the job-auctioning, cronyism, nepotism and even vice of recent generations will now be repudiated.

What is not clear, however, as the council ends, is that the moral revival and the tightening of doctrinal and ceremonial formulas in the face of protester opposition will be sufficient to save for the papacy the position of importance and sometimes even dominance which it has enjoyed in Europe since the high Middle Ages and even back to Charlemagne seven and one-half centuries ago. There are, on the contrary, many signs that the day has ended when a pope like Innocent III (1198–1216) could see himself as the arbiter of both public and private morality and when other pontiffs could depose kings and emperors.

The final benediction services here, on December 4, 1563, have terminated a meeting which has gone on, with interruptions, since December 13, 1545. Following a slow start at the first session (1545–1547), the council picked up momentum in a second round (1551–1552), and now in this final year has concluded on so vigorous a note that it is plain that this will go down as the most important of the twelve-century series of ecumenical assemblies.

What may be seen in time as a main action of the council has occurred almost by inadvertence. That is the fact that the council allowed itself to be summoned into existence by a pope (Paul III, the former Cardinal Alexander Farnese) and that it will now submit its actions for ratification to another Roman pontiff, Pius IV, the erstwhile Cardinal Giovanni Angelo de' Medici (no relation to the Florentine Medicis). It is a foregone conclusion that Pius will rubber stamp the council's reforms and formulas but the mere act of submission to papal authority emphasizes that at least one vast part of Christianity has not rejected Peter's fifteen-century-old Roman throne.

This may well even prove to be the council's most crucial act for the greater share of northern Europe is now on record in opposition to continued papal dominion over the Church. That has been true now since the Twenties in much of Germany and Switzerland, in England and Scandinavia since the Thirties and in young Queen Mary's Scotland for the past three years.

With the council solidly on the side of sixty-four-year-old Pius IV, and with so much of northern and western Europe in spiritual revolt against the Vatican, many political observers are expressing fear here that the Continent faces more than rival church belltowers, sermons and religious exercises, and that there may even be an expansion of the recent military combat. While the council was in session the emperor tried to help the pope and his council by putting troops into the field against protesters, trying to get them to attend the council submissively, and there was even fighting here on the edges of Trent; but the emperor's guns accomplished little. A few protesters were here under a safe conduct for the second session in the Fifties but they agreed with very little the council did. They left and did not come back. In a situation such as this some Cassandras are saying that Europe may even see a religious civil war complete with battles fought with artillery and that this could rage on for decades. European Christianity was united for 1,000 years up to 1520 but how it can come back together again in coming years or even in centuries is hard to see at the council's conclusion. These are some reasons being emphasized here:

1) The council rejected the Rev. Mr. Luther's idea that every man should be able to find his own way to God through study of the Bible without the sacraments, Mass, elaborate Church organization of bishops and popes, and much else that has characterized European religion since the high Middle Ages. On the contrary the council listed seven Sacraments as a key part of orthodox devotion, insisted on the Mass as the central act of worship, and endorsed other popular practices of recent centuries (belief in Purgatory, reverence for saints and their relics) which northern reformers have been sweeping into discard.

2) The council answered reform demands for expanded freedoms by indicating to the contrary that it favored an Index of Forbidden Books. There was no final action on this today but the pope is expected to issue such a listing soon. With the success which Johann Gutenberg's printing invention has had in Mainz, Germany, and with similar presses now turning out books in Cambridge, England, and even as far away as Mexico City in the New World, it is taken for granted among impartial observers here that any limitation on the people's right to read will meet with an explosive reaction in the new free climate of the north and west.

As the council closes, preparations are under way to get the assembly's rulings adopted as official governmental policy inside the small countries of the Italian peninsula and in Poland. Council administrators see no trouble in accomplishing this but there are straws in the wind suggesting that Spain will endorse the council conclusions only to "the extent that they do not infringe the rights of the king." In France it is doubtful whether Queen Mother Catherine de Médicis, the regent, will consent to countersign the council declarations at all. Fifty-four-year-old John Calvin of Geneva, a native Frenchman, has been making gains in France, and Catherine de Médicis has acted gingerly with regard to him. Somewhat the same situation is true in Scotland where 21-year-old Queen Mary, herself a devout follower of the pope, is not doing much to oppose the protester John Knox, a papal foe now widely followed by parliament and people. With rulers calling the turn between the reformers and the papal party in much of the rest of northern Europe the

Scottish queen's strange situation is causing much comment here and no one offers a guess as to how it will turn out for Mary, Queen of Scots.

As the Trent council ends, both of the main figures who have ruled Europe for half a millennium—the emperor and the pope—are in notable decline. With so many small states in middle and northern Europe affirming their own national and religious independence some pessimists here have been speculating that the old Europe, a continent united against the Southeastern Moslem threat—the Europe of the Crusades, one in nationality and one in faith, will not be seen again for generations, if ever.

With the council's rulings falling on so many deaf ears in north Europe, and with papal bulls and excommunications now of scant interest in much of Britain, Switzerland, Germany, the Netherlands and Scandinavia, it is hard to realize that it is only seventy years since Rodrigo Borgia (Pope Alexander VI) divided South America between Portugal and Spain. Already the Eastern bulge of that new continent is speaking Portuguese while Spanish is the language aborning of the Andes. Yet no one on the margins of this council dares predict that popes will have that kind of civic power soon again.

Mention of Borgia popes brings to mind one area on which the council, the Scottish John Knoxes, the Luthers and the Calvins all agree: that the papacy and much of the rest of Church organization in recent generations has been a scandal for men of piety; they have been cockpits in which self-seekers have used bribery and other high crimes to enrich their families in mockery of Christ and Peter. Now, if you can believe council edicts, and if you can trust signs coming from Vatican Hill, that sad day for Christian faith is drawing to a close.

Travellers up from Rome have marvelled here in recent months that the tone now inside the Vatican palace is more like that of a stern monastery than of the flamboyant Renaissance court of a few years back. Pope Paul IV who died four years ago at 83 is given the credit as the churchman who made the change. He reigned for only four years but the Curia and the College of Cardinals were unrecognizable when he finished with them. Paul cut out the sale of high Curial offices. When he took Peter's throne there were 113 bishops in Rome, hangers-on like the noblemen in the courts of Paris and London. By the time Paul died all but a dozen of the Rome bishops had been shipped back to home dioceses. Paul packed the College of Cardinals with priests without princely connections, clergymen known only for old-fashioned virtues.

The effect that will have on future papal elections is plain. Old-timers on the Seven Hills are saying that it is hard to believe that it is little more than half a century since Alexander VI's notorious daughter, Lucrezia Borgia, ran the Vatican briefly in July 1501 while her father was absent from the city.

Here at the council the same fresh breeze has been blowing in the person of 25-year-old Archbishop Charles Borromeo, a nephew of the current pope, Pius IV. Reverend Mr. Borromeo was not even a priest until this past year but in short order he has been ordained, promoted to bishop and then raised to the wealthy archdiocese of Milan. In one sense this seems to reflect the same kind of family favoritism which shocked Father Martin Luther when he visited Rome on business of his order, the Augustinians, in 1510. But in Archbishop Borromeo's case there is a difference. He dominated the final session of the council during this past year. It was in good part thanks to him that austere new codes for clergy and laity were pushed through committees and passed on the council floor. His uncle, the pope, has made the young archbishop the Vatican's number two officer, its secretary of state. No one here doubts that the youthful prelate will see to it that Trent reforms are no dead letters on the Tiber banks, in Milan or anywhere else his long arms can reach. A rich youth, the new Milan archbishop has attracted attention for the monklike simplicity and even severity of his life style.

One curiosity of this council has been that many of those uppermost in the minds of the 200 or so delegates never appeared:—

The former *Father Luther,* the rebel priest who set off this century's extraordinary religious explosion, died at 63, a year after this council convened, but in the intervening seventeen years the council fathers never have ceased to wrestle with the Lutherian ideas, accepting some (the need of reform), rejecting others (de-emphasis for the sacraments, elimination of the Mass, an end to Rome leadership).

Fifty-four-year-old *John Calvin,* the Genevan, whose reforms have all but eliminated singing and dancing from his Swiss community and, on the other side, Spain's late *Ignatius of Loyola* who died seven years ago at 65 but whose influence has been immense here and may even grow as the Vatican puts Trent decisions into effect.

This Ignatius of Loyola was a soldier who underwent a religious conversion after a grave battlefield wound. Three decades ago on Montmartre in Paris he brought six other "companions" together with him inside a new religious order, the "Company of Jesus." Organized along military lines with Ignatius as "general" of the company for life, the band placed itself at the pope's direct service. From seven the "company" has grown to a group of hundreds of zealous and well educated priests, a formidable body whose influence was felt strongly inside the council as early as the 1551–1552 meetings. Some of the observers here are predicting that Loyola's Jesuits will use the council's decisions and their own fervor to stem the advance of protester ideas all through Italy, Spain and Eastern Europe.

This council ends with many questions unanswered and with a few guesses about what is to come:

One question is whether men like Archbishop Borromeo and the followers of the late Paul IV really can succeed in making the Vatican a spiritual center with no more highbinders like Innocent VIII (still remembered for making a cardinal of the seventeen-year-old son of Lorenzo de Médicis, the Magnificent), Rodrigo Borgia (father of six) and Julius II, the soldier-pope of 1503–1513 who told his sculptor, Michaelangelo, to depict him not with a book but with a sword. Many who have known the Rome of recent generations doubt there can be any such change, but there are others who insist that this council and Archbishop Borromeo will work the miracle.

And what of many other matters such as the small one of what is to become of Pope Julius' Swiss Guards? These were formed in 1505, two years into Julius' reign, to push the French out of Milan. If the Vatican does indeed become a monastery will the Swiss go back to their cantons? Or, as has so often happened in the long Rome history, will they linger anachronistically beside the papal throne? Only history will answer that.

And what about all the books and paintings, all the creations of modern Renaissance art, all the works of Michaelangelo, of Raphael, of Fra Angelico and of Benvenuto Cellini, which have made the Vatican library and museums intellectual and aesthetic show places during the past century? Will the "monks" of a changed Vatican disperse them or will they stay together as a unique treasury of this era's creations? No one offers a forecast.

Finally, will Europe regain the unity of the pope-emperor centuries or has a new day of free individuals and small sovereign states been born instead? If it be the latter what will become of the great crusades against the East—against the Mahometans? Will architects and engineers continue to throw up great cathedrals or will their skills go to some different type of construction? Will protesters or Romans win in the end, or will a third mentality triumph in their steads? Few here make a guess but as the last candles go out on Trent's altars all have the feeling that this council has been a turning point in the story of Europe and of the known world.

Barrett McGurn was described in *The Saturday Review* by the Jesuit Father John LaFarge as "one of the greatest reporters of religion of our century." As the *New York Herald Tribune's* expert on Roman Catholic affairs he covered the election of Pope Pius XII in Rome as a cub reporter in 1939 and then headed the paper's Rome bureau from 1946 to 1952, and 1955 to 1962. During his thirteen Rome years for the *Herald Tribune,* Mr. McGurn reported every major Vatican event including the election of Pope John XXIII and the preparations for John's ecumenical council of the Sixties.

Mr. McGurn is the author of *A Reporter Looks at the Vatican* (Coward McCann, 1962) and *A Reporter Looks at American Catholicism* (Hawthorn, 1967). He scored a world scoop on Pope Paul VI's plans to visit America in 1965, winning the Front Page Award of the New York Newspaper Guild, and the Silurians' prize.

Mr. McGurn was president of the association of foreign correspondents (Stampa Estera) in Italy in 1961 and 1962 and president of the Overseas Press Club of America, the organization of American foreign correspondents from 1963 to 1965. Since 1966 he has served as a United States government spokesman in Rome, Saigon and Washington. He is currently spokesman for the U.S. Supreme Court.

King's Medical Heretic Upsets Orthodox Physiologists

Dr. William Harvey Demonstrates That Blood Does Circulate

By LAWRENCE G. BLOCHMAN

Not only does the spirit of revolt continue to grow in Parliament despite King Charles' assent to the Petition of Right last June and the assassination in August of the arrogant Duke of Buckingham, but it is finding an echo in the Royal College of Physicians. In fact, I predict that a revolutionary tract by Dr. William Harvey, M.D., the king's physician, will create an uproar in orthodox medical and other scientific circles before the end of this year 1628.

Dr. Harvey's monograph will declare, in defiance of what has been commonly accepted as truth for 1500 years, that the same blood flows through the arteries and veins, is pumped to the extremities by the heart and is pumped out again when it returns, over and over again. Where the blood originates is not at issue here (Aristotle believed it came from the liver). For centuries doctors generally agreed with Galen that the heart was a furnace of sorts, the source of the body's heat, and that the blood was conveyed from the liver to the right ventricle of the heart and that it was purified by passing to the left ventricle through invisible pores in the septum that separated the two ventricles. That explained the difference in color of the two kinds of blood. The blood that went through the arteries, Galen said, was mixed with air from the lungs and something he called "vital spirits"; the pulsation of the arteries was due, he said, to the expansion and contraction of these spirits.

A Cambridge professor who taught Dr. Harvey at Caius College (and who has asked to remain anonymous) tells me that Harvey is not the first to question Galen and his worshippers. He pointed out that a

Spanish physician named Miguel Serveto, who lived mostly in France and wrote under the name of Servetus, had disputed Galen's invisible pores only seventy or eighty years ago. Servetus proved that the blood did not ooze through the septum but was pumped through the lungs by the right heart and sent back to the left heart via the pulmonary vein. Unfortunately Servetus also wrote some pantheistic pamphlets criticizing the doctrine of the Trinity and was burned at the stake by John Calvin's orders at Geneva in 1553—proving, said my Cambridge don, that physicians should stick to their nostrums and leave politics and religion to the scoundrels and the saints.

I received a definite impression that my scholarly friend did not think too highly of Dr. Harvey. His reference to politics was an undisguised crack at Harvey for having been too buddy-buddy with royalty. Not only was he physician to the controversial present king but was also physician extraordinary to his father, King James. I undertook therefore to investigate Dr. Harvey's standing as a physician before seeking an interview with the man himself.

I found London doctors divided in their opinion of Harvey. There may have been some jealousy involved on the part of those whose practice didn't include such highly placed and well-heeled patients as were treated by Dr. Harvey. The late Lord Chancellor, Sir Francis Bacon, or more properly Viscount St. Albans, was one of Harvey's patients—before he was convicted of bribery and removed from office in 1621, as one colleague was quick to point out. The Earl of Arundel, diplomat and patron of the arts, was also a patient.

However, one physician I interviewed (and who also asked that his name be withheld) declared: "Just because he makes his rounds on horseback with his man following behind on foot with his pills and instruments doesn't make Harvey a genius. In fact, I wouldn't give tuppence for one of his prescriptions, although some apothecaries get quite high prices for a Harvey formula."

As most people are aware, it is standard practice for a London apothecary to collect and sell doctors' prescriptions for their own profit.

Under close questioning, my anonymous informant admitted that Dr. Harvey did possess some skill as a surgeon. He had performed a rather spectacular operation in which he removed a woman's breast. He was also able to put his theories to practical application: he caused a large tumor to disappear by putting a tight ligature around the neck of the growth and cutting off the blood supply.

I wrote to Dr. Harvey requesting a personal interview and was given a date some three weeks off. In the meantime I managed to attend a number of his lectures on the circulation of the blood given at the College of Physicians.

I was surprised to find him quite a small man, round faced with a dark, almost olive complexion. He had a full head of jet-black hair, just beginning to be touched with silver at the temples; after all, he was fifty years old. He was highly spirited in his presentation and walked about the platform as he lectured, gesturing to make his points as though to overcome the hostility he sensed among many of his auditors. He reminded me of a diminutive game cock, challenging all disbelief.

His demonstration of the flow of blood in the veins toward the heart was most convincing. He put a ligature around the arm of a student and as he tightened it he called attention to the bulging veins on the side of the tourniquet *away* from the heart. He produced a magnifying glass so that the students could mount the platform and look at the tiny knots under the skin in the engorged veins which Harvey explained were valves which kept the blood flowing in one direction (toward the heart) instead of backing up toward the fingers. This experiment, Dr. Harvey said, was first performed by the Italian anatomist Hieronymus Fabricius with whom he had studied for four years in Padua at the turn of the century.

At another demonstration Dr. Harvey made an incision in a student's artery and showed that the blood spurted in rhythm with the pulse and that the tempo was synchronized with the systole (contraction) of the heart. He then tightened a ligature around the arm on the side nearest the heart and the blood stopped spurting.

At the conclusion of this session one student asked what to me seemed an embarrassing question: "You say it's the same blood that flows outward through the arteries and comes back through the veins," the question went. "Can you explain to us, doctor, how the blood gets from the arteries to the veins?"

A titter ran through the audience, followed by an expectant hush. Dr. Harvey smiled slightly, waited for silence, then looking straight at his questioner replied: "That, sir, I cannot explain. At this point in scientific history only God can comprehend the transfusion from one system of blood vessels to the other. God alone also understands the source of the motive power which causes the heart muscles to contract and dilate.* Are there other questions?"

---

* The question was not answered until nine years after Harvey's death when the Italian microscopic anatomist Marcello Malpighi, born the year Harvey's historic

There were, but they seemed politically motivated, and Dr. Harvey turned them neatly aside. He was not physician to the king solely because he had been physician extraordinary to James I, the king's father, but because the king gave him access to the royal game preserves for his animal experiments which would be the basis for his next scientific study.

When I finally was received by William Harvey for a private interview, I noted that his personal appearance at close hand was even more impressive than my first perception. His forehead was higher and broader, his eyebrows were fuller and darker, and his well-trimmed beard reminded me of the actor-poet-dramatist Shakespeare I remember seeing at the Blackfriars Theatre when I was a very young man.

Dr. Harvey had nothing more to say on what medical men consider either a lunatic's hallucination or the most revolutionary concept in physiology for many centuries.

"My work on the study of the movements of the blood is finished," he said. "I have observed the phenomenon of circulation in living dogs, pigs, snakes, frogs, fishes and slugs—even in oysters, insects, transparent shrimp and chicks before they are hatched. I have nothing more to say on the subject. Read my book if you want to learn all that I know."

"What is the title, doctor?"

"*Exercitatio Anatomica de Motu Cordis et Sanguinis in Animalus.*"

"It's in Latin, then?"

"Naturally."

"I don't know Latin, doctor."

"Unfortunate, but I don't propose to teach you, beyond giving you the title: *Treatise on the Anatomical Movements of the Heart and Blood in Living Creatures.* Be sure you obtain a competent translator."

"What research occupies your interest now, doctor?"

"I am preparing a work to be published in ten or twenty years—whenever I complete the research to my satisfaction. It will concern the generation of living things and will, I hope, bear out my thesis, *Omne vivum ex ovo.*"

"Sorry, doctor, but my Latin—"

"Ah, yes. I had forgotten the lacuna in your learning. All living things spring from the egg. Or what stands as surrogate for the egg in mammals."

---

treatise appeared, discovered the capillaries, the microscopic links between the two networks. Although the motive-power of the heart beat is now recognized to be electric, its biochemical origin is, in this year 1974, still known only to God.—*Editor.*

"And you expect your research will span two decades, doctor?"

"Possibly less, since the king has placed the animals of the royal deer parks at Windsor and Hampton Court at my disposal. There is a practical side, you see, to my royalist politics."

After a few polite interchanges I thanked the good doctor and took my leave.

I obtained one of the first copies of *Motu Cordis* that arrived from Frankfurt where they were printed. The first translation by a friend who is a Latin scholar was set before my eyes shortly before I sat down to write this review of the man and his work. I think it would serve to further characterize the man if I reproduced verbatim a few lines from the title page and the dedication. The title page reads:

EXERCITATIO ANATOMICA DE MOTU CORDIS ET SANGUINUS IN ANIMALUS

GUILIELMI HARRVEI ANGLI

Medici Regii e Professoris Anatomica in
Collegio Medicorum Londonensi

I call the reader's attention to the fact that he ranks his title of the king's physician ahead of that of his academic title. The dedication on the next page gave me pause.

Serenissimo & Invictissimo

CARLO MAGNA

Brittaniae, Franciae & Hyberniae Regi,
Fidei Defensori.

I can just hear the Parliamentarians' rude remarks when they read the dedication to the Serene and Invincible Charles the Great. And the Duc de Sully who once called the king's father the wisest fool in Europe must have something equally biting to say about King Charles when he notes the inclusion of France in his kingdom.

There were in all nineteen pages of introductory matter, largely designed to satisfy some ego or other, but only fifty-three pages of the text that will, I predict, revolutionize the science and practice of medicine in the next one hundred years in these islands, regardless of what happens in that other revolution shaping up between the Stuart king from Scotland and the English parliament.

Dr. William Harvey, in those fifty-three pages, has upset orthodox medical men anus over alphabet by stating the following well-founded conclusions, all of them logically based on experiment:

1. That the heart, not the liver, is the point from which the blood is distributed throughout the body in a "motion, as it were, in a circle."

2. That the heart is a muscular sac whose contraction (not dilation) drives the blood outward and simultaneously produces the pulse in the arteries.

3. That the arteries contain blood exclusively, not air.

4. That the blood returns to the heart in the opposite direction via a system of separate vessels—the veins—and is the same blood.

5. That the blood from the right heart reaches the left ventricle of the heart *not* through Galen's "invisible pores" but via the pulmonary artery to the lungs (where it is purified) then back to the right heart via the pulmonary vein.

6. That the flow of blood is continuous—until it is halted by death when the heart stops contracting.

7. That there is mathematical proof of the hypothesis that the blood moves "in a circle." In his masterly ninth chapter the pompous little scientist proudly answers the cynical question of the stupid mastiffs snapping at his heels. Measuring the hearts of numerous cadavers, Harvey determined that the left ventricle when dilated can hold a little more than two fluid ounces of blood. In contraction the left ventricle could contain about 16% less—so that at each contraction it would expel about one-fourth of an ounce of blood. Beating at the rate of seventy-two per minute—or slightly over 1000 systoles in half an hour—the heart would pump from ten to fifteen pounds of blood in that time, an amount that is at least half again the amount of blood that the average man contains in his entire body. Dr. Harvey established the fixed ratio of blood to the total weight of a body by measurements obtained from butchers. He found that when the throat of an ox—or a pig or a sheep—is cut, the entire blood content of the carcass is drained in fifteen minutes, and that the amount is fairly constant in relation to the weight of the animal. Using the same ratio for man,* Harvey calculated that the amount of

* Three and one-half centuries after Harvey scientists have fixed the ratio of blood content to body weight at about 5 percent—or about 7½ pounds for the average man.—*Editor.*

blood pumped by the heart in half an hour would exceed the total of man's blood supply by anywhere from 30% to 100%. Since there is no apparent space in the body to absorb the excess blood (and the excess would be compounded every half hour) it must be obvious to any rational creature that the same blood circulates over and over again.

The prime topic of talk in the taverns and drawing rooms today continues to be the assassination of the Duke of Buckingham and the king's increasingly bitter and stubborn struggle with Parliament which seems certain to end in his proroguing the Commons, if not in actual civil war. However, I venture to predict that in the centuries ahead when Charles and all the House of Stuart will have been chased back to Scotland and when the name of the disgruntled officer who did away with Buckingham is forgotten—what was his name, by the way? John something? Could it be Felton?—the work of the cocky little royalist physician will not only be remembered but celebrated by the unborn generations of scientists who will have been freed from the myths of the Galenists.

Salve, Guilielmi Harrvei!

Larry Blochman's concern for the world of William Harvey dates back half a century when as police reporter for the late-lamented *San Diego Sun* he watched the coroner's pathologist delve more or less competently into the secret interior of a local Chinese who had been killed in a Tong war.

A graduate with the class of 1921 from the University of California (Berkeley, of course; UCLA was a junior college then), he worked on English-language newspapers in the Orient (Tokyo, Shanghai, Manila, Singapore, Batavia [now Jakarta] and Calcutta) and in France. He has been free-lancing since 1927, except for forty weeks in Hollywood and four years with the Office of War Information where he directed the European, African, and Middle Eastern broadcasts of the Voice of America.

His books dealing with medicine include a biography of Dr. Squibb, a physiology for teenagers (*Understanding Your Body*), a book on massage (*Wake Up Your Body*), one on laboratory medicine (*Doctors Anonymous*), collaborations on leprosy (*Alone No Longer*) and behavior therapy (*Help Without Psychoanalysis*), and a translation from the French (*In Search of Man* by André Missenard, a disciple of Alexis Carrel).

He is the creator of the fictional pathologist-detective Dr. Daniel Webster Coffee who for twenty-five years has appeared in the pages of *Collier's, This Week, Ellery Queen's Mystery Magazine,* three books and a television series.

Blochman has been a member of the Overseas Press Club since the first year of its founding. He has been a member of the Board of Governors several times and a vice president once. He is also author of the OPC round-the-world bar guide, *Here's How!*

Freedom of Press Sustained by Obscure Publisher

As reported by JOHN WILHELM

A printer and editor of the *New York Weekly Journal,* John Peter Zenger, thirty-eight-years old, was found not guilty by a twelve-man jury today, August 4, 1735, of charges of publishing seditious libels against the Royal Colonial government of New York.

This is the first time the principle of truth has been successfully employed as a defense in the colonies even though the publication of the allegedly libelous statements in question was admitted by Zenger's attorney, the distinguished Andrew Hamilton, of Philadelphia.

Crowds in the small courtroom in New York's City Hall cheered when the jury foreman announced the verdict, and the group of spectators and counsel moved along Nassau and Broad streets to the nearby Black Horse Tavern to discuss the important new development. Zenger himself was returned to the gaol until formalities authorizing his release could be drawn.

It is widely held among the townspeople of New York that Zenger did not write the articles in question, but was merely the printer of them. It is believed that James Alexander, a local attorney of prominence and a man of wealth, had the skill in rhetoric to be the author of most of the articles concerned. And in fact, with a group of friends, had financed Zenger in establishing the *Weekly Journal* in opposition to the established newspaper, the *New York Gazette,* which rarely if ever deviates from a line of support for the king's appointed governor.

But only Zenger's name appeared in the *Journal,* and it was Zenger, an immigrant from Germany with an imperfect command of English, who was, perforce, the object of any libel suit by the crown attorneys who were lacking any evidence that others participated in the publication.

The matter is seen by observers here as a strong political blow against the unpopular Governor Cosby and his administration, but the acceptance of the judicial aberration of the jury against the advice of the presiding judge in freeing Zenger as a legal principle is far from clear. In fact, jurists contend it will have no effect in the foreseeable future on cases of libel or freedom to print. The long-run historical effect, however, may be great, as the case is bound to be studied widely both in the colonies and in the capitals of Europe as it has attracted much attention.

Zenger had been imprisoned on November 17, 1734, and held in custody since then, but presumably will be released tomorrow. The *Weekly Journal* has been published throughout this time by the wife of the accused, Anna Zenger, and an employee. Mr. Zenger was unable to raise bail of £400.

The verdict came as a surprise to both the Chief Justice of the Province of New York, James Delancey, and the Attorney General of the King, Richard Bradley. The latter felt he had only to show publication of an admitted libel to convict the defendant, and the Justice had instructed the jury to this effect.

The defendant had been charged with publishing false news and seditious libels with "wicked malice against the administration of the Royal Governor, William Cosby, Captain General and Governor-in-Chief, and to traduce, scandalize and villify the governor and the ministers and officers of the king, and to bring them into suspicion and ill opinions of the subjects of the King George II residing within the province."

Complaints brought against Zenger by the Crown involved information issued for printing and publishing two statements with apparent libels against the governor and his administration.

One report that had particularly offended the governor was contained in an issue of the *Weekly Gazette* which alleged the governor permitted sailors from a French warship to come ashore and gather information about the defenses of the bay, and another issue accused the governor of arranging for only his favorites to attend council meetings.

Hamilton, who was Zenger's lawyer, an eighty-year-old man who is erect in carriage and with a persuasive manner before the jury, startled the court by replying to these charges:

"May it Please your Honour; I am concerned in this Cause on the Part of Mr. Zenger the Defendant . . . I cannot think it proper for me (without doing Violence to my own Principles) to deny the Publication of a Complaint, which I think is the Right of every free-born Subject to make, when the Matters so published can be supported with Truth; and therefore I'll save Mr. Attorney the Trouble of examining his Witnesses to that Point; and I do (for my Client) confess, that he both printed and published the two News Papers set forth in the Information, and I hope in so doing he has committed no Crime."

The prosecuting attorney then stated that as Mr. Hamilton had admitted fact of publication, he moved that the witnesses be discharged as there was no further occasion for them to testify, and the jury should bring in a verdict of guilty as charged.

Mr. Hamilton. "Not so neither, Mr. Attorney, there are two Words to that Bargain. I hope it is not our bare Printing and Publishing a Paper, that will make it a Libel: You will have something more to do, before you make my Client a Libeller; 'scandalous, and seditious,' or else we are not guilty. . . .

"May it please Your Honour; I agree with Mr. Attorney, that Government is a sacred Thing, but I differ very widely from him when he would insinuate, that the just Complaints of a Number of Men, who suffer under a bad Administration, is libelling that Administration. . . .

"I was in Hopes, as that terrible Court, where those dreadful Judgments were given, and that Law established, which Mr. Attorney has produced for Authorities to support this Cause, was long ago laid aside, as the most dangerous Court to the Liberties of the People of England, that ever was known in that Kingdom; that Mr. Attorney knowing this, would not have attempted to set up a Star-Chamber here, nor to make their Judgments a Precedent to us: For it is well known, that what would have been judg'd Treason in those Days for a Man to speak, I think, has since not only been practiced as lawful, but the contrary Doctrine has been held to be Law. . . ."

Mr. Attorney. ". . . The Case before the Court is, whether Mr Zenger is guilty of Libelling His Excellency the Governour of New York, and indeed the whole Administration of the Government? Mr. Hamilton has confessed the Printing and Publishing, and I think nothing is plainer, than that the Words in the Information are 'scandalous, and tend to sedition, and to disquiet the Minds of the People of this Province.' And if such Papers are not Libels, I think it may be said, there can be no such Thing as a Libel."

Mr. Hamilton. "May it please Your Honour; I cannot agree with Mr. Attorney: For tho' I freely acknowledge, that there are such Things as Libels, yet I must insist at the same Time, that what my Client is charged with, is not a Libel; and I observed just now, that Mr. Attorney in defining a Libel, made use of the Words, 'scandalous, seditious, and tend to disquiet the People'; but (whether with Design or not I will not say) he omitted the Word 'false.' "

Mr. Attorney. "I think I did not omit the Word 'false': But it has been said already, that it may be a Libel, notwithstanding it may be true."

Mr. Hamilton. "In this I must still differ with Mr. Attorney; for I depend upon it, we are to be tried upon this Information now before the Court and Jury, and to which we have pleaded 'Not Guilty,' and by it we are charged with Printing and publishing 'a certain false, malicious, seditious and scandalous Libel.' This Word 'false' must have some Meaning, or else how came it there? I hope Mr. Attorney will not say, he put it there by Chance, and I am of Opinion his Information would not be good without it. But to shew that it is the principal thing which, in my Opinion, makes a Libel, I put the Case, the Information had been for printing and publishing a certain 'true' Libel, would that be the same thing? Or could Mr. Attorney support such an Information by any Precedent in the English Law? No, the Falsehood makes the Scandal, and both make the Libel. And to shew the Court that I am in good Earnest, and to save the Court's Time, and Mr. Attorney's Trouble, I will agree, that if he can prove the Facts charged upon us, to be 'false,' I'll own them to be 'scandalous, seditious, and a Libel.' So the Work seems now to be pretty much shortened, and Mr. Attorney has now only to prove the Words 'false,' in order to make us Guilty."

Hamilton then referred back to the Magna Carta and English common law to prove that freedom to express justifiable truth had been accepted in earlier times.

The Chief Justice Delancey, a young man recently appointed by the governor, objected that Mr. Hamilton could not offer truth of a libel as a defense and said "The Court is of the opinion you ought not to be permitted to prove the facts in papers" and offered long citations of supporting evidence.

Hamilton then appealed directly to the jury:

"It is not the cause of the poor printer, nor of New York alone, which you are now trying. . . . It may in its consequences affect every freeman that lives under a British government on the main of America.

"It is the best cause as it is the cause of Liberty, and I make no doubt but your upright conduct this day, will not only entitle you to the love and esteem of your fellow citizens, but every man who prefers freedom to a life of slavery will bless and honour you, as men who have baffled the attempt of tyranny, and by an impartial and uncorrupt verdict you have laid a noble foundation for securing to ourselves, our posterity and our neighbors, that to which nature and laws of our country have given us a right, the liberty both of exposing and opposing arbitrary power by speaking and writing the truth."

The jury adjourned for deliberations, and then Thomas Hunt, the foreman, returned a verdict of "Not Guilty" which shocked the judge but provoked cheers from onlookers crowding the courtroom.

Governor William Cosby, who was named to govern the New York colony by George II and arrived in the city of several thousand population on August 1, 1732, had previously been governor of the island of Minorca where his subjects had accused him of unfairly seizing properties and had protested to the British Board of Trade. In his new post in New York, he had developed some substantial enemies prior to the Zenger trial including the man serving as acting governor before his arrival, Rip Van Dam, from whom he demanded part of Van Dam's stipend.

Other opponents of the governor included the previously mentioned James Alexander and William Smith, both prominent attorneys in the colony and men of wealth, and Lewis Morris Jr., all of whom feared their interests were imperiled by the new governor's actions. They had differences over a disputed election in Eastchester where the sheriff had allegedly disenfranchised numerous voters to prevent Morris from winning an election.

It is widely known that this group, anxious to have a means of communication with the public other than the *New York Gazette* published by William Bradford, a man of substance, but in close alliance with the Colonial government, had supported a new publication.

They had encouraged the establishment of a newspaper by John Peter Zenger, who had served eight years as an apprentice to Bradford, beginning as an ink-stained printer's devil, until the end of his apprenticeship when he left Bradford to become an itinerant, wandering about the colonies. He had been born in the Rhineland of Germany in 1697, and come to the American colonies in 1710 as a youth. His English was faulty and he never mastered it to the extent he could be called an editor. But he is considered a fine printer and publisher, and his second wife, Anna, helped with the operation of the shop and the putting together of the weekly publication, the *New York Weekly Journal*.

It was widely held that Zenger was assisted and encouraged in publication of the *New York Weekly Journal* by a group headed by Alexander, who is a brilliant writer and a scholarly lawyer although his strength did not lie in court appearances. Many suspect that most of the articles in the Journal ridiculing the royal government and Governor Cosby were in fact written by James Alexander, but proof of this was not introduced at the trial, if in fact it could be proven at all. Cosby himself stated:

"Mr. James Alexander is the person whom I have too much occasion to mention. . . . No sooner did Van Dam and the late Chief Justice (the latter especially) begin to treat my administration with rudeness and ill-manners than I found Alexander to be at the head of a scheme to give all imaginable uneasiness to the government by infusing into, and making the worst impression on, the minds of the people. A press supported by him and his party began to swarm with the most virulent libels."

Governor Cosby first ordered that Zenger be charged with sedition and libel by a grand jury upon accusations brought by Chief Justice Delancey, but that jury failed to act, and so did a second jury subsequently. The governor did succeed with having certain issues burned in public but was forced to call upon slaves to do so as officials declined.

On November 17, 1734, Zenger was arrested by the sheriff with a warrant sworn by the governor and his council, and held on a charge of "seditious libel." Although he signed a statement saying his total wealth amounted to ten pounds, bond was fixed at the unusually high sum of £400 which Zenger was unable to post.

After a public defender was named for Zenger, James Alexander and others approached the famous Philadelphia Lawyer, and former Attorney General of the colony of Pennsylvania, Andrew Hamilton, to represent Zenger in court. Fortunately, he agreed and was able to persuade the jury to his argument that truth was an element to be considered in a charge of sedition and libel. The convincing of the jury was not in fact a legal landmark, but more of a recognition of a political situation which later was to lead to thought in developing other laws, as the case was widely studied in all the colonies and in England as well.

The finding of the jury clearly did not reflect the laws of the colony at that time. The Chief Justice had agreed with the Attorney General that the New York law was based on the 1606 Star Chamber case, *de Libellis Famosis,* which concluded that true statements could be libelous. The implication was that truth was no defense if a libel had in fact been printed.

But Hamilton in his defense was doing more than arguing that sedition had to be false as well as malicious and damaging to the government.

He was in fact pleading that the people had certain rights to criticize their government, and this line of argument had found willing listeners in the twelve-man jury. This was a development in political affairs that was equally important to separate reasoning that certain freedoms belonged to the printer of a newspaper, which may have been a lesser and ancillary conclusion in the view of the jurors.

It is to be remembered that selection of the jury for the Zenger trial was begun by a court appointed attorney, generally considered friendly to the governor. This public attorney originally pled Zenger not guilty, and did move for the striking of a jury. This process called for the clerk of the court to select the names of forty-eight free-holders, from whom the defense and prosecution could each eliminate twelve names leaving twenty-four from whom the final twelve could be selected.

At first the clerk produced a list of names including non-freeholders and markedly containing names of former magistrates and tradesmen in the business of supplying the government. Zenger's friends objected to this device, and a new list of properly drawn freeholders was prepared on July 30, 1735.

The key to the defense of Zenger was a conclusion, probably reached by James Alexander, himself an attorney of note but not a trial lawyer of any great appearance, that the public defender named for Zenger be replaced by a more able counsel.

One of them had suggested the name of Alexander Hamilton of Philadelphia, a man considered perhaps the best lawyer in all of the colonies. Hamilton had had a distinguished career as Attorney General of Pennsylvania from 1717 to 1726, Speaker of the Assembly of Pennsylvania from 1729 to 1739, and had been associated with James Alexander in many law cases. He also had brought suit for libel against William Bradford and the New York Gazette in an unconnected and earlier case, where Bradford was accused of defaming the Pennsylvania Assembly. Thus he was familiar with many of the participants in the Zenger case.

However, Hamilton was nearly eighty years of age, suffered from gout, and his health made it doubtful if he would agree to serve. Still, he was straight and erect in carriage, with a persuasive courtroom manner, and it was plain to all that his intellectual powers were sharp and his mind keen.

Upon being written to by Lewis Morris Jr. upon the advice of Alexander, who joined in the plea for Hamilton to come to New York to serve as counsel for Zenger, Hamilton wrote back that he was interested and would like to see all the papers involved. Upon perusing them, he agreed to take the case.

In 1735 the town of New York was a community of some 10,000 inhabitants grouped in homes built about the Fort, the governor's house, and the City Hall, built in 1700 at the corner of Nassau and Wall streets. The courtroom where Zenger was tried was in the City Hall. Nearby were the King's Arms and the Black Horse taverns, where those who could not crowd into the courtroom adjourned to hear details of the case and debate it.

Political ideas of the time came from such British publications as reprinted in the *New England Courant,* the *Massachusetts Spy,* and the *Boston Post.* Many were reprints of Whig journalists in England such as the "Cato" papers which dealt with such daring concepts as freedom of speech and even reflections upon libeling.

The defense of Zenger as conceived by James Alexander was based on much of this thinking, and was evident in many of the articles Alexander apparently authored for the *Weekly Journal* although none were ever under his name nor even provable as his. There also were attacks reputed to him upon Governor Cosby, who had become his political antagonist shortly after his arrival, due to disputes over land ownership, voting rights and Crown appointments and fees. Alexander and his group felt uneasy about their position under the new governor. The governor's side has never been fully presented to the public, but it is evident that he was intent upon making a maximum financial gain from his position as governor.

Alexander and Hamilton in writing in court took the position that the public had a right to criticize their government, even in a royal colony, and they suggested that making an offense of seditious libel was really a device to protect the king and his ministers. Hamilton proposed that although this might be appropriate law in England, it might not be in the colonies where settlers were largely surviving through their own struggles to make a living and defend themselves.

Further, Alexander and Hamilton argued that there were limits to power of the state to destroy individuals, and that citizens were not obligated to support a governor, uncriticized, if he was about to damage a province or colony. There was no other way to bring a minister of the Crown to justice, he indicated.

Hamilton pressed for free speech and implicitly for freedom of the press although this concept was not expressed as such. Only later, it was felt, would the latter concept be formalized.

The victory which freed Zenger, however, was in fact a political defeat for the governor and was not recognized as the first step toward the right of freedom of the press.

Nevertheless, the *Weekly Journal* had reprinted an item which said: "The liberty of the press is a subject of great importance and in which every individual is as much concerned as he is about any other part of liberty."

Thus the doors of the gaol swung open, the humble printer who bore the title of editor of the *Weekly Journal* walked free and was able to resume publishing the *Weekly Journal* which his wife had produced during his incarceration.

John R. Wilhelm, Dean of the College of Communication, comes from an extensive background in professional journalism. He is head of one of the six degree colleges of Ohio University. Its School of Journalism is third largest in the nation, and its School of Radio-Television is one of the largest in the world. Before coming to Ohio University in 1968, he directed the world-wide news-gathering network of the McGraw-Hill Publishing Company for the forty-five publications of that company.

For nine years previously, he had served as a foreign correspondent in both Europe and Latin America for both newspapers and magazines and as an NBC commentator. He was a war correspondent during World War II.

As head of McGraw-Hill World News, he directed a world-wide organization of eighty-seven staff correspondents located in twenty-one cities, both foreign and domestic, such as London, Moscow, Bonn, Paris, Hong Kong, Tokyo, Milan, and Mexico City. This organization also has over one hundred fifty special or string correspondents in other cities throughout the world. The company-maintained service provides McGraw-Hill editors with half a million words a week.

Mr. Wilhelm holds an AB degree from the University of Minnesota where he studied journalism. Thereafter he was a police reporter for the City News Bureau in Chicago, a general assignment reporter for the *Chicago Tribune,* night manager for the United Press in Detroit, on the United Press cable desk in New York and served as a war correspondent for the *Chicago Sun* and later as a European staff correspondent for that newspaper. He joined McGraw-Hill in 1947 and served as McGraw-Hill news bureau chief in Buenos Aires and in Mexico City before returning to New York in 1955 as editor of the World News Service. He also was NBC's correspondent during this time.

He was president of the Overseas Press Club of America (1959–60). In 1961 he was given the University of Missouri Honor Award for Distinguished Service in Journalism.

Mr. Wilhelm is the author of two books on Mexico, one book on the Caribbean and numerous studies of foreign correspondence, a field in which he is a recognized international authority. He is married to Margaret Maslin Wilhelm, who was a Red Cross girl in Europe at the time he met her during the war. They have four children.

The Wright Brothers Begin Era of Powered Flight

As reported by ANSEL E. TALBERT

Man grew wings today, December 17, 1903, for the first time in history and from now on can compete with the angels.

Two young bicycle builders and former newspapermen from Dayton, Ohio, named Wilbur and Orville Wright made four flights this morning in a flying machine of their own design and manufacture over the rocky beaches near Kitty Hawk. All four were into the teeth of high, gusty winds having velocities of between twenty-four and twenty-seven miles an hour, and in biting cold weather which has frozen every pond and puddle in this area.

They are the first flights on record in which a heavier-than-air flying machine lifted from the ground under its own power, flew forward without any speed reduction and landed safely at a point as high above sea level as the one from which it started.

The inventors who built the machine and made the flights are remarkable men from an equally remarkable family. Their seventy-five-year-old father, the Right Reverend Milton Wright, who is a bishop of the United Brethren Church, and for many years the editor of a publication called *The Religious Telescope,* also found time to invent a typewriter. An older brother, Loren Wright, invented, patented, and sold a hay press.

In addition to building and selling a bicycle of their own design which they named the "Wright Special," Wilbur and Orville designed and built several printing presses, on one of which they produced a full-sized weekly newspaper called *The West Side News.* They later converted this into a five-column daily, *The Evening Item,* and have helped a Negro friend—Paul Lawrence Dunbar, the poet—to found a magazine written entirely by members of his race. This was printed on the Wright Press.

The amazing performance today of the two young Daytonians (Wilbur is thirty-six-years old and Orville is thirty-two) comes only eight days after the latest failure of the larger, more elaborate and more costly flying machine of Professor Samuel Pierpont Langley to fly in tests near Washington, D.C. Prof. Langley, secretary of the prestigious Smithsonian Institution and a former assistant to the director of Harvard Observatory, is a distinguished astronomer, physicist, and mathematician who for several years has devoted the major part of his time to conducting powered flight experiments.

The two Wright brothers have only a high school education, although Orville once planned to enter Yale. They have sharpened their naturally inquisitive minds by newspaper reporting and editing, and by voluminous reading in their father's library of several thousand volumes dealing with almost every subject under the sun.

The four flights they made today, after a brief and not so successful "hop" three days ago with Wilbur aboard the flying machine, lasted from twelve to fifty-nine seconds. The flights covered distances ranging from 120 to 850 feet, which would have increased materially had the Wright brothers and their flying machine not been struggling against high and gusty winds.

Although all were completed successfully, there were several times during their progress when an accident appeared to be imminent, due to the gusts and the unfamiliarity of the two "flyers" with their machine operating under the power of its twelve to fourteen-horsepower engine. Since Wilbur had exhausted his seniority by taking off three days ago, Orville made today's first flight lying flat on the flying machine's lower wing beside the engine, while his brother ran alongside the craft to steady it before it left the ground. After that, the brothers alternated.

The last and longest flight of the day took place just before noon with Wilbur at the machine's controls. After about 800 feet had been covered in flight, the flying machine began pitching as kites sometimes do when flown in strong winds.

It then darted downward and made a hard landing. The frame supporting the front rudder was broken at the time of landing, but the main part of the machine was not injured at all. Repairs could have been completed by tomorrow, except for a sudden and unexpected disaster which overtook the flying machine while it was resting quietly on the rocky and sandy soil after the fourth flight.

This happened while the brothers were discussing their epochal exploits with five local residents who witnessed all of them, and accepting congratulations with their customary modesty and reticence. A howling gust caught up and overturned the frail machine, which is built of pine and ash with two cloth-covered wings, and then turned it over and over until it was completely wrecked.

J. T. Daniels, who was out three days ago for the first powered trial, and counts the Wright brothers as close friends—as do all the other witnesses—was nearest to the flying machine except for Wilbur. Both tried to hold the machine until the others could join them, but failed. Mr. Daniels became entangled in the structure and was upset and dragged along, getting some bad bruises and scratches but suffering no major injuries.

The flying machine is an almost complete wreck and cannot be repaired here for more flights. The Wright brothers are saddened by the accident and what it has done to their plans for this season, but they are in no way really discouraged. They say that all their past experiments with kites and gliders and their theories of how to build a successful flying machine were proven today on the sands of Kitty Hawk. They already have plans for a new "practical flyer."

The one wrecked today represents a joint investment by them of about $1,000 including tickets for both from Dayton to Kitty Hawk and return. This sum does not, however, include any wages at $16 a week which skilled bicycle mechanics would have been paid had they done most of the work on the flying machine's construction instead of the two brothers.

Had such wages been paid, Wilbur and Orville say that the cost would have been about $2,000. The flying machine's four-cylinder engine, which they designed and constructed at their Dayton bicycle shop after failing to find one for sale anywhere which suited them, burns kerosene fuel costing 15 cents a gallon.

The Wright brothers' achievements are certain to give great satisfaction to their friend, Professor Octave Chanute, this nation's great authority on gliding and other related aeronautical matters, who visited them at their camp here in October, and watched some of their preliminary gliding flights. The professor is scheduled to address the annual meeting of the American Association for the Advancement of Science in St. Louis later on this month and doubtless will have something to say about today's events, although he had left before they took place.

The flights also are certain to please Bishop Wright, a widower who lives in Dayton. The Wright brothers say that it was their father who first excited their interest in building a flying machine. When they were boys, he gave them a toy called a "hélicoptère" which was made in France. A twisted rubber band in it rotated propellers so as to make it rise upward and strike the ceiling of their home.

When the two brothers left Dayton together on September 16 with their flying machine used today broken down for shipment and assembly at Kitty Hawk, their father's parting words to them were:

"Here is a dollar. Be sure to wire me when you are in the air."

This is the first thing which the brothers did this afternoon after they collected the wreckage of their flying machine, cooked their own lunch in the building which they erected themselves as a living and sleeping quarters, and then carefully washed, dried, and put away the dishes.

They also took time to thank Mr. Daniels and the other witnesses, W. S. Dough, A. D. Etheridge, W. C. Brinkley, of nearby Manteo, N.C. and a youth named Johnny Ward, of Nags Head, for all the volunteer assistance which the brothers received.

Although Orville read of the most recent failure of Prof. Langley's "aerodrome" to fly on December 11 when he was hurrying back from an emergency trip to Dayton to obtain a new set of solid tool steel propeller shafts, neither brother expresses anything but the highest regard for the professor, with whom they have corresponded. Prof. Langley is reported to be in seclusion, deeply hurt by the ridicule and abuse to which he has been subjected, because of his two failures in man-carrying powered flights after initial successes with a steam-powered model.

Instead of expressing envy over the fact that Prof. Langley had funds amounting to around $70,000 to back his work, in contrast to their own meagre resources, they say that the knowledge so learned a scientist believed powered, man-carrying flight to be possible was an incentive and an inspiration to them.

The Wright brothers have not said so, but it is possible that they are taking a bit of good-humored satisfaction from the certainty that today's flights will confound Professor Simon Newcomb, whom many regard as the most distinguished and knowledgeable scientist in the United States. Prof. Newcomb, the only American citizen since Benjamin Franklin to be elected to the French Academy of Science, carefully explained less than two months ago in an article in *The Independent* immediately following an earlier failure of the "Langley aerodrome" that heavier-than-air human flight was impractical, if not completely impossible.

Prof. Newcomb said that even in the unlikely event a flying machine got off the ground carrying a man, the following would happen, unless all scientific knowledge was wrong:

"Once he slackens speed, down he begins to fall. Once he stops, he falls a dead mass. How shall he reach the ground without destroying his delicate machinery?"

Prof. Newcomb's views have had the full support of many other distinguished men of science in this country.

One of the most articulate of these has been Rear Admiral George W. Melville, chief engineer of the United States Navy. In numerous comments, and in a recent article in *The North American Review*, he has argued that the idea of successful heavier-than-air flight by man is absurd.

It is now time to describe the events leading up to today's flights, and to explain how the Wright brothers, two largely self-educated journalists and bicycle builders, have succeeded in teaching themselves how to fly in a machine of their own invention, where some of the world's supposedly most learned scientists failed even to grasp the idea of human flight.

The explanation lies mostly in the characters of the two men involved. They are men of great faith and imagination, who have been willing to use the tools and techniques of science without becoming part of the scientific establishment to the extent of adopting its prejudices, or perpetuating its mistakes. One might say that they have the true spirit of science, in that they recognize what sometimes is called a "scientific truth" to be only hypothesis based on the best data or evidence available at the time.

Their active interest in solving the secrets of human flight in a heavier-than-air machine—initially aroused by their father and his toy "hélicoptère" gift dates back eight or ten years to before the mid-1890s.

For centuries other men had dreamed of flying like birds, and a number actually attempted to do so, but without success. Aside from stories of the gods and heroes of Greek and Roman mythology, there are historical references telling how Simon the Magician, for example, fell to his death in Rome 1,800 years ago, and of others coming after him who were lucky if they only broke a leg. During the past century, Sir Hiram Maxim and Sir George Cayley were among the builders of flying machines of one size or another.

But, it was the internationally-known series of gliding exploits of the late Otto Lilienthal of Germany, who was killed in a crash of one of his gliders in 1896, which really stimulated into action the imagination of first Wilbur, and then his younger brother. Lilienthal made hundreds of glides from hilltops and high places in his native land. Reading about these convinced the Wright brothers that the road to success lay in putting power to a glider, rather than building a flapping wing craft or ornithopter to imitate the birds.

Fired by Lilienthal's experiments and some of his theoretical conclusions, the Wright brothers wrote to the Smithsonian Institution in Washington to ask what scientific data were available on the subject of heavier-than-air flight. It turned out that there was very little tested information so they decided to go ahead and find out what they could by their own labors.

Controlling any flying machine in the air to do the bidding of its operator or "pilot" obviously was going to be a major problem. It was Wilbur who got the basic idea for latitudinal control of the "Wright Flyer" just demonstrated here, while idly twisting a cardboard box.

Lilienthal tried to control his gliders by shifting his weight during moments in the air, but it was the inadequacy of this method which contributed to the accident causing his death. Chanute and an associate named Morril some years ago obtained a patent for a horizontal rudder intended to give a glider or any other flying machine its longitudinal control.

Wilbur Wright, looking at what happened when he twisted the box, envisoned a flying machine with a biplane wing. He recognized that if the operator of such a machine could easily warp or twist the curvature of the wing tips at will during flight, he could alter and control its performance. Consequently, four years ago in Dayton, the two brothers constructed a large biplane kite having wings which could be warped from the ground by controls. They put it into the air hundreds of times to prove that their theory was right.

The following year, they built their first full-scale glider embodying the same principles, and brought it here to the lonely dunes of Kitty Hawk for testing during the Fall season. First they put it aloft as a kite, in light winds, to try out some of their still untested controls, from the ground. Then, it became a man-carrying kite in winds of over twenty-five miles an hour. This gave the two brothers the chance of actually getting off the ground in their creation, and seeing how it responded to the various devices and techniques of guiding movements they had devised.

They tried out a fixed horizontal "rudder" mounted in front that initially had to be adjusted on the ground, but which they later made controllable. They were able to warp the wings for lateral control by an ingenious wire arrangement actuated by their feet. Finally, they made about a dozen free glides from hilltops which kept them in gliding flight for a total of about two minutes altogether, and caused them to doubt that performance tables Lilienthal compiled before his untimely death were accurate.

In the spring of 1901, primarily to get many hours of control experience at minimum risk, the Wright brothers designed and built their glider number two. This had a wing spread or span of twenty-two feet, a total area of 290 square feet and a structural weight without its "pilot" of 108 pounds. Its wing curvature, however, appeared to cause pitching which the front horizontal "rudder" or elevator could not balance, when the machine was used in high winds as a man-carrying kite. Although they made many more successful glides than during the season previous, they were disappointed that their glider's "lift" was less than one-third of what they had expected it to be from preliminary calculations.

During the ensuing winter, in Dayton, they carefully reviewed all the data and experience they had accumulated, and then designed their third and much larger glider. This one had numerous improvements and refinements, including a pair of fixed vertical "fins" to give it greater directional stability.

Its wing span was thirty-two feet one inch and it weighed 116.5 pounds. During the year's late summer, they made nearly 1,000 glides in it here at Kitty Hawk, amounting to about twenty hours of free flight. Their experiences with its performance caused them to replace the two fixed vertical "fins" with a single larger movable rudder, also in the vertical plane. After two months of gliding and experimenting, they were completely confident that they had only to add a light and powerful engine to achieve the world's first powered heavier-than-air flights.

The engine of the Wright brothers' flying machine, which is hardly damaged at all by today's accident, is as remarkable as the airframe which it pushes forward in the air. The two brothers also designed and built this themselves, with the extremely able assistance of one of their Dayton bicycle shop employes, named C. H. Taylor. Before they went to this trouble, they tried to locate an engine in the United States and abroad which would meet the requirements their calculations showed they needed—but to no avail. Then, they tried to interest some of this nation's most prominent builders of automobiles and horseless carriages in turning one out to their specifications, but again failed completely.

The Wright brothers felt that they had to have an engine which would weigh no more than 200 pounds and deliver at least eight horsepower. They were both amazed and delighted when the one they built from their own design, with little to guide them, turned out sixteen horsepower in its initial tests. They found out in further trials that it could be counted on for the steady twelve horsepower which it produced during today's four flights.

For fuel, as already noted, it burns a kerosene by-product of oil refining, costing 15 cents a gallon. Since the tank holds somewhat less than that amount, fuel cost was not a major expense this morning. When they came to Kitty Hawk in September of this year, they sent their flying machine by rail from Dayton to Elizabeth City, N.C. in boxes, and purchased a five gallon can of kerosene from the boatman who took them in his ship to Nag's Head, the nearest port to Kitty Hawk.

Technically speaking, the Wright brothers flying machine engine is a horizontal four-cylinder one of four-inch bore. The cylinders are iron units, individually cast, and fitted into a solid cast aluminum crankcase. This extends to form a water jacket around the cylinder barrels. Mr. Taylor and the Wright brothers took turns in machining the crankshaft from a solid sheet of armor plate that was one and nine-sixteenths inches thick.

A low-tension generator of the horseshoe type having an inducted electromotive field provides the ignition. The pistons are lubricated near the end of a stroke by small engine oil cups.

The hot spark needed to start the engine comes from a starter box outside the flying machine. It uses four dry-cell batteries and a home-made induction coil that was made at the Wright bicycle shop in Dayton. Water for cooling the engine flows through a thermo-siphon from a long and narrow radiator that is mounted on one of the wire "struts" of the flying machine's center section. Here also is mounted the fuel tank which takes the kerosene to the engine by means of a gravity-flow system.

It might be thought that, after the development of their concept of flight, the engine provided the greatest challenge to the ingenuity of the Wright brothers. While they now modestly admit that the engine indeed was a considerable achievement, and praise Mr. Taylor's work on it to the skies, they both agree that their prime problem was to design airscrews or "propellers" which would not waste the engine power. The entire project almost certainly would have failed had this not been accomplished. This field of experimentation may hold the clue to why Professor Langley and others did not succeed.

Initially, the Wright brothers turned to ship propeller formulae for a solution. But, they quickly found that the existing ones were inexact, and had little relevance to performance in the air. It dawned upon them, in discussing the problem, that an "air propeller" would simply be a wing surface turning in a spiral direction. With this in mind, they worked out their own formula.

The brothers checked this out with the greatest possible care during a series of tests in Dayton, during which their air propellers were mounted on a test stand in such a manner that their performance could be measured exactly. In this endeavor, one more invention of the Wright brothers proved useful. It is called a wind tunnel, and they made it by knocking out the ends of a large box used for shipping laundry salt. They actually have built two of these and in them tested the lifting qualities of over 200 wing sections.

Their wind tunnel tests showed them that they had a combination of engine power and propeller thrust which was at least one-third more efficient than any similar one ever developed by such noted scientists as Professor Langley and Sir Hiram Maxim. A Wright air propeller delivered 66% of the power their motor expended in twirling it.

These facts caused them to decide that two propellers would be better than one in their actual flying machine, and that the "airscrews" should turn in opposite directions to neutralize the torque or twisting effect of whirling machinery, which with one propeller, would tend to force the machine to one side.

Here their wide experience in building new-type chain drive bicycles was of great help to them. In completing the machine destroyed by the winds today, they used a heavy tubular shaft to take the power from its engine, and transmit it directly to two large sprockets.

On these were fitted chains, almost exactly like those on the newest bicycles, with each chain running to a sprocket for each propeller. One of the chains was twisted and crossed in the middle to form a figure eight, for the purpose of reversing the direction of one airscrew.

The final events leading up to today's flights were filled with drama and excitement. By the middle of the summer just passed, the two brothers finally were satisfied with the power and performance of their engine and with the efficiency of their airscrews or "propellers."

Their 1903 model engine-powered flying machine had been constructed so as to have measurements and characteristics similar to the 1902 glider.

There were important improvements: The front elevators had been doubled, and they had controls which allowed the "pilot" to deflect their surfaces and also change camber or curvature. There was a much better routing and arrangement of the control wires causing the main wings to warp at the wish of the machine's operator; for the first time a cloth covering was used on both the top and bottom surface of each wing. The new "propellers" were mounted back of the wings so that they pushed rather than pulled the flying machine ahead.

Because of the rough nature of the terrain, the Wright brothers designed for their invention's launching platform, a sixty-foot-long monorail which can be moved about at will so as to launch into the wind. Up to the moment of leaving this for actual flight, most of the flying machine's weight combined with that of its operator rested on a jettisonable cradle to which a ball-bearing hub was attached. The undercarriage for landing had skids somewhat like the runners of sleds in which small boys do "belly busting" slides down snow-covered hills.

The two brothers left Dayton for Kitty Hawk by railroad on September 23, and made the final stages of their journey by ship and horse-drawn cart, carrying their boxed-up flying machine and its launching equipment. They had built a shed at their camp here in 1901 and enlarged this in 1902 to hold their largest and newest glider. But the winds and the weather of the previous winter had put the shed off its foundations, and the two brothers decided to put up a new building near it which could serve as a workshop and assembly room, as well as housing for their assembled invention during bad weather.

The new headquarters of this year is a large frame structure, with hinged doors and a tarpaper-covered roof. Just as it was being completed, a sudden storm, with near-hurricane winds of over seventy-five miles an hour struck, and threatened to take the new roof with it. Orville snatched up a ladder, a hammer and some nails, and with his back to the wind, made it secure.

Because of the storm and other adverse weather conditions, the Wright brothers were unable to start actual assembly of their flying machine until October 15. Soon afterward, Dr. Chanute dropped in for a few days, but left for St. Louis. On November 6, they decided to send the propeller shaft back to Dayton for some repairs and alterations which kept it from them until November 20.

At this point, the weather turned bitterly cold, with winds bringing snow flurries down from the Hudson Bay area. On November 28, the flight program suffered another setback. The two brothers, who are perfectionists in all they do, noticed a tiny crack on one of the tubular propeller shafts, and decided that both shafts would have to be replaced by stronger ones of solid tool steel, which also would be of smaller diameter.

After a hurried conference, it was decided that Orville should hurry back to Dayton with all possible speed and work personally with Mr. Taylor in turning out the new shafts. This was done, and Orville was on his way back with the shafts on December 11, when he read in the newspapers of that day the details of Professor Langley's spectacular failure.

Nothing daunted, on the following day, which was last Saturday, the Wright Brothers cemented and screwed into place their machine's new shafts, only to find that the weather was too calm for attempting a flight. Because of the machine's kite-like characteristics, and the added weight of its operator, they had calculated that they needed at least at first, to fly into a steady wind to get off the ground properly.

The Sabbath always is a day of rest and worship for the Wright brothers, and they treated last Sunday in their customary manner, reading and talking at their camp. On Monday, the winds still were not right in their opinion for a flight to start from level ground, but their impatience to begin led them to decide to place the monorail track up the side of Kill Devil Hill on a nine degree slope. Three years ago, they had made their first uncertain glide from the same slope, and it turned out to be a success.

As a signal to members of the Coast Guard Life Saving Station nearby, they ran up a small flag, and five station members came over to help them carry the flying machine and its track to the starting point. Monday's helpers were Mr. Daniels and Mr. Dough already mentioned, Robert Wescott, Thomas Beacher and Benny O'Neal.

It had been agreed that the one of the Wright brothers who was not operating the flying machine should run along the track during its launching and hold the wing level as long as possible to lessen the possibility of an accident. When they tossed a coin to see who flew first, Wilbur won, and wearing his rumpled working clothes and a cloth cap, he climbed onto the lower wing and lay down prone as he had on previous glider flights. In this position his hips fitted into a sort of saddle or cradle and by moving it he was able to manipulate the wings and rudder.

A restraining wire held the flying machine steady in place while the engine was started. When Wilbur released this, the flying machine shot forward so rapidly, due to the power of its motors and the downward slope of the hill, that Orville had time only to take a few running steps before he was left behind. About forty feet along, the machine lifted to the accompaniment of a loud cheer from all watching.

But, either because of nervousness or unfamiliarity, Wilbur appeared to nose the flying machine upward too steeply. After climbing for a moment or two, it seemed to lose speed and drop downward at the nose with somewhat of a jerk. The hours Wilbur has spent in motorless flight in previous years came to the rescue, and he swiftly maneuvered the elevators as to cause the machine to sweep down the hillside instead of crashing.

It made a swerving landing about 105 feet from the point of takeoff, and Orville's stop-watch showed that his brother had been in the air only about three and one-half seconds. One of the skids broke when it dug into the sandy soil, and there also were some minor breaks in the framework.

The brothers would not call this operation a flight, because it was not from level ground, but they were happy about it because it showed them that their launching method almost certainly was safe and practical.

Orville commented: "On the whole, we are much pleased, and we shall proceed."

By yesterday afternoon, the skid and all other damaged parts had been fully repaired, and the monorail track had been set up on entirely level ground about 100 feet from the Wright brothers workshop. Last night, the wind began to rise and temperatures dropped below freezing. The two brothers were too excited over today's prospects to sleep, and during today's early morning hours they kept indoors, hugging a stove which they had fashioned out of a large carbide can, in order to keep warm.

At 9 A.M. today, the winds still were stronger and more gusty than the two brothers considered ideal for their first real attempts at flight, but when the same conditions prevailed an hour later, they decided not to wait longer. Up went the flag once again to signal the life saving station men, and over to the camp came today's five observers and voluntary helpers.

At 10:30 A.M., after the track had been adjusted so as to face the flying machine directly into the wind, it was Orville's turn to climb aboard. While the engine was being warmed up in the biting cold air, he called to Wilbur: "Everything's ready?"

When Wilbur nodded his assent, Orville released the wire. This time, because of the resistance of the strong wind of twenty-seven miles an hour, the flying machine began to move along the track slowly. It kept to the track for forty feet with Wilbur having no trouble in staying alongside. Then it lifted, and one of the life savers took the first photograph of powered human flight when it was about two feet from the ground, with Wilbur still running hard along the right wingside. This is being developed hopefully. The gusty currents and the not completely satisfactory balance of the machine's elevator caused it to dart to an altitude of 10 feet at one moment and down to a few inches a second or two later.

It made a somewhat hard landing in the sand 120 feet from the starting point after being airborne for twelve seconds, but suffered no damage. It takes only a moment to calculate that the "Wright Flyer" had a speed of ten feet a second against a wind speed of thirty-five feet a second —and would have flown 540 feet in twelve seconds on a relatively calm day.

The record of the first flight in the history of the world was broken repeatedly this morning as the two brothers alternated at the controls. Wilbur, on the fourth and final flight, actually covered 852 feet in fifty-nine seconds.

At this moment, the Wright brothers, two brown-haired and blue-eyed young Americans are preparing to return to Dayton to tell their father and all their family members and friends about their experiences.

They have no flying machine, but they have something much greater and more valuable in their sole possession.

It is the secret of human flight, something which no other persons have heretofore possessed.

Ansel E. Talbert was the first newspaperman to fly over both North and South Poles and float across the North Polar region on Ice Island T-3; was one of the first two U.S. newsmen to fly as a passenger at 1,400 m.p.h. in the Concorde supersonic transport, and was one of the passengers on the first supersonic crossing of the Atlantic by an airline-type aircraft, in September, 1973.

A graduate of Columbia University and the Columbia Graduate School of Journalism, his past positions were as Military and Aviation Editor and syndicated columnist for the *New York Herald Tribune*; Vice President of the Flight Safety Foundation. A former USAF Lt. Colonel, one of his assignments was as Assistant to the Military Attache, American Embassy, London.

He has written numerous articles for *The Daily News* of New York and *The American Legion Magazine*. He was a regular patricipant in the Imperial Press Club, a program broadcast weekly on WQXR and *The New York Times* network, and the CBS television program, Longines Chronoscope. He wrote *Famous Airports of the World* (Random House) and was co-author of *The Grand Original—Randolph S. Churchill as seen by his friends* (Houghton Mifflin). In 1972 he was the winner of the TWA Award for the best writing on aviation in any aviation or aviation-oriented magazine.

He curently is a columnist and associate editor at American Traveler Inc., a publishing firm specializing in aviation and travel magazines. (See also *Who's Who in America.*)

New Political System Installed in Russia

As reported by LEON DENNEN

The Romanov dynasty suddenly crumbled, almost without a shot, on March 15, 1917, after a reign of three hundred years.

Czar Nicholas II abdicated his throne just one week after some 90,000 striking workers, mostly women, converged on the center of Petrograd with the immemorial Russian wail of *Dai nam khleb:* "Give us bread!"

The swift collapse of the monarchy, although unexpected, was actually the final act of the revolutionary drama that began to unfold in Russia in the winter of 1914, following the outbreak of World War I.

Plagued by the incompetence and corruption of the court camarilla and by military blundering and inefficiency, Russia was being bled white by the unequal war against the Kaiser's vastly superior army. The sinister role and influence of Czarina Alexandra and her "spiritual" mentor, the Siberian "monk" Gregory Rasputin, had exasperated even the officer class and the aristocracy whose support had been largely responsible for the suppression of past revolutionary outbreaks.

The Romanov Empire seemed to be falling apart. The Czar's government was split by petty feuds. Transport and communications were reduced to chaos. In the cities people were hungry and famine took a frightening toll even in the peasant villages, the producers of Russia's staple diet: bread and potatoes.

Starvation was a grim reality for millions of Russians. The cry for *khleb* (bread) in the provinces was even louder than in Petrograd.

I shall never forget the women of Rovno in the Empire's Ukrainian hinterland—the patient, long-suffering Russian women with furtive eyes and sunken faces who seemed to be eternally in search of bread.

On bleak winter days, from dawn to sunset, they kept a stoic vigil before bakeries and food shops that never opened. They waited for hours in the bitter cold only to be told that there was no bread or potatoes to be had. They grumbled, they cursed their fate—and they waited.

Occasionally, in desperation, the famished women of the hinterland would break into a food shop or a bakery—despite the terror of the harsh "Pharaohs," the Czar's police who ruled the remote provinces. Those lucky enough to find a crust of bread or a few frozen potatoes would run home holding their loot tightly in their hands. The next day their vigil started all over again.

In the capital of Russia, more industrialized and more sophisticated, demonstrations and strikes were a more frequent occurrence. The Petrograd demonstration of March 8 which sparked the Russian Revolution was, on the whole, undramatic and uneventful. The newspapers described it as a "local non-political" incident—a protest against bread rationing introduced by the government. Several bakeries in the center of Petrograd were raided and there were some clashes with the "Pharaohs." But the mounted Cossacks—the Czar's traditional and loyal defenders who had massacred strikers in the past—were surprisingly passive.

Under orders of their officers, the Cossacks told the strikers to disperse. But they did not use their whips and refused to charge the crowd. Instead, they rode gently through the marching columns, laughing goodnaturedly and even fraternizing with the demonstrators.

Some marching women carried red flags with inscriptions that called for the overthrow of the Czar: "Down with Autocracy!" But in Petrograd, as in the provinces, the desperate cry was, "Bread for the hungry."

Nicholas was at his military headquarters at Mogilev (450 miles south of Petrograd), playing the role of active Supreme Commander, when the first demonstrations occurred in the capital. Long isolated from the people by the Czarina and her hand-picked ministers, he was out of touch with all that was happening in Russia. He actually believed that the demonstrations were instigated by the docile and well-fed members of the spurious State *Duma*—Nicholas' feeble excuse for a semi-parliament—a caricature of a representative assembly which he had created reluctantly after the revolution of 1905.

Urged by the Czarina to be "firm" and "show authority," the Czar, in reply to an alarming telegram from his frightened Minister of Interior, wired from Mogilev: "First, dissolve the *Duma*, the main source of trouble; second, suppress the riots at any cost, with the full use of military force."

But even an order from the God-anointed *Batiushka* ("Little Father") could no longer stem the tide of revolt or change the course of history.

On March 9 the "local non-political" incident snowballed into a strike of 200,000 workers and students. This time the police opened fire in the Nevsky Prospect, killing some demonstrators. A high police official was shot. But the soldiers and Cossacks again behaved with restraint.

The March Revolution (or "February Revolution") thus started with a demonstration of starving masses and culminated in the refusal of the soldiers and Cossacks to quell the incipient revolt which spread like wildfire on the following days.

It was indeed "one of the most leaderless, spontaneous, and anonymous" revolutions of all times.

Russia's capital, though pivotal, was not, however, decisive in Nicholas' demise. To grasp the full import of the "March miracle" that heralded one of the great turning points in human history we must take a closer look at the provinces where much of the high revolutionary drama was enacted.

Petrograd, remote from the life of the ordinary Russian, was only one city in the immense Eurasian empire. It constituted only 1/75 of the country's inhabitants the vast majority of whom venerated Russia as "holy" and derided her as punitive—who regarded Russia at once as a loving *Matushka* ("Little Mother") and a harsh stepmother.

For some days after the Czar fell, the fate of the Revolution continued to hang in the balance until the provinces had been heard from. How did the common people in the hinterland look, talk and act on the eve of the Revolution? What animated Russians in some of the remote provinces?

How well I remember the wild joy that the news of the stirring events in Petrograd brought to Rovno, a district capital in the Ukrainian province of Volhyn. No one who did not witness the euphoria of March 1917 in the provinces can know what it was like—no one who lived through it will ever forget it.

Rovno was typical of the "prison of nations" of Imperial Russia—a multi-national city where the Pole hated his Russian overlord and both humiliated the Jew.

The surrounding countryside was dotted with tiny thatched peasant villages—mere slashings in the primeval woods—built of clay around the wooden church with its bright painted cupolas. They were inhabited by Ukrainian peasants who were eternally at war with the city slickers.

Frequently on market days the peasants—instigated by the Czar's police and lavishly supplied with vodka—would go on a "big drunk," execute pogroms and loot Jewish and Polish shops. Thus did Czarist officialdom maintain the "balance of power" in the Empire.

John Reed, who visited Rovno as a war correspondent in 1915, left a fairly accurate description of its "shabby largeness, wide streets half paved with cobbles, dilapidated wooden sidewalks, rambling wooden houses, and the swarming uniforms of its minor Czarist officials."

There was another Rovno Reed did not see—the city of revolutionaries, anti-Czarist conspirators and secret meetings. Twice a week the "evil smelling" cab drivers, carpenters, shoemakers and tailors would meet in a peasant's hut on the outskirts of the city and, along with students, teachers and other intellectuals, plot the overthrow of the monarchy—and dream of freedom.

Then, on the cold and rainy day in March 1917, the beautiful dream became reality. The *revolutsia,* unexpected, bewildering and even frightening, suddenly released the strangled hopes of the people.

Ancient hatred and long-age enmity were forgotten as Ukrainian peasants with cropped heads, long-bearded Jews in caps and Polish *pans* with waxed mustaches danced in the muddy streets along with soldiers and students.

Emaciated women, wrinkled and bent, and girls prematurely aged with bitter work and eternal humiliation forgot their hunger, shed tears of happiness and embraced strangers in the streets.

"Christ is here," they cried. "The truth has dawned in Russia."

Many *muzhiks* (peasants) who rushed to the city in alarm believed that the Revolution had actually liberated the Czar—the "bearer of the people's truth"—from the clutches of his wife, the former German princess, and the court conspirators. They were convinced that Nicholas had been a prisoner of the *Nemka* (the German woman) who sold out Russia to the Kaiser.

These wild rumors circulated among the common people in the provinces long after the Czar's abdication. "Curses on the *Nemka,*" cried the town folk and villagers, "but the Czar, God's deputy on Russian earth and the Savior's own choice, is still Czar."

The mystique of the *Batiushka* ("Little Father") was deeply rooted in Russia's hinterland. Centuries of oppression and poverty had not eradicated the magnetism radiating from the mitre-crown.

Had Nicholas acted with any sort of determination in the crucial days of March he might have stopped the revolutionaries. But the monarchy was already desperately sick. Nicholas' regime was so worm-eaten that it needed a rude blow to bring down the Romanov dynasty. It was delivered by the striking women in Petrograd on March 8.

Was the Czar as evil as he is generally depicted? According to Alexander Kerensky who knew him well, Nicholas himself was not an evil man. He was by all accounts a loving father and devoted husband.

But, as Kerensky told me, he was timid, only half-literate and "totally unprepared for the job of Czar." The son of a cruel and rough despot, Alexander III, Nicholas loved to surround himself with strong courtiers, who often turned out to be charlatans and adventurers. He was completely under the influence of his wife, Alexandra, who apparently saw herself as Catherine the Great, another minor German princess who once ruled Russia as an absolute monarch.

The former Princess Alice of Hesse-Darmstadt, a German granddaughter of Queen Victoria, though much stronger than the Czar, was a high-strung woman given to mystical exaltation that bordered on the pathological. After marrying Nicholas in 1894 she went "native" with a vengeance. She became the pillar of the Russian church and patron of the most reactionary politicians.

The Czarina Alexandra never learned to speak or write Russian adequately, but she considered herself a judge of the *muzhik's* character and of the "Russian soul." A fanatical believer in the autocratic power of the Czar, she was convinced, with typical German arrogance, that "Russia loves the whip."

Alexandra's overriding passion was the Czarevich Alexis. The heir to the Romanov throne was afflicted with hemophilia (hemophilia was hereditary in the House of Hesse) and it seemed that he could not survive without a miracle. Alexandra, according to Kerensky, believed not only in miracles but in magic.

Many Russians also yearned for a miracle in the bleak days of the war. Great fervors shook the people. Wonder-working "holy men" and self-torturing "saints" roamed the country preaching strange gospels.

Scores of such "holy men" invaded the Ukraine. One in particular— "St. Ivan the Ugly," as the awed peasant women called him, lovingly— stands out in my memory. He was a toothless hunchback with long black hair reaching to his shoulders, who walked barefoot and hatless even on the coldest winter day.

No one knew where "St. Ivan" came from but his fame as a miracle-maker spread quickly through the province of Volhyn. Peasants flocked from the villages to Rovno to get a glimpse of the "holy man." Despite his reputation, no one ever saw him perform a miracle.

On two occasions, on market days, I heard him "speak in tongues" and saw him do a weird dance, a sort of dervish or Holy Roller contortion, twisting and shaking his deformed body while the awed peasants knelt in the snow and crossed themselves.

"St. Ivan" was, in his own way, also a revolutionary. He appeared in the province with the glad tidings that he had come to liberate the "suffering people" from the "German She-Devil." Although he preached treason, so venerated was the hunchback that the police did not dare to arrest him for fear of provoking bloody riots.

The most celebrated wonder-worker was, of course, Gregory Rasputin who, unlike "St. Ivan," became a pillar of the monarchy.

"We got acquainted with a man of God, Gregory, from the Tobolsk Province," the Czar scrawled in his diary in November 1905. It was a fateful entry, indeed. The "man of God" was none other than the astute Siberian peasant Rasputin, a giant of a man with hypnotic eyes and a bald scar on his head, the result of a beating he received for horse stealing.

"Our Friend," as the Romanov couple came to refer to Rasputin, apparently possessed hypnotic powers and he exercised his healing gifts on the Czarevich. It seems that he was able to stop the boy's bleeding and thus saved his life on several occasions.

This extraordinary circumstance gave the dissolute peasant a hold on Alexandra, who was convinced that he had been sent by God to save the dynasty and the autocracy. She began to take his advice in everything, including the conduct of state affairs.

Rasputin became the favorite "saint" of Petrograd's highest society, where mysticism and spiritualist *seances* had become the fashion. His hypnotic eyes and powerful physique played havoc with the sensibilities of the bored ladies of the Czarina's entourage, who vied with each other for his favors. It became the *chic* thing to shower presents on the "man of God," which he quickly squandered in riotous and lusty living.

Knowledge of Rasputin's scandals spread throughout Russia and became the favorite subject of guarded comments in the salons of the rich and the hamlets of the poor. In the provinces even youngsters read penny pamphlets, distributed by the underground, describing the amorous "Adventures of Grishka Rasputin and the *Nemka*." When there were no police in sight, they used to sing:

> The frightened Czar issued a proclamation:
> Freedom for the dead—Prison for the living.
> Russia, Russia, I grieve for you;
> Grishka Rasputin has ruined you.

Even after Rasputin had been dead for some time Alexandra cherished the hope that the "saint" was praying for her family "in the world beyond." A day after the monarchy's fate had already been sealed by the March 8 demonstration in Petrograd, the Czarina wrote in a letter to Nicholas:

"My darling, I let you go with a heart torn by anxiety . . . But what can I do? Pray . . . and pray again. *Our dear friend in the world beyond also prays for you.* Only, darling, be firm. Show some authority, that's what the Russians need. You have been kind. Make them feel your fist now."

Rasputin was killed by Prince Yusupov, who was married to the Czar's niece, in order to save the monarchy and Russia, in December 1916. "The bullet which killed him reached the very heart of the ruling dynasty," said the great poet Alexander Blok. The personal tragedy of the Romanovs and the fate of Russia were closely intertwined.

As Russia's defeats in the war against Germany mounted, rumors flooded the nation that there was treason in "high places"—that Alexandra was the spearhead of a pro-Kaiser conspiracy in Petrograd. Two of her protégés, the War Minister Sukhomlinov and the Minister of Interior Protopopov, were commonly believed to be traitors in the pay of Germany.

Grumbling in the provinces against the "traitors" in Petrograd increased. Bitter crowds milled helplessly and hopelessly in the streets, frequently clashing with the police. Their angry talk was like the intermittent roar of waves which alternately break with a splash and pause for breathing space.

The Germans and their Austro-Hungarian allies were rapidly advancing toward the Ukraine. Long files of stretchers bore groaning wounded men to the overcrowded hospital trains which stood on the tracks of Rovno without locomotives. There was a shortage of doctors, medical personnel and even bandages.

Thousands of refugees—many of them bearded old Jews and mothers (with babies in their arms) who had been expelled from their homes—squatted in the snow, stolid and bewildered among their bundles and rolls of bedding. As they retreated before the Germans, the Russians cleared the country of every living thing, destroying houses and scarce food supplies.

The Russian peasants fought valiantly for their *Batiushka* and died in droves behind their officers. But rifles and ammunition were as scarce as bread, potatoes and bandages. Soldiers shared one rifle, so that men often had to wait for arms until their comrades were killed.

The army's losses were immense. In the first year of the war alone Russia lost more than four million men in killed, wounded and prisoners.

By 1916 the Russian army was no longer capable of waging war. In fact, it ceased to be a fighting power.

Who was responsible for the defeats? The Czarina, obviously, said the common people.

There were, of course, many complex reasons—social, economic, political and sheerly human—that brought about the collapse of the Romanov dynasty. Yet there is little doubt that it was the suspicion of treason in the Czar's palace—even more than the demonstrations of the hungry women and conspiracies of the revolutionaries—that was the immediate cause that triggered the March Revolution.

The full text of the Czar's abdication did not reach Rovno until March 23. Telephone and telegraph communications were disrupted by the war and rail service was completely disorganized by the advancing Germans. Local newspapers had long ceased to appear because of censorship and the shortage of paper and newsprint.

However, as usual in Russia, the grapevine worked faster than the communications media. The city was filled with rumors. Some even said that the Czar had finally decided to divorce the Czarina and exile her to a convent in Siberia.

Little groups of people, covert revolutionaries and students, practically camped at the railroad station in the hope that some stray train, bringing newspapers from Petrograd or Moscow, would manage to reach the city.

In the early morning, greeted by a thundering "hurrah," a panting and puffing train finally crawled into the station. Its rusty engine was a riot of red—red wreaths, red banners and streamers with inscriptions that announced the Revolution.

I can still see the fat little engineer who suddenly emerged from his cabin wearing, of all things, a red broad-brimmed lady's hat with long feathers. To the crowd's cheers, he tossed a bundle of newspapers. They were several days old but they told the story.

The liberal newspaper *Rech* carried on its front page the news of the abdication. "Not wishing to become separated from our son," Nicholas told his subjects, "we bequeath our heritage to our brother, the Grand Duke Michael Alexandrovich. . . ."

But the same issue of the newspaper carried the news that Michael had declined the throne. For the first time in three centuries Russia was without a God-anointed *Batiushka*.

Perhaps my most vivid recollection of this historic moment is the face of an old Russian soldier when he first learned that Nicholas was no longer Czar. He was a tall, spare, venerable-looking peasant of about sixty with a long flowing beard streaked with gray and dressed in a soldier's uniform that made his appearance ludicrous. His right arm was clasped around a soldier of about seventeen—his son, as I later learned—with a red face covered with pimples.

The old man and the boy were standing in a circle of soldiers, many of them wounded men using make-shift crutches, who were listening to a long-haired student shouting hoarsely about the Revolution in Petrograd. The soldiers were silent and sullen as the student harangued them; there was hardly a trace of emotion on their passive faces.

"*Grazhdanie,* Citizens, the Autocrat has fallen," the speaker roared. "Long live freedom!"

But the soldiers were suspicious. It seemed incredible that the *Batiushka* was no longer autocrat of Russia. Was it a police ruse, a provocation like Black Friday in 1905?

Suddenly the old soldier stepped forward. He fell to his knees in the snow, crossed himself and began to cry. Amidst sobs, he addressed his sullen comrades:

"Brothers, soldiers, freedom has come to Mother Russia. We, the people, are poor and oppressed, burdened like slaves. The German woman is sending us, soldiers, to the slaughter like cows. They think we're beasts, not human beings. Now the truth has dawned in Russia."

The silent, impassive soldiers began to stir. Here was someone of their own, speaking their own language, who was not afraid to berate the *Nemka*. They looked cautiously about them. Sensing doom, the Czar's "Pharaohs" had vanished from the streets.

After a tense moment of indecision, cries suddenly pierced the air:

"Long live freedom!" The old soldier, crossing himself again, rose to his feet and started to walk toward the main street. His comrades followed him.

All moved forward in that solemn and majestic order peculiar to the Russian people. The demonstrators marched to the city jail to liberate the political prisoners. Someone in the crowd began to sing the haunting revolutionary funeral march which was last heard in the streets during the revolution of 1905:

> You have fallen, victims in a fatal struggle
> For the love of the people.
> You have sacrificed all for the people,
> For its life, its honor, its liberty.

When the demonstration reached the prison gate it was met by Colonel Nicholas Kossonogov on a white horse at the head of a detachment of mounted Cossacks.

In Rovno, as in most towns and villages of Russia, only a few functionaries of the Czarist regime actually attempted to resist the Revolution with arms. One of them was Kossonogov, a retired Cossack colonel who was the director of the city's Classical *Gymnasium* and teacher of the "patriotic" subject of history.

A tall, fierce-looking man with a pointed mustache dyed pitch-black, he was one of a myriad of Czarist bureaucrats dispatched to the provinces near the war zone to keep an eye on the restive national minorities.

The inhabitants of the city first became aware of Kossonogov's ever-watchful presence during the trial of two Jewish students whom he accused of spreading "defeatist propaganda." "Legal defenders of our Holy Russia," he thundered in the courtroom, "it is my patriotic duty to destroy this dangerous race of revolutionaries. I shall banish all Jews to hell or to America."

Along with the bull-necked *Ispravnik* (chief of police) who was hated throughout the province for his venality and cruelty, Kossonogov was a leader of the Black Hundreds, a league of arch-reactionary monarchists who were the chief instigators of pogroms.

Now Kossonogov decided to make history instead of teaching it. Discarding the traditional blue frock-coat of a *Gymnasium* teacher, he was attired in the uniform of a Cossack officer with a row of decorations on the padding of his chest and a curved silver sword dangling at his side.

"In the name of the Czar, disperse," the colonel shouted when the demonstration, led by the old soldier, approached the prison. "The Jews are fooling you. You will be punished for your disobedience."

"You are lying about the Jews," replied the old man. "We no longer have a Czar."

"Brothers, Cossacks, save *Matushka* Russia. I order you to fire."

The Cossacks shuddered in obedient movement and raised their rifles. But Kossonogov was fighting for a lost cause. As in Petrograd, the Cossacks did not fire. They sensed that something strange was happening in Russia.

The crowd surged forward, carefully bypassing the Cossacks.

The frightened prison warden immediately released ten political prisoners whom the soldiers carried on their shoulders to the center of the town.

As they reached the golden-domed *Sobor* the church bells suddenly began to peal with a deafening roar. Father Aleksey, attired in churchly vestments, stood at the head of a procession of men and women carrying ikons and chanting hymns to the accompaniment of the bells.

I can still see this gentle-faced *pope* (priest) of the Russian Church as he was sprinkling holy water right and left. He was a big man with reddish whiskers that almost reached to his knees. He held no high office of authority in the Church but, like Dostoevski's "elder," Father Zosima in *The Brothers Karamazov,* was respected for his holiness and wisdom. He was particularly famous for his booming voice, a basso profundo, his admirers claimed, that even the great Fyodor Chaliapin might envy.

Now Aleksey was sprinkling holy water and thundering away: "Christian soldiers, the solemn hour has come. Holy Russia is free. In the name of God, the Father, God, the Son and God, the Holy Ghost, I bless thee Revolution."

But the strangest sight of all was the chief of police, the *Ispravnik.* Bareheaded, he carried an ikon and walked meekly behind the priest as though he hoped to be shielded by Aleksey's broad back. His lips were moving imperceptibly as though he, too, was blessing the Revolution. Out of uniform and its glittering array of medals, the man who only yesterday terrorized the province, the "Hangman" seemed to have shrunk to insignificance. The *Ispravnik* was now wearing an ordinary soldier's gray overcoat with a red ribbon in its buttonhole.

One could recognize the reactionaries of yesterday by the ostentatious dimension of their red ribbons in their buttonholes. The Czar's chief allies had abandoned him overnight.

Nicholas' demise, in the provinces as in Petrograd, was marked by few excesses. In the past, great upheavals in Russia had frequently resulted in savage massacres of national and religious minorities. But the Revolution was sacred. Even criminal elements were too overjoyed to loot or kill.

Although the Revolution had been consciously awaited longer than any other in history, it caught even the most dedicated anti-Czarist conspirators unawares.

Many of the better known revolutionary leaders were in exile or in Siberia. These included such moderate Mensheviks as Julius Martov, Irakly Tseretelli, Fyodor Dan, the anti-Marxist Social Revolutionary Victor Chernov and the Bolsheviks Lenin, Trotsky, and Stalin.

Even those who managed to elude the Czar's secret police—the *Okhrana*—and were living underground in Petrograd, failed to see the handwriting on the wall. They were convinced, Alexander Kerensky told me, that "there will be no revolution for a long time."

Lenin, the arch-revolutionary was also skeptical. On January 27, 1917 —less than two months before Nicholas' abdication—he predicted in a lecture to young workers in Switzerland that his generation will most probably not live "long enough" to see the day of revolution dawn.

Though leaderless, the people, nevertheless, rejoiced in their new freedom. "There is a Revolution in Russia," said a poet, "and all Russia is one vast public forum." Petrograd's liberal newspaper *Rech,* always a staunch advocate of law and order, complained that the country was fast beginning to resemble the American "Wild West" at the turn of the century.

But the ordinary man's ability to absorb revolutionary slogans diminishes in proportion to his hunger. As the revolutionary fervor abated after the first weeks of euphoria, a myriad of social, economic and political questions demanded an answer. The people were still hungry. The Czar was gone but the new rulers in Petrograd and the old generals were continuing the disastrous war.

"Trust in God," says a peasant proverb, "but take care of your garden." Freedom (*svoboda*) is fine, said the *muzhiks*, but a peasant cannot live without land.

Land-hungry peasants came to Rovno and other cities from their villages to demand an answer to the crucial question: "Is it true that the

Revolution was already dividing the *pomieshchiks'* land among the peasants?" To them the Revolution heralded, above all, the long-awaited day when the land would be their own.

The bulk of the Czar's army were peasants. Soldiers by the thousands began to desert the trenches for fear that they would not reach their villages in time to receive their share of the land.

They looked hopefully to the "educated people"—teachers, journalists, lawyers and assorted intellectuals—who had started all this revolution business. But they looked in vain. The "educated People," as Wladimir Woytinsky said, were "more the bards" of the Revolution than organizers of victory. After years of conspiring and dreaming they were more skilled in defending the principles they cherished than in fitting them to the cruel realities of life.

The "educated people" were too busy creating political parties— Ukrainian nationalists, Polish nationalists, Jewish Socialists (Bundists), Zionists, Mensheviks, Social Revolutionaries, Anarchists, Zimmerwaldists. They made speeches, issued proclamations and paraded endlessly in the streets—each party under its own red banner and its own slogans.

When news of Nicholas' abdication filtered into the provinces, the Czarist officials, in most cases, took the path of least resistance. They meekly handed over authority to spontaneously organized Citizens' Committees (*Grazhdanskiye Komitety*).

However, there was not much agreement in the Committees—broad coalitions of all parties—except for the monarchists. Each political party insisted on the wisdom of its own special program and suspected its opponents of harboring bourgeois or chauvinist views. Each had its own priorities.

The debates and the disputes in the Rovno Citizens' Committee went on fruitlessly and endlessly for several weeks. Finally a Solomonic compromise was reached: to send a delegation to Petrograd to seek instructions from the wiser heads in the capital. Each party was to designate a member of the delegation.

Once again there were speeches and parades, as the delegation, with marchers singing revolutionary songs and a brass band playing the *Marseillaise,* was accompanied to the chaotic railroad station to wait for a train.

By the time the provincial envoys reached the capital, Petrograd already had two rival "governments"; and the quarreling members of the Rovno delegation became partisans of one or the other faction. Though both governments resided in the Tauride Palace—an ornate structure built by Catherine the Great for her lover Potemkin—they were worlds apart in their social and political outlook.

The Provisional Government, made up mostly of members of the old *Duma,* represented Russia's enlightened and liberal bourgeoisie which, while opposed to the autocracy, had a vision of Russia as a sort of constitutional monarchy.

The Soviet (Council) of Workers' and Soldiers' Deputies organized almost simultaneously by the left-wing parties to act as a watchdog on the "bourgeois" members of the *Duma,* had already coalesced into the powerful "Executive Committee" of the Soviet when the Rovno delegation reached Petrograd.

Prince Georgi Lvov, the first Prime Minister of the Provisional Government, was an enlightened aristocrat, a gentle and deeply religious follower of Tolstoy who despised Rasputin and the autocracy. But as Prime Minister, despite his great moral authority, he was completely submerged in the chaos unleashed by the Revolution.

The key members of Lvov's government, Foreign Minister Pavel Milyukov and War Minister Alexander Guchkov, had as little contact as the Prime Minister with the workers and soldiers who had made the Revolution and who recognized only the Soviet, *their* Soviet, as the source of all authority.

The Provisional Government thus found itself—even before it began to function—with little popular support and was entirely dependent for its authority upon the Soviet.

Local Soviets soon mushroomed throughout Russia. The Rovno delegation, split into pro-Soviet and pro-government factions, in no time vanished from history altogether.

Some of its members drifted back to the city to form a Soviet of Workers' and Soldiers' Deputies to which the "Peasants" were now added. Others received mandates from the Provisional Government to turn the Citizens' Committees in the whole province of Volhyn into Municipal Administrations (*Gordskoye Upravleniye*) and to act as an arm of the government.

The inevitable tug of war developed between the provincial Soviets —which represented the more primitive, politically inexperienced masses easily swayed by the most attractive promises—and the Municipal Administrations which were backed by more sophisticated liberals and Western-minded intellectuals.

This, with some minor variations, was also the situation in Petrograd. Most moderate Socialists, the "bards of the Revolution," who were still in control of the Soviet's Executive Committee in Petrograd, were convinced that, according to the Marxian gospel, Russia was not yet "ripe" for full-fledged socialism. As the Mensheviks saw it, Russia first had to go through the stage of capitalist industrialization and bourgeois democracy. Therefore, instead of assuming authority as a government, they preferred to play the role of back-seat drivers for the Provisional Government.

Until Lenin's Bolsheviks gained a majority in the Petrograd Soviet in the month of October, despite the divided control of the State, there was some measure of cooperation, however sporadic, between the two rival "governments." For a period in May several Socialist members of the Soviet even joined the Provisional Government as ministers.

The saintly Victor Chernov, the anti-Marxist Social Revolutionary, became Minister of Agriculture. The Marxian Mensheviks Tseretelli and Skobelev agreed to serve as Ministers of Posts and Telegraphs and of Labor.

But from March until May 1917 the bridge between the two parts of the dual system of power—the Provisional Government and the Soviet—was Alexander Kerensky, a moderate Social Revolutionary and a former member of the *Duma,* who was for a time the Minister of Justice in the Provisional Government and a Vice Chairman of the Petrograd Soviet.

A brilliant orator and lawyer, Kerensky, at thirty-six, was widely known in the remotest parts of Russia as the people's tribune and fearless defender of political prisoners in Czarist courts. He was idolized by the people in the provinces long before they had heard Lenin's name. Suddenly his name was on all lips and his picture on all walls.

To many of his countrymen Kerensky appeared to personify Carlyle's "Ablest Man," the hero of new Russia. Within weeks he became Minister of War and by the beginning of July he replaced Prince Lvov as Prime Minister.

As Minister of Justice, Kerensky immediately introduced sweeping political and social reforms. Under his guidance, the Provisional Government proclaimed freedom of expression, freedom of association and the right to strike. All discrimination based on class, nationality, or religion was abolished. The Jews, long the most oppressed minority in Russia, were given complete equality.

For the first time in her history, Russia was looking toward the ideals and responsibilities of a political democracy—ideals that had guided her growing ranks of revolutionaries since the *Dekabrist* (Decembrist) rising of liberal officers in 1825.

But the Provisional Government, though guided by high ideals, was indecisive and weak. Having set its sights on a Constituent Assembly— which the programs of all Russian political parties, including the Bolsheviks, had demanded—to be elected by a nationwide franchise, it delayed important decisions such as land reforms and ending the war.

This policy, however justified juridically, was politically disastrous, for the government lost much support among the peasantry. The land-hungry *muzhiks* could no longer be appeased by legal arguments. Soon, in Volhyn and other provinces, they took the law into their own hands, looting and burning the manors of the *pomieshchiks,* often along with their luckless owners. They began to distribute the land without waiting for permission from the "educated and wealthy gentlemen" in Petrograd.

Equally crucial was the question of the non-Russian nationalities. About 60% of the Empire's population were non-Russians. More than 18% were Ukrainians, 6% Poles. 5% Byeolorussians, the rest Jews, Balts, Georgians, Tatars, Bashkirs, etc.

These subjects of the Czar had not only been oppressed by virtue of class, but had further been discriminated against as members of various nationalities. For decades the harsh policy of forceful "Russification" provoked unrest and revolt among the non-Russians. But the Czarist government stubbornly upheld the idea of a highly centralized Russian state—"one and indivisible Russia."

The moderate politicians in the Provisional Government were reluctant to take binding action on this issue until the convocation of the Constituent Assembly. Many of them, like Milyukov, also believed firmly in "one and indivisible Russia."

But even the Socialists, including Kerensky, who advocated a Russian Federation in which all nationalities would have their autonomy, insisted on postponing all decisions until the Constituent Assembly met.

Thus, Lenin outbid them all. He dispensed promises lavishly and boldly: land to the peasants, independence to any nationality that wanted it and, above all, immediate peace to the war-weary people.

By March 1917 the Russian army, as the French General Pétain warned, was "nothing but a façade that would fall to pieces if it makes a move." Yet the myopic Allies—Britain and France—exerted strong pressure on the Provisional Government to step up its war effort.

Lenin, unlike Kerensky, was not interested in peace with honor. As he saw it, the defeat of Czarism would be "the very least" evil that would come from the war. Lenin felt it was to the advantage of the masses that Russia should be defeated.

Even before he had reached Russia from his exile in Switzerland— a full month after the Czar's abdication—Lenin announced that he intended to sign a separate peace with the Germans.

Meanwhile, food shortages increased and the peasants lost confidence in the Provisional Government. They refused to accept the new money (named *kerenkys* after Kerensky) even for frozen potatoes. They demanded old Czarist rubles or gold. On occasion, when the militia tried to force them to accept the *kerenkys* the peasants protested that they were being robbed by the new *barins* (lords) from Petrograd.

Wounded soldiers and deserters (many of them carrying rifles) continued to stream to the cities. "Out of the trenches and obscure holes and corners," N. Sukhanov reported, "had crept utterly crude and ignorant people whose devotion to the Revolution was spite and despair, while their socialism was hunger and an unendurable longing for peace."

The desire for peace became the obsession of millions in Russia's provincial cities, towns and villages.

This was Lenin's trump card. The war, in his view, was a product of capitalism and imperialism. Therefore, said his Bolsheviks (who now, on Lenin's insistence, began to call themselves *Communists*) "turn the imperialist war into a civil war."

Although people in the provinces hardly knew Lenin's name, his views on the war, spread far and wide by soldiers deserting from the front, were catching on.

Walking past Rovno's jail one day, I came upon this scene: a motley crowd of the "crude and ignorant" people were listening attentively to a soldier who was speaking to them through the bars of an open window. He had been jailed, he said, by Kerensky's officers because he was opposed to the imperialist war.

This was probably not the real reason, since hundreds of deserters roamed the provinces unmolested. But the soldier obviously had been at the front, where he had been subjected to the propaganda of Lenin's agents.

"Comrades, Brothers," he shouted through the bars, "I am for comrade Lenin. I am Bolshevik. Away with the war. Down with the Provisional Government! All Power to the Soviets!"

"Who is Lenin?" the people asked. "Who are the Bolsheviks?" Few knew. But the soldier was against the war and that made him a hero.

The crowd stormed the prison and, as was by now customary, carried the soldier on their shoulders to the headquarters of the local Soviet in the center of the town. They "elected" him chairman of the Soviet in place of the bespectacled intellectual, a moderate Menshevik, who preached the continuation of the fight against the Kaiser all the way to Berlin.

This was the first official emeregence of Bolshevism in Rovno although, as subsequently became clear, Lenin's propagandists had long been active at the front and in the provinces.

The fact is that until the sailors of Kronstadt, inspired by the Bolsheviks, made their first armed assault on the Provisional Government in Petrograd in the month of July few people in the provinces knew anything about Lenin.

There were the usual rumors, of course. Some said that Lenin was a Communist (a word they had never heard before) and therefore a German. Monarchists and Black Hundreds who, after several months of lethargy were beginning to stir, claimed that the little man with the narrow eyes and broad cheekbones of a typical Mongolian-Slav was a Communist—therefore a Jew. (Lenin's real name—Vladimir Ilyich Ulyanov—was as Russian as Romanov.)

The peasants with their fixation on the Germans even believed that Lenin had been sent to Russia by the Kaiser to restore the *Nemka* to the throne.

Ironically, it was Lenin's most prominent ally, Leon Trotsky, a Jewish intellectual with a goatee and pince-nez, who replaced Kerensky as the hero of the hinterland. "Trotsky is a real *Pravoslavny* (a true Orthodox Christian)," the common people said. "Unlike Lenin, who is a German, Trotsky is a real Russian who wants to divide the land among the peasants."

The rumors about Lenin were based, in a large measure, on the manner in which he returned to Russia from Switzerland on April 16. Burning with impatience to reach Russia, Lenin, after exploring every device to make his way across the war lines, finally made a deal with the Kaiser's government which gave him a "sealed" train to travel through German territory.

The Germans, of course, engineered his return to Russia because they knew that Lenin wanted to stop the war. They saw a chance to exploit the weakness of their enemy. They obviously hoped that Lenin's return to Russia would multiply confusion and weaken the country's will to fight.

But was Lenin a German agent? Alexander Kerensky, in scores of conversations and interviews I had with him, insisted that Lenin was a "paid agent" of the German General Staff who had crippled the Provisional Government by "a stab in the back." Lenin "had no moral or spiritual objection to promoting the defeat of his own country," Kerensky said.

German agent or not, Lenin returned to Petrograd with a proprietary interest in the Revolution. He was not there when the Czar fell but he was determined to finish the job by subverting the fragile post-Romanov democracy in Russia, destroying the Provisional Government and establishing a Dictatorship of the Proletariat.

He had nothing but contempt for his principal adversaries, the moderate Socialists, who wanted to lead liberated Russia toward a modern Western-type democracy.

Even before he set foot in Petrograd's Finland Station, Lenin, in *Letters from Afar,* wrote in his instruction to Bolshevik comrades:

"Our tactic—complete distrust, no support for the new government. Kerensky is especially suspect. . . . No deals with other parties."

Lenin was essentially a pragmatist rather than a theoretician. He had the supreme ability to pursue any means to achieve his goal. Immediately upon his arrival in Petrograd he embarked on a campaign to regroup the forces represented in the Soviet—by uniting the extreme radical elements, strengthening their activity and isolating the moderate Socialists who were still a majority in the Executive Committee.

One day after he reached Petrograd, on April 17, Lenin made two speeches—one to the Bolsheviks and another at a joint session with the Mensheviks—in which he outlined a ten-point program commonly known as his "April Thesis."

He again condemned the conflict with Germany as an "imperialist war" and demanded "no support" for the Provisional Government. He warned against the "illusion" of a parliamentary democracy: "Not a parliamentary Republic but a Republic of Soviets of Workers', Soldiers' and Peasants' Deputies in the whole country." His "Theses" also called for the confiscation of all landlords' estates, nationalization of all land and the elimination of the army and police.

Lenin's views were totally unacceptable to the moderate Socialists.

They saw his program as "anti-Marxian" and unrealistic, one likely to plunge Russia into civil war, anarchy and chaos.

"Lenin has raised the flag of civil war," said Joseph Goldenberg-Meshkovski, for many years Lenin's comrade-in-arms. He has "announced his candidacy for the vacant throne of Bakunin," the apostle of world anarchy.

The Bolshevik leader was not impressed. Civil war and chaos are, after all, a professional revolutionary's stock-in-trade.

Lenin was for "Revolutionary Virtue"—with himself as the embodiment of Virtue. He was dreaming of a Dictatorship of the Proletariat that would "make the Russian Revolution a prologue to world revolution."

To achieve this goal it was necessary to transfer all political power from the democratic Provisional Government to the Soviet and then remove the Soviet from the control of the moderate Socialists and place it under the control of the Bolsheviks.

Consequently, the struggle for the world revolution required that the Bolshevik Party become the ruler of Russia.

Here, in fact, we come to Lenin's most distinctive innovation in revolutionary theory and practice—the substitution of a disciplined party of professional revolutionaries for the working class as the motive force of revolution.

Despite some opposition in his own party, Lenin persisted. He began to set up in each district and factory of Petrograd an organization "capable of acting as one man" and bound to the Central Committee of the Bolshevik Party with strong ties, so as to counter the considerable influence of the moderate Socialist parties.

In defiance of a resolution of the Executive Committee of the Petrograd Soviet, Lenin established a Red Guard, consisting of workers and soldiers who belonged to the Bolshevik Party.

He also dispatched propagandists throughout Russia who began to form armed Red Guard units in the towns and villages of the provinces.

Such was Lenin's authority—and persistence—that the All-Russian Conference of Bolsheviks that was held in May overwhelmingly approved his extremist program, which it had rejected three weeks before. From that time the Bolsheviks embarked on a campaign to seize power by discrediting the Provisional Government and extending their influence in the Soviet, the army and the navy, where Leninist propaganda urged the troops to desert and fraternize with the Germans.

The slogan was "All Power to the Soviets." In Petrograd on May 16 (a month after Lenin's return from Russia), demonstrating crowds, led by the Bolsheviks, chanted "Down with the Provisional Government" and "All Power to the Soviets." By June demonstrators with similar slogans invaded the streets of Rovno, Zhitomir, Lutsk, Kovel and other towns of the Ukraine.

Throughout Russia the lines began to form for a struggle between the Bolsheviks and the Provisional Government.

Circumstances favored the Bolsheviks. The temporary character of the Provisional Government and the duarchy of power exercised by it with the Petrograd Soviet, precluded any decisive action on the numerous vital questions that faced it. Lenin took full advantage of the situation.

The first open armed struggle of the Bolsheviks and their allies against the Provisional Government occurred in Petrograd on July 15— three months after Lenin's return to Russia.

It was a "Reconnaissance in depth"—to test the readiness of the masses for the final battle of which Lenin never ceased to dream.

The masses were not ready, however, and the Bolsheviks were dispersed by troops and workers loyal to the Provisional Government. Lenin escaped to Finland and some of his co-conspirators were arrested.

But Lenin's "Reconnaissance in depth," though it failed, upset the precarious balance of forces in the country, as it was meant to do. (The Bolshevik leader firmly believed in the theory that even "defeat in action is victory.") His bold attempt to seize power with the help of the Kronstadt sailors alarmed the conservative and liberal circles who were associated with the anti-Socialist army officers. On September 9, they, in turn, attempted a *putsch* under the leadership of General Lavr Kornilov, the son of a Siberian Cossack.

Kornilov, who had been appointed by Kerensky as Commander-in-Chief of the Army on July 31, was one of the few Russian generals who tried desperately to restore discipline in the army after the havoc created by Bolshevik propaganda. But he was not a popular general and his *coup* likewise failed when railwaymen loyal to the Provisional Government refused to transport his troops.

However, Kornilov's attempt to seize power provided Lenin with a new battle-cry: "The Revolution is in danger."

Kerensky still believed that there were "no enemies on the left" and that Lenin, however violent in his speech, was basically a Socialist.

He therefore made one more attempt to come to terms with the "err-ing brothers" and pardoned the Bolsheviks ostensibly as a reward for their help in the struggle against Kornilov.

Lenin contemptuously rejected the olive branch of the moderates. He instructed his propagandists to denounce Kerensky's government as a "government of national treason" and "counter-revolutionary conniv-ance."

There was, of course, not an atom of truth in the Bolshevik claim that Kerensky was an accomplice of Kornilov. This did not deter Lenin who made a science of the maxim that the "end justifies the means."

There is little doubt that Kornilov's attempted *coup* was the turning point in the fate of the March Revolution. It polarized opinion into left and right and, as always in the process, squeezed out the middle.

Kerensky, having discovered to his sorrow that there were also ene-mies on the extreme left, now had to fight for the life of Russia's new-born democracy against the extreme right as well as on the left.

Bolshevik propagandists, many of them armed sailors from Kronstadt, were hurriedly dispatched from Petrograd to the provinces to denounce Kerensky as Kornilov's collaborator and preach Lenin's gospel of "All Power to the Soviets." They were better organized and better rehearsed than their moderate Socialist opponents.

Since they were sailors—seldom seen in the provinces—who had come directly from Petrograd they obviously knew the real truth. People still remembered the revolt of the sailors of the cruiser *Potemkin* in 1905 and regarded all sailors as revolutionary heroes.

Moreover, Lenin's propaganda had the "authenticity" of an oft-repeated falsehood: "The Provisional Government sold out to the capi-talists. Kerensky got a bribe of ten million rubles—Czarist gold rubles, not worthless *kerenkys*."

More and more frequently the sailors in the provinces—lavishly sup-plied with vodka by their Bolshevik leaders—resorted to violence.

"Down with Kerensky! Down with the Constituent Assembly!" cried Lenin's agitators.

"Long live the Constituent Assembly!" replied the moderate Social-ists. "Lenin is a German agent. His promise of land, peace and freedom is a fraud."

The Bolshevik slogan "Down with the Constituent Assembly" was a reflection of Lenin's new policy.

The calling of a Constituent Assembly had figured prominently in the

Bolshevik program before the party gained a majority in the Petrograd Soviet. In the period of April–October 1917 one of the most consistent charges levelled in Bolshevik propaganda at the Provisional Government had been that it was unjustifiably postponing elections to this body. Now, however, the determination of the Leninist majority to ensure Bolshevik hegemony made the concept of a democratically elected Assembly that would give Russia a democratic constitution—an anachronism from the Communist point of view.

The hinterland was confused and bewildered by the whirlwind of charges and countercharges. The Kornilov episode had a disastrous effect on the morale of the provinces. It opened up the old wound—distrust between the common people and the "educated" liberal bourgeoisie, the new *barins*.

The Provisional Government's anti-Bolshevik campaign after the *coup* in July petered out so far as the masses were concerned and Bolshevik influence increased again. Hardly known in March, when the monarchy toppled, Lenin's followers had succeeded by October in gaining control of many local Soviets.

In Volhyn and other provinces they infiltrated the militia and, as in Rovno, managed to capture the prisons and court houses, where they installed "Revolutionary Tribunals" to try anyone suspected of counter-revolution. They increased their Red Guards with deserters from the front.

While the moderate Socialists and their allies dreamed of a democratic constitution and waited for elections to the Constituent Assembly the Bolsheviks were relentlessly undermining Russia's fragile democracy.

Even before Lenin and Leon Trotsky staged their successful *coup* on November 7, Bolshevik-dominated Soviets were virtual rulers in many towns and villages in the provinces. The municipal administrations were in a state of complete paralysis and many of their more far-sighted officials went into hiding.

The balance of forces in the Petrograd Soviet had also shifted radically. By October the Bolsheviks had a majority in the Executive Committee and Trotsky was elected chairman, a post he held in the revolution of 1905.

Events were fast approaching a climax. Though he spoke in the name of the proletariat, Lenin, in fact, had little faith in the revolutionary fervor of the masses. In November 1917, the greater part of the proletariat was exhausted by the months of hardship and confusion it had already endured. Lenin realized that a majority of the apathetic workers would not lift a finger either to overthrow or to help the Provisional Government.

The main targets of his frantic propaganda, therefore, were the soldiers, especially of the Petrograd garrison, and the sailors of the Kronstadt naval base and the Baltic Fleet.

In Petrograd and at the front, said Woytinsky, "deadly poison had been injected into the troops. At first it worked slowly, but gradually the infection penetrated deeper and deeper into the blood, brains and heart of the army."

The war-weary peasant lads in soldiers' or sailors' uniforms were no longer able to make a distinction between Kornilov, Kerensky and the moderate Socialists. To them they were all members of the same gang.

The heroes of March became the villains of November.

However, the most important single fact that contributed to the overthrow of the Provisional Government was undoubtedly the Bolshevik victory in the Petrograd Soviet and the formation of its Military Revolutionary Committee.

Frightened by Kornilov's attempted *coup*, the Military Revolutionary Committee was, ironically, created on October 22 at the suggestion of the Mensheviks. It was to have served as an organ of cooperation between the Soviet and the Petrograd garrison. But the Bolsheviks packed it with their members, appointed Trotsky as chairman—and thus gained control of all the troops in the capital loyal to the Soviet.

The Executive Committee of the Soviet had by now left the Tauride Palace and moved its offices to the Smolny Institute, formerly a finishing school for girls of the nobility, which became Trotsky's headquarters and the spearhead of the anti-government conspiracy.

The organization of the *coup* against the Provisional Government was thus conducted openly under the banner of the Soviet. This was immensely useful to Lenin, since many soldiers, especially workers, still had doubt about the Bolsheviks. They would respond to a call from *their* Soviet but not to an appeal from the Bolshevik Party.

On November 7, 1917, the tide of Russian history turned again. Swiftly the Bolsheviks seized power, setting a pattern of Communist exploitation of a genuine revolutionary situation that has been standard strategy ever since.

Two days before the *coup*, on November 5, Lenin and his adherents met secretly in the home of the journalist Sukhanov (his wife was a Bolshevik) to prepare a plan for action.

Lenin was impatient. He feared that the Constituent Assembly might produce a majority for the moderate Socialists. He was eager to start the uprising before the nation's voters spoke out against the Bolsheviks in a democratic election.

Lev Kamenev and Grigori Zinovyev, two of Lenin's key lieutenants (Stalin played only a secondary role at the time), insisted that a *coup* was premature. But Lenin, the undisputed leader of a monolithic and disciplined party, stubbornly persisted; he carried the day as usual. He won a large majority at the meeting. The Bolsheviks' hour had arrived.

The new era opened in the history of Russia—and the world—with a shot from the cruiser *Aurora*. The Kronstadt sailors, under the leadership of the Bolsheviks Dybenko and Raskolnikov, were in open revolt. The democratic Provisional Government was doomed.

Trotsky, who organized the insurrection, boasted that the cruiser fired only a blank. The *Aurora* "thundered," he said gleefully. "The boom and flash of a blank fire are much bigger than from a loaded gun. The curious onlookers jumped back from the granite parapet of the quay, fell down and crawled away. . . ."

But the *Aurora's* shot echoed throughout hungry, confused and war-weary Russia.

During the night of November 7, while Kerensky was out of the city attempting to rally a force of loyal troops, the sailors and Lenin's Red Guards, led by Antonov-Ovseyenko, surrounded the Winter Palace where the Provisional Government was waiting for the Prime Minister's return with reinforcements. The government was deposed and most of its ministers were arrested.

"When we came out on the street we were surrounded by a shouting and threatening mob," reported S. L. Maslov who replaced Victor Chernov as Minister of Agriculture.

"Where is Kerensky?" the mob screamed.

But Kerensky was not to be found. The biggest prize among the members of the Provisional Government slipped through Lenin's grasp.

There are, of course, many versions of how the "heroic" Bolsheviks "stormed" the Winter Palace. The romantic Trotsky, the irreconcilable knight-errant of world revolution, makes much of the "Art of Insurrection."

The fact is, however, that there was no serious fighting and only a few people were killed in the attack on the Winter Palace. Like the Czar's regime eight months earlier, the Provisional Government also fell almost without a shot.

Lenin gambled and won. He knew how to take advantage of the fact that Russia, in his own words, was the "freest country in the world."

Lenin's *coup* was complete and, unlike the March Revolution, it was achieved without the support of the masses. On November 7, the revolutionary crowds were small. Lenin did not need the workers. "We acted as a compact military force," he said. Like the Czars, the Bolsheviks resorted to the traditional techniques of coercion which the Russian people thought they had forever destroyed.

Lenin, like Robespierre, believed in revolutionary terror. Was it not Robespierre who said that "terror without Virtue is bloody and Virtue without terror is powerless?" Lenin also believed in virtue.

Soon reports coming to the newspapers began to paint a picture of terror and despair in the towns and villages of the hinterland. They described chaos and anarchy. The militia in every town was being removed and replaced by Red Guards.

"The appearance of these rascals is almost invariably a sign of robberies and murders," an eyewitness reported.

Terror hung over Rovno. One day a sign appeared on a building in the center of the city which read: "Extraordinary Commission to Fight Counter-Revolution." This was the first emergence in the Volhyn province of the *Cheka*, Lenin's notorious secret police which replaced the Czarist *Okhrana* as the terrorist arm of the government.

A young pickpocket known as "Motke the Thief" was installed as chief of the *Cheka* by a special emissary of Feliks Dzerzhinsky, the fanatical Polish "poet" who became head of the dreaded organization in Petrograd.

Hitherto only political prisoners were released from jail. But Motke's first act was to liberate convicts with criminal records and appoint them as his lieutenants.

Soon there were widespread arrests in the city and even executions. The joy of the March Revolution turned into sorrow, hope into fear.

But for Motke and his *Chekists* Lenin's seizure of power was indeed liberation. He could now levy *kontributsia* (a special revolutionary tax) on rich and poor alike. He could loot in the name of the Dictatorship of the Proletariat.

As Danton is reported to have said on his way to the *guillotine*, "In times of revolution power will always go to the biggest scoundrel."

But Motke's reign of terror, as it turned out, was short. He was killed in broad daylight by Kozlov, chairman of the Soviet and self-appointed commander of the Red Guards—the same soldier who had been sprung from jail because he preached the transformation of the imperialist war into a civil war but who was actually, as it became known later, a convicted arsonist.

The local Soviet, which regarded itself as the legitimate representative of the Bolshevik Party, apparently resented the *Cheka's* right to exact *kontributsia* without sharing the loot. Motke, with a mandate from Dzerzhinsky himself, turned a deaf ear to the Soviet's warning. One day he made the fatal error of breaking into the house of a wealthy Russian widow who, unknown to him, was Kozlov's mistress. The widow screamed. She ran out into the street shrieking that a Jew was trying to rob and kill a good Christian, a true *Pravoslavny.*

Suddenly out of nowhere an enraged Kozlov appeared pointing his rifle at Motke.

"Comrade," the ex-pickpocket cried, "don't shoot. I am a Bolshevik, like you. I am only doing my revolutionary duty."

"You lie," replied Kozlov. "I am not your comrade because you are a Jew and a Communist. Only a Christian can be a Bolshevik."

Kozlov thereupon split Motke's skull with the butt of his rifle.

It took a long time for the Kozlovs of Russia to realize that Lenin, who was more interested in world revolution than in Russia, had changed the name of the Bolshevik Party to the Communist Party. They identified the foreign name Communist with Germans, Jews, "Menshevik bloodsuckers" and "fat bourgeois Social Revolutionaries."

In Volhyn and other provinces, the elections to the Constituent Assembly went on despite the terror, so great was the people's urge for freedom. As Lenin foresaw, a majority of Russians were against the Bolsheviks. They voted for democratic Socialism but not for Communism.

The Assembly on which the Provisional Government had set so much store was duly elected and out of 707 seats the Bolsheviks won only 175. With 370 seats, the moderate Social Revolutionary Party gained an absolute majority. Some thirty-six million Russians took part in the elections and less than nine million voted for Lenin.

These were the first, and the last, free elections ever held in Russia.

The Constituent Assembly finally met in Petrograd on January 18, 1918, under the chairmanship of Victor Chernov, but it held only one session. The following day it was stormed and dispersed by Dybenko's sailors. A mass demonstration, mainly of workers, in favor of the Assembly, was put down by Lenin's Red Guards who killed many of the demonstrators.

The Bolsheviks had no intention of handing over power to a democratic body in which they were a minority.

Trotsky was jubilant. "The simple, open, brutal breaking up of the Constituent Assembly," he said, "dealt formal democracy a finishing stroke from which it has never recovered."

The ideals of the March Revolution died in less than a year.

With the wide world as his beat, many countries, capitals and people have become familiars of Leon Dennen, for twenty-five years a foreign correspondent and columnist for the Newspaper Enterprise Association.

He is the author of *Trouble Zone, Where The Ghetto Ends, The Soviet Peace Myth* and wrote, among other things, the chapter on Yugoslavia for the *Cavalcade of Europe,* an earlier Overseas Press Club book. He translated from the Russian David Dallin's *Soviet Russia's Foreign Policy* as well as a number of plays and short stories, including works by Vladimir Mayakovsky and Isaac Babel.

Dennen was born in New York City. "However," he writes, "my parents, who once campaigned with Eugene Victor Debs in the United States, returned to their native Russia before the outbreak of World War I. Stranded by the war, they subsequently took a leading part in revolutionary events, especially in the vast province of Volhyn." Dennen was a first-year student in the Classical *Gymnasium* when the Czar fell.

Boyd Lewis, himself a noted foreign correspondent, as President and editor of the Newspaper Enterprise Association, recently wrote about Dennen:

"What a story this man has to tell when his books are published. Roving postwar Europe from one scene of crisis and conference to another he quickly became a page-one reporter with a gift for telling the news behind the news and the news plus its significance.

"Friends of long standing were now in places of power: Von Brentano in West Germany, Leon Blum in France, Di Gasperi in Italy.

"The mayor of West Berlin, a frequent stop on Dennen's global beat, was now Ernst Reuter, who owed his life to Dennen's efforts during the war.

"Willy Brandt, now Chancellor of Germany, has told in his biography *Reuter* how Dennen saved Reuter and other German anti-Nazi freedom fighters. When Turkey broke relations with Germany in 1944 elements in the Turkish police connived with Nazi agent Franz von Papen to scoop up anti-Nazi Germans refuged in Turkey and to deliver them to the Gestapo in Bulgaria. Dennen obtained the intervention of President Inonu to save Reuter and many others from betrayal.

"Years later the Bonn government pinned the Officer's Cross of the Order of Merit of the Federal Republic on the chest of this son of a Ukrainian Jewish socialist newspaper editor.

"In my many years as an editor I have never known a writer with a greater capacity for analysis and association of events in far away places.

"On March 6, 1953, Dennen caused a journalistic sensation. On that day—just twenty-four hours after Josef Stalin died—Dennen wrote of a rift between Russia and Red China.

"At a time when the world's foreign offices were assuming that Moscow and Peking were unshakable allies, his dispatch in the *World-Telegram and Sun* created a front page sensation. Confirmation from other sources was slow to come *but come it did.*"

Twice, in 1958 and 1960, Dennen was cited by the Overseas Press Club for the "Best interpretation of foreign news in the American press."

Adolf Hitler and the Forces
That Catapulted Him to Power

As reported by SIGRID SCHULTZ

Born in Austria in 1889, Hitler seemed meek indeed to everybody who met him in the days when he slipped into Munich in 1913. According to the German historian, Werner Maser, he had left his native country because he did not want to serve in the Austrian Army. He was not a draft dodger, but he left because he considered himself a member of the German race and infinitely superior to the members of the sundry ethnic groups united under the Emperor of Austria-Hungary. In his autobiography he claimed that he had been terribly poor in his student days in Vienna. This was not true. He had enough money to spend countless evenings at the Opera House, glorying in the music of Richard Wagner and the tales about the supposedly heroic Germanic gods. In the same period he also went to lectures by anti-Semitic leaders who were spreading their theories all over the Austrian capital.

When the war broke out in August, 1914, he rushed to seek the permission of the King of Bavaria to serve as a volunteer in a Bavarian regiment. It was granted, and from that moment on he became a super-patriotic German and shared the dream that moved all Germans, from Kaiser Wilhelm II on down: the dream of foreign conquests which would make Germany the most powerful country in Europe.

Though the men at whose side he fought in some of the most bitter battles in France described him as "about the sloppiest Corporal in the outfit," who refused to accept the rank of a sergeant, because he did not want to boss other people—(he said), he turned out to be an exceptionally brave dispatch runner. This earned him the regular Iron Cross early in the war. Thanks to the devotion and energy with which Captain Guttmann, who was Jewish, went to bat for him, Hitler also won the important Iron Cross First Class, which the authorities did not like to give to mere privates or corporals.

Most of his comrades made fun of Hitler because he indulged in a good deal of day dreaming. But on one occasion he surprised them no end by claiming that some day he would hold the "high rank" of a deputy in the Bavarian Diet. His wartime superior, Captain Fritz Wiedemann, when telling me of the incident years later, admitted that he, too, had snickered because Hitler did not show the slightest trace of the self assurance or energy expected of a politician, but then he discovered that the Austrian went to a great deal of trouble to find newspapers and magazines of all kinds. He studied everything that was being written by or about General Erich Ludendorff most closely. He was certain the General would succeed in throwing the Americans and the British back into the Channel, as he had promised to.

Hitler's idol failed him. While he and the German armies were still fighting on August 8, 1918, Ludendorff decided that the war was lost. Instead of asking the Kaiser to sue for an armistice immediately, Ludendorff summoned his own clique of officers, Barons of Industry, including the Steel King Fritz Thyssen, the Coal King Hugo Stinnes, and a few fanatical Pan Germans, to secret conferences. They organized what may well be called "the conspiracy of the German Military-Industrial Complex." It was a crafty one indeed. The gentlemen felt that their Kaiser might be overthrown. This did not worry them because they thought that a German republic would probably secure easier terms from the victors than His Imperial Majesty. At the same time, they worked out schemes that would enable them to finish off the republic when they felt like it and to prepare for a war of revenge against the Western allies. After putting over secret deals with the Communists in ·Moscow and signing an official treaty with them, they mapped out plans to exploit the fear of Communism that moved the "bourgeois Western world."

By October 3, 1918, they felt their job was done and Field Marshal von Hindenburg and General Ludendorff shocked the Kaiser by demanding that he sue for an armistice immediately, but he obeyed.

As far as the Ludendorff group were concerned, they refused to accept the idea that Germany's defeat was final. Nor did a certain Corporal Adolf Hitler.

On the day of the Proclamation of the German Republic, November 9, 1918, and when Germany surrendered two days later at Compiègne, he was in a military hospital in Pasewalk near Berlin recovering from a mustard gas attack in which he was caught in Flanders on October 13, 1918. Five years later, when writing in his "Mein Kampf," he was still emoting wildly, spewing vitriolic hatred of Jews and Socialists, blaming them for Germany's defeat and concluding with a dramatic-sounding line: "I decided to become a politician."

As soon as he was well enough to travel, Hitler rushed back to revolution-torn Munich to search for his wartime comrades, many of whom had been demobilized.

A miraculous change took place in his life; thanks to the Iron Cross First Class that was pinned on his shirt, he was welcomed as an important character by some of the snootiest anti-republican, anti-Semitic, monarchistic officers on duty in Munich. He quickly forgot the gratitude he owed the Jewish Captain for securing that decoration for him. The very first speech he delivered at a Munich street corner to try out his oratorical talents was a violent denunciation of all Jews, charging that they had not fought as bravely in the war as other Germans. He knew this was a lie, but in the atmosphere prevailing in Munich in those days, his speech was applauded which was all that counted as far as he was concerned.

There never was a more systematic opportunist than Adolf Hitler, nor a more pliable hypocrite. For four years, while he served in the army he never made an anti-Semitic crack within the hearing of his superiors, Wiedemann said. As soon as he discovered that one could secure advantages by co-operating with anti-Semitic groups, he quickly became one of the wildest of the lot and the Reichswehr officers who had been impressed by his Iron Cross First Class went to work to reward him; so did a bibulous, popular, amusing poet Dietrich Eckart and a tough military organizer, Captain Ernst Roehm, a notorious homosexual who knew where some of Bavaria's secret funds were hidden and who had political ambitions.

The Reichswehr officers and the poet noticed that their protégé was poorly educated: the latter spent long hours teaching him racist theories, the art of formulating snappy lines to impress the mob and actually improving his grammar. The former sent him to "indoctrination courses" they had set up to teach the Kaiserist version of history, traditional militarist lines, anti-Communist propaganda but above all, hatred of the new-born German Republic. He paid scant attention to the rather spectacular assassination of the moderate Socialist chief of the Bavarian state, Kurt Eisner, a Jew, by a Count Arco-Valley, which was followed by the outbreak of a Communistic revolution, run mostly by weird, highly inefficient intellectuals. In his "Mein Kampf" Hitler was careful not to mention the fact (checked and confirmed by the historian Werner Maser), that he had served as a spy for the shockingly bloodthirsty group of units from sundry "Free Corps" which the Reichswehr sent to Bavaria on May 2, 1919 to oust the Communists. They killed Reds and hundreds of men and women who had nothing to do with the Soviets, until even the most ardent anti-Republican military chiefs in Bavaria begged the Berlin government to withdraw them as fast as possible, which it did.

By then the Constitutional Assembly elected by order of Friedrich Ebert, acting as President of the emergency government which assumed the bitter task of seeking to lead defeated Germany back to peace, was working overtime devising a new Constitution in Weimar. Studying the speeches of its members that appeared in the press, Hitler's two close advisers, the poet Eckart and Captain Roehm came to the conclusion that he would prove a crafty political leader in the new political set-up.

On one occasion the poet said: "Hitler must have had a number of tough horse traders among his peasant forebears from whom he inherited not only his somewhat heavy-set, awkward figure, but an incredibly sharp memory, an extra ability to sense the other fellow's weak points, to seize every opportunity that came his way, to wait patiently until the opportunity he foresaw reached the right point and then to exploit it with utter speed and ruthlessness to gain the advantage he craved."

The old man's analysis of the way Hitler's mind operated was to prove pretty accurate all through the years, especially since he added, chuckling, as if he approved of his protégé's attitude: "Old-time horse traders had no moral or ethical inhibitions, nor will Hitler ever allow any to handicap him in his determination to reach his goal." When asked what that goal was, the poet replied indignantly: "Naturally, a greater Germany that will have gotten rid of all Jews, is what I am teaching my pupil to work for."

One of Hitler's jobs, while he was still on the payroll of the Reichswehr, was to attend meetings of all political hopefuls throwing their weight around Munich in open or secret meetings which gave him the perfect chance to shop around for the right political "vehicle" for himself, as Eckart and Roehm had instructed him to. By September 1919 he had picked the "German Worker's Party," because its moving spirit, a locksmith Anton Drexler, was anti-Semitic and anti-Marxist and because its relatively small group of loyal followers were little fellows who he felt certain would be easy to boss. They were, especially with the help of Roehm and Eckart pulling wires behind the scene. Hitler started out as number 7 on the Board of the Party. By January 1920 he was its Propaganda Chief. He worked out the basic program he wanted so fast, with Anton Drexler and an economist Gottfried Feder, whose purpose in life was to "abolish slavery to the payment of interest," that he was able to call his first spectacular mass meeting for February 24, 1920 in the famous Beer Hall of the "Hofbraeuhaus."

Renting that hall cost more money than the Party had, which worried its official chairman who resigned in protest. This was exactly what Hitler wanted to happen. Though he yammers endlessly in "Mein Kampf" about poverty, he knew he could count on funds from Roehm who was still with the Reichswehr and close to the highly influential General Ritter von Epp. Some 2000 citizens turned up and listened patiently for four hours while Hitler roared out details about the twenty-five point program aimed at making the Fatherland more powerful than ever. It was a weird mixture designed to lure all kinds of people to the party, from super-Nationalists to violent anti-Semites. Some of the points were directed against capitalism and bound to meet with the approval of glowing Communists.

On that first evening some listeners dared to protest against a few points, only to be thrown out by strong-arm squads. Two of them were on duty: Hitler had brought one along and Captain Ernst Roehm had brought another. That set the pattern for Hitler's future rallies: clubbing down dissenters became hallowed tradition, with brown-uniformed Storm-troopers, known as the S.A., taking care of the chore—which many of them considered an enjoyable sport.

Finding that the original title of his party sounded too "proletarian," Hitler changed it to "the National-Socialist German Workers' Party." This was to make it easy for him and his fellow-agitators to play both sides of the street, stressing "Nationalism" in certain areas, and "Socialism" in others, depending on what was more popular with the audience. Poet Eckart shortened the title to the more harmonious sounding "Nazi" Party.

Hitler, his bodyguard and his budding S.A. engaged in countless fights. On one occasion he beat up and injured the main speaker of a rival group so badly that he and some of his helpers were put on trial, sentenced to four weeks in prison and forced to serve that sentence despite the fact that most German judges spared no effort to distort the law in favor of men who spouted the Nationalist line, the way Hitler did.

This incident did not prevent upper crust Germans from beginning to show an interest in the Nazi party. Occasionally some of the old-timers in the party complained that he was too rough and bossy. He considered himself the big moneymaker of the party because people paid for tickets to hear him thunder out his standard speech at all party rallies and even at a number of social functions, including tea parties. Thanks to this popularity, he had no trouble forcing the Board to name him Chief of the party and to grant him the "dictatorial powers" he demanded.

Hitler's self confidence rose sky high when the famous ace of World War I, Capt. Hermann Goering, the successor of Richthofen, and a fellow student of his at the Munich University, Rudolf Hess, dropped their studies in order to become his chief lieutenants, and help him fight his way to absolute power. Goering was to tell me proudly, many years later, that he was the one who suggested the title "Fuehrer" for Hitler in 1921. Millions of Germans were to swear loyalty to that "Fuehrer" for almost a quarter of a century.

LUDENDORFF'S MILITARY-INDUSTRIAL COMPLEX PULLED WIRES FOR HITLER

The leaders who had plotted together with General Ludendorff in August and September of 1918, had foreseen that any government which succeeded that of the Kaiser would have to move fast to obtain vast amounts of food for the German population as soon as it came to power if it were to become stable and popular. The masses had been forced to live on near-starvation rations for two winters. The shortage of food was harrowing in the fall of 1918 and the following years and a number of members of the "industrial complex" decided to use hunger as their ally in their fight against the newborn republic.

Two days after its birth, a few arms manufacturers and other big plant owners presented staggering bills to the government's financial expert, claiming that the imperial authorities had failed to pay them. They demanded immediate payment, knowing that the republic would find itself in a difficult financial position if it paid them the full amount.

They finally condescended to accept payment of the equivalent of

300,000,000 gold dollars in installments. The government paid, hoping to establish friendly relations with industrial leaders who were getting ready to revive the export business which had enriched Germany before the war.

The export business boomed all right, but the successful exporters who belonged to the Ludendorff clique made sure that very little money came back to Germany, helping to precipitate one of the worst inflations any country ever experienced. The German economist, Kurt Pritzkoleit, summarized the methods some of them used in his book *The New Masters*: "Heavy industry took up credits in paper marks, invested them in finished goods which they exported, and placed the payments they collected in Swiss and other foreign banks to use that money to buy lucrative businesses abroad." The speculators enriched themselves to a fantastic degree. They falsified their books so adroitly that the tax collector could get almost no money out of them.

The inflation made it impossible for the government to buy food abroad and relieve the misery of the people, as the anti-republicans had hoped. When the government threatened to try some of the speculators for illegal operations, they threatened to lock their plants and fire all the workers if it continued to "annoy" them. Consequently, the hungry people blamed the government for the shortages from which they were suffering and began to listen eagerly to Nazi hate mongers, Communists and other enemies of the republic. They blamed the inflation and the shortage of food on the reparation payments the French and others demanded since German authorities never fully exposed the sinister activities of the big and little speculators in the early days of the Weimar Republic.

Believing that the "hunger campaign" of the industrialists had compromised the republic, groups of militarists decided that the time had come for them to stage a "putsch." This one was to become known as the "Kapp Putsch" and was staged by the Ehrhard Brigade and other units which were encamped in Doeberitz, near Berlin, on March 20, 1920. It proved a spectacular failure, partly because President Ebert and others they meant to arrest had been tipped off in time and had left the German capital, mostly because, for the first and last time in the country's history, the people turned against the military leaders. They remembered how the Kaiser and his Generals had lied to them for four years and decided to join the nationwide strike which the labor union leaders were organizing. Less than ten days after they had strutted into Berlin, the Putschists found themselves forced to retreat to Doeberitz.

The rear guard attracted world wide attention by shooting point blank into a dense crowd that was standing quietly watching their departure. Many were killed and injured in plain sight of foreign correspondents looking out of the windows of the Hotel Adlon.

General Ludendorff had been slightly involved in the "putsch." His reaction to its failure was to lead to the major turning point in the life of Adolf Hitler, a man about whose existence he did not even know at the time. Shortly after the Putsch the general told the brother of the "Potash King" of Germany, and other members of his group, that the failure of the "Putsch" showed clearly that the attitude of the German people had changed. No high ranking German officer, no member of the former reigning houses would be able to overcome the distrust of the voters for quite a while to come. In order to regain absolute control, he and his friends would have to go hunting for a proletarian, a man who stemmed from the lower classes, who spoke the language of the masses but was a glowing patriot. If properly trained, he would be able to win the confidence of the general public and become the absolute dictator of the country, while obeying his orders and those of his group.

Ludendorff surprised his listeners by stating that he himself was ready to train a talented proletarian if he, or they, succeeded in finding one. He was certain that in view of his special knowledge, a pupil of his would become the all-powerful dictator of Germany and rid the country of the Socialists and other "peace mongers."

The mighty ex-General took off for Bavaria, where nationalists of all political shades and backgrounds were throwing their weight around. For a while he avoided meeting one of the local rabble rousers, Adolf Hitler, being repelled by the fact that a number of highly unsavory characters, including at least one man who was accused of being a pimp, were on his team and enjoyed his special friendship. So did some refugees, from Baltic lands, who rated high in Ludendorff's estimation since the days when a section of the Kaiser's General Staff had prepared plans for the conquest of Western Russia, years before Ludendorff carried them out. (They were the secret "pre-Peter plans," i.e. plans aiming at the reduction of the Russian Empire to the size it had been in the days before Peter the Great!") Among them was a Baron Erwin von Scheubner Richter who enjoyed the General's confidence. He obtained his permission to introduce Hitler to him, after assuring him that his friend was as passionately devoted to the idea of big conquests for the Fatherland as he was.

The Fuehrer was struck dumb with emotion when his wartime idol condescended to speak to him. This sudden silence was striking because, though he never confided his real secret thoughts to anybody, he was probably one of the most talkative politicians who ever lived. A German reporter, who was a Nazi in those days, told me that the only time in his life that he saw Hitler listen silently to anybody, for hours on end, had been when he and Ludendorff got together alone, in the home of a discreet acquaintance in a nearby suburb or some out of the way pub. Eckart, the poet, was listened to patiently by Hitler, but for much shorter periods.

After Ludendorff came to the conclusion that Hitler showed a far-above-average ability to understand complicated military and political moves, thanks to his sharp memory, the two men went in for long meetings. They were kept secret because cagey Hitler wanted to be the only one of his group to garner extra knowledge from the General.

When, in the beginning of 1923, Germany's Steel King Fritz Thyssen called on Ludendorff, he boasted that he had found his ideal "proletarian" and that he was training Adolf Hitler for the post of dictator of Germany. After attending a rally at which the Fuehrer spoke, he gave Ludendorff the equivalent of 25,000 gold dollars for the Nazi Party, which was a fabulous sum in those days when Germany was racked by an inflation that became worse at a terrifying rate.

The moment the General told Thyssen and other key members of the Military-Industrial Complex that he had selected Hitler as Germany's future dictator, was the most important turning point in the Austrian's career up to then. It meant that in the eyes of countless people he no longer was a low-class rabble rouser, but a man who had inherited some of Ludendorff's prestige and deserved money from them, to help him carry out his and their plans. Thyssen admitted that he had given Hitler a total of one million gold marks in the twenties and early thirties. Quite a number of other contributors helped pave the road for him, not out of generosity but because his and their goals were the same: more power for themselves and Germany.

The Coal King, Stinnes, told members of the U.S. Embassy in September 1923 that "a man of simple origin" was being trained in Bavaria and would soon emerge into the limelight as the country's dictator. He did emerge into the limelight in 1923 but, not as a dictator!

That "simple man" undertook a pilgrimage to Bayreuth in October to honor the memory of Richard Wagner, get acquainted with his family and especially with Houston Steward Chamberlain, the author of the book *Foundations of the Nineteenth Century* (published in work started the racist fever that marked the first half of and convinced Kaiser Wilhelm II, his generals, and millio Germans that as members of the German Aryan race, they h to rule the world and to look down on the Jews. Hitler's anti-Semitism rose skyhigh after his talk with Chamberlain. So did his conceit after the old man heaped fulsome praise on him. He returned to Munich convinced that there was nothing in the world to prevent him from doing everything he wanted to as the racist "Semi-god" had told him.

He and some of his younger lieutenants turned reckless and decided that the Nazis and allied groups of veterans were strong enough to march on Berlin and overthrow the Ebert government, the way an Italian, by the name of Mussolini, had marched on Rome in 1922 and had become the supreme master of that country. They thought it smarter not to tell Ludendorff about their plan, but went ahead to organize a "putsch" to force the Bavarian government to cooperate with them.

MUNICH BEER HALL PUTSCH INTRODUCES NEWCOMER HITLER TO FOREIGN NEWSPAPER READERS

That "putsch" was a two day affair that took place on November 8th and 9th, 1923, in the course of which 19 men were killed, and scores were seriously injured. Details about Hitler's histrionics in the Beer Hall and his behavior while the police and some 3,000 armed Nazis were busy shooting it out in a street battle, figure in almost all books about him. He ran from the scene, not pausing for a second to see if he could help any of the wounded, but traveled to a nearby resort, Uffing, to hide upstairs in the home of the American-born mother of his chief for the foreign press, Ernst Hanfstaengl, known as "Putzi." The latter's junoesque sister, Erna, on whom the much slighter Hitler had a crush for quite a while, told me that she had never seen a man as frightened as he was.

By February 1924, when he and his fellow-putschists had to face trial, he had fully recovered all of his braggadoccio and arrogance. The trial turned out to be a superb propaganda show for Hitler. The judge rarely tried to curb Hitler's impertinence and on a number of occasions he allowed him to rant on for four hours at a stretch. The failure of the putsch did not prevent him from roaring out his boast that he was certain to become Germany's all-powerful dictator and that the Reichswehr, its officers and soldiers, would back him.

The Germans, rich and poor alike, relished his outbursts. Even the supposedly democratic newspapers reprinted some of them verbatim, claiming that their readers were intelligent enough to see through the lies. The reason why Hitler found such a warm echo was that the inflation was nearly at its peak at the time of the putsch and Franco-German relations were very bad. But at the end of November, Dr. Stresemann succeeded in forcing Germany's financial experts to introduce reforms that put an end to the inflation and he came to an understanding with the French. Conditions were improving at a fine clip, but in February 1924 distrust and bitterness were still rampant, and readiness to wallow in hatred of the government and the foreign occupation forces was strong.

Instead of sentencing the Nazis to prison, the kind judge ordered them detained in the comfortable fortress of Landsberg-on-Lech, where Hitler was treated like a beloved, honored guest. He was allowed to receive visitors as often and as long as he pleased. They ranged from the famous professor of geo-politics, General Karl Haushofer, who would come up from Munich and supplement the knowledge Hitler had acquired as Ludendorff's "pupil," to members of German minority groups from Poland, Czechoslovakia, etc. as well as Austrians seeking instructions on how to serve the German and Nazi cause in their parts of the world, to racists and Jewbaiters who, as Rudolf Hess stated a few years later, discussed plans that called for the persecution of Jews.

How seriously the racial problem preoccupied him while in Landsberg is obvious in his main opus, *Mein Kampf,* which he dictated while there and which was to become a kind of "Bible" for the Nazis. He echoed Chamberlain's line about the "superiority of the Aryan race, to which Germans belonged, over all other races." He denounced and threatened Jews more ferociously than they had ever been threatened before, except in the darkest Middle Ages. He stressed "Germany's right" to more land.

In fact, *Mein Kampf* should have left no doubt in the minds of peace-loving Germans and other politicians about the ruthlessness, the all-consuming ambition of the author. But at the time the book appeared, he seemed rather unimportant and none of them proved anywhere as alert as peace lovers should be.

Hitler was released after serving only nine months of a five year sentence and returned to Munich a few days before Christmas 1924. He had worked hard but had also enjoyed a kind of sabbatical in Landsberg, during which he had mapped out all kinds of schemes for himself. They were crafty ones!

He was really an actor, a dissembler by nature, as those of us who watched him through the years, know. Back in Munich he played the role of the reformed character who abhorred violence so well that Bavaria's Premier allowed him to call a political rally for February 27, 1925 to set up a new Nazi Party. The first had been banned after the Beer Hall Putsch.

Four thousand men turned up at the rally. There was no reformed character around. For two hours Hitler carried on in his wildest style, denouncing the Weimar Republic, the Jews, the Marxists more violently than ever. The audience went berserk with joy, and the Nazi Party was reborn with Hitler as its boss.

The Bavarian Premier was furious about the way Hitler had fooled him. He wanted the Austrian troublemaker deported back to Austria, but only Kaiserist judges were on duty in Germany. They ruled that Hitler could stay. The Premier of Bavaria and those of most other states then forbade him to speak in public for a number of years.

Undaunted, he went after men in other parts of Germany whom he had met earlier and induced them to start small centers in their home towns, and he gradually developed a nationwide Nazi network. He held rallies in the states in which he was allowed to speak, and former S.A. men who had enjoyed strutting around in parades in the past, in front of their admiring womenfolk, were delighted to have a chance to perform again.

Hitler had won the warm sympathy of a number of dethroned princes, as well as that of the Duke of Saxe-Coburg, who ranked as important because he was related to the Royal family of England.

The presence of any kind of princeling on the rostrum beside Hitler made the rally seem extra glamorous to the run-of-the-mill Germans and far more impressive than meetings called by the leaders of the Weimar Republic, who felt duty-bound to inform their audiences about serious problems that had to be faced and discussed carefully before decisions were taken. Centuries of feudal rule had left their impact on the minds of a great number of Germans who considered the political home-work self-respecting citizens of a free society are expected to do a painful, bewildering chore. That "young fellow" Hitler made it abun-

dantly clear that he despised the Republic and it did not take long until
enthusiastic admirers of his went to work to encourage him by shouting
the slogan: "Fuehrer befiehl, und wir folgen Dir" or "Fuehrer, issue
your orders and we'll obey you!" whenever they met him.

Hitler did need encouragement in 1925 and 1926. Progress was slow,
partly owing to the improvement of conditions in Germany, but above
all because he was determined to forge ahead on his own, without asking Ludendorff or Captain Roehm to help him secure funds from industrialists who were financing groups that opposed the Weimar Republic.

LADIES TO THE RESCUE!

There were a number of ladies among those who helped him while
he was hunting for a friendly industrialist, even though he had ruled
that women must be kept out of politics! Not only did they throw parties
to give him a chance to meet important men who, they hoped, would
join the Nazi Party and improve its finances, but some of them gave him
money of their own. Others handed him jewels and antiques which
were so valuable that a Swiss financier accepted them as security for a
loan. Some of the ladies proved generous behind the backs of their hus-
bands! Lady donors I met were enthusiastic about the way the Fuehrer
played the role of "the attentive cavalier" when with them, and while
the handkissing business was routine, they raved about "the deep soul-
ful look with which his big blue eyes would stare deep into their eyes."
In time, he added a touch of hypnotical hardness to the expression in
his slightly protruding bright-blue eyes when staring at people who were
being introduced to him. A surprisingly big number of supposedly tough
American businessmen were as impressed by that stare as the ladies.

Two couples worked hardest to help Hitler in 1926. One of the
couples, the wealthy publisher Hugo Bruckmann and his wife, won the
race when she succeeded in talking the multimillionaire coal magnate
Emil Kirdorf into "conferring" with Hitler in the Bruckmann home in
Munich in July 1927. The Fuehrer delivered his customary four hour
speech, but knowing that the 80-year-old man's main goal in life had
been, and still was, to cut wages and make workers work overtime, he
tailored it to appeal to him. He stressed that his party would protect the
rights of employers and keep workers "in their place." The multimillionaire approved.

Hitler's days of plenty started when Kirdorf joined the Nazi Party and donated 300,000 marks as a starter. Thanks to Kirdorf, he met many of the key figures of "heavy industry" and they applauded his speeches enthusiastically. He also made Hitler write a memorandum about his plans for the German economy which was distributed secretly to important leaders.

Unable to resist the temptation of playing a double game, Hitler had his number two man, Gregor Strasser, who was deeply concerned about the plight of German labor, campaign in industrial areas and lure workers into the Nazi Party. There was no telling, said opportunist Hitler, when allies in Labor ranks might prove useful! When Kirdorf heard about Strasser's activities, he branded the Nazi Party as "leftist" and resigned from it.

That meant nothing to the Fuehrer: other "angels" had come his way and bigger sums of money than ever were pouring into the coffers of the Nazi Party or disappearing into his own pockets. Captain Goering was back in Germany and was busy improving the Party's relations with key officers in the Reichswehr, while Hitler was having a grand time because the leader of the Nationalists, "Newspaper King" Dr. Alfred Hugenberg, who had been one of the directors of the Krupp Armament plants in wartime, confided some military secrets to him. They intensified his hope that Germany would soon speed up the preparation for the war of revenge against the victors of 1918!

Hugenberg told him about German plants which the militarists and industrialists were re-converting into special armament plants in violation of the disarmament provisions imposed on Germany under the terms of the Versailles Treaty. What enchanted him and Hitler even more, was that the money needed for these conversions had been obtained from American bankers who did not bother to find out exactly for what the huge sums the Germans were borrowing were to be used.

The reason Hugenberg was revealing true details to Hitler was that he wanted to induce him to plot with the military and industrial complex that was planning a major campaign to prevent the government from signing the "Young Plan" which had just been drafted and which ruled that Germany had to continue to pay reparations. Hitler naturally agreed to make common cause with the Nationalists, but insisted that every move his Nazi Party made to help be given ample publicity.

The leaders of the Weimar Republic took the first threats of the new allies calmly. They had good reason to be proud of their achievements and especially those of Dr. Gustav Stresemann, the most brilliant Foreign Minister Germany had in this century. Thanks to him Germany reached agreements with the Western powers and the League of Nations which seemed to be harbingers of peace.

Dr. Stresemann died on October 3, 1929. The New York stock Market crashed three weeks later, precipitating the world wide depression.

Hitler ruled that the time had come for the Nazi Party to overthrow the government and to seize power and for him to be appointed Chancellor of Germany.

He had many S.A. and S.S. units scattered all over the country. Most of them went into action immediately, clashing with the local police forces and poorly trained semi-military units of Socialistic and democratic organizations.

Hitler and his subleaders kept increasing the savagery of the onslaught of their armed followers in countless German towns and ports. In Berlin a number of S.A. units, who belonged to the more moderate Nazi wing, gave them a rude surprise. Searching for a soupkitchen, some unemployed S.A. men noticed a super-elegant car, parked near the center of town, decorated with all kinds of insignae showing that it belonged to the Fuehrer. They found out that it was a brand-new car, for which Hitler had just paid the fabulous sum of 40,000 marks! The indignant, hungry men thought of all the food this money could have bought and their S.A. units demonstrated against the Fuehrer, demanding his ouster. Regular street battles took place between them and the really bloodthirsty, black-uniformed S.S. which moved quickly to punish the men who dared to try to stage a revolt against the Fuehrer.

Hitler had sensed that there was unrest in the ranks of his armed forces and had sent a cry for help to Captain Roehm, who had written him a letter in 1925, before he left for Bolivia, promising to return to Germany if his "beloved" Fuehrer ever needed him. He kept his promise—and by the end of 1931 he had restored iron discipline in the ranks of the S.A. and S.S., and increased their numbers to an enormous force of 400,000 men.

GERMAN INDUSTRIALISTS LAVISH MILLIONS ON HITLER

By the end of 1931 the number of unemployed Germans had risen to over 5,600,000. Industrialists were closing plants faster than Republican authorities believed justifiable, claiming that they had no funds left to continue production; but they had ample funds when it came to financing their friend Adolf Hitler and his Party.

In his many secret conferences with them, he had trotted out the favorite theory of his first teacher, General Ludendorff, about the importance of conquering vast Eastern lands to provide "living space for the German people" and raw materials which Germany lacked. The barons of industry remembered the happy months of the spring of 1918, when Ludendorff's armies had sallied forth and seized areas in Russia at their request to obtain minerals, etc. they wanted. Certain key-men in the Ruhr knew that the plotters of the Reichswehr, including General Kurt von Schleicher, had perfected plans with the same goal in mind in the twenties when the German military leaders and the Russian military had been close secret allies.

To strengthen the position of the man who shared their dreams, they made sure that he had enough money to survive the depression, and to put over some of this scheme at a time when most party leaders were handicapped by lack of funds. The "Steel King" Fritz Thyssen admitted that he himself gave Hitler a total of one million marks in the course of years. He held that the Fuehrer's industrial protectors gave him 2,000,000 marks between 1930 and 1933; which is certainly too low a figure, since an army of 400,000 S.A. and S.S. men also cost money.

Generous gentlemen in the pro-Nazi Camp, who wanted the Nazis to cut a fine figure, gave them funds to enable them to take up quarters and establish their offices in the elegant Hotel Kaiserhof, just a few minutes walk to the Wilhelmstrasse, the Chancellory, the German White House and other government buildings. Furthermore, at the very height of the financial crisis, one of Munich's famous palaces was put on the market for 1,500,000 marks. German and Dutch admirers of the Fuehrer put over the deal for him and since he considered himself a master architect, he himself supervised the transformation of the palace into the very impressive National Headquarters of the Nazi Party.

THE MILITARY TO THE RESCUE!

Thanks to their extra funds, the Nazis staged big election campaigns and won a good number of them in German states and towns. Their party had 25,000 dues-paying members at the end of 1925; by the end of 1931 they numbered a little over 800,000 and one year later they passed the 1,400,000 mark! And every party member knew what some S.A. men would do to him if he failed to pay on time!

General Kurt von Schleicher, the number two man in the War Office who belonged to the clique which had plotted with General Ludendorff in August and September 1918, felt that the sporadic civil war between the Nazis and the defenders of the Republic represented a waste of national energy and by the fall of 1931 he decided that the only way to end it was to help Ludendorff's "star pupil" Hitler secure a post in the government. The only man who could appoint him was President von Hindenburg.

Schleicher asked Captain Roehm to find out whether Hitler and Goering would like to be granted an audience with the President. The reply was an enthusiastic "yes" and on October 10, 1931 the Fuehrer and the Air Force Captain were received by the old gentleman. Hitler pontificated for almost an hour, boasting that his plans would make Germany more powerful than ever, and then he repeated some of the pet lines of Hindenburg's wartime partner Ludendorff.

"That man represents a danger for Germany," the President told Schleicher, after ending the audience abruptly. He said firmly that he did not want to have anything whatsoever to do with the "private from Bohemia." It was not that he confused the various parts of Austria, but in the eyes of real Prussians like Hindenburg, Bohemians were unreliable characters, who lacked the discipline a Prussian considered vitally important. He obviously meant to stress his distrust of the man. That distrust still pre-occupied him in the last days of his life (August 1934) when he talked about it to the surgeon Professor Sauerbruch, who was at his bedside, and muttered regrets about ever having forgotten it, "even for a very short while."

Back in the fall of 1931 when Schleicher, whom I knew fairly well, told me about the failure of the Hindenburg-Hitler meeting he had arranged, he was still impressed by the insight the President showed when he asked him why he considered Hitler dangerous: "He is dangerous because a nation always has to pay for the recklessness, the lies of gambler types like him, if the people fall for them. Hitler shows the first signs of megalomania; he'll get worse, fast. He is a little like Ludendorff who never had sense enough to stop at the right time and the right spot. But Ludendorff was a real military man, which that private from Bohemia is not. The trouble is, we have lots of well-meaning fools, who'll fall for a megalomaniac thinking he is a great patriot!"

It never dawned on Hitler that his pontificating might have repelled Hindenburg. He told some of the Nazi bigwigs that he feared the President was not as alert as he should be, because he apparently failed to realize how important a man, he, Adolf Hitler, was. The opportunity to show him that he was strong enough to be a rival of his came Hitler's way in the first months of 1932 when Hindenburg allowed himself to be talked into running for a second presidential term. Chancellor Dr. Heinrich Bruening and the members of his cabinet had been unable to find a candidate who was half as popular as Hindenburg. Since he was in his mid-eighties, Bruening agreed to campaign in his place.

Brash 43-year-old Hitler, who was still a "stateless citizen," rushed to acquire German nationality just in time to step forward and claim the Presidency, together with two other rivals of Hindenburg. Since he had scored a major success when he addressed millionaires at the Industrie Klub in Düsseldorf in January—which meant extra donations—the Nazi Party was rich enough to have its chief flown around the country in a private plane to address mass meetings in twenty-one cities. The debut of a plane in an election campaign impressed the people, but Hindenburg had been their national hero for almost twenty years and he won 53% of the vote on April 10, 1932, while the "new German" Hitler garnered 36%.

Even though he lost, the election proved mighty useful to Hitler: it had carried his name into townlets and villages where it had never been heard before. To Bruening, who had scored the victory for Hindenburg, it was to spell tragedy. A very few weeks after he had toured the country, assuring the Germans that despite his age, Hindenburg's mind was crystal clear and that he was an ardent supporter of the Weimar Republic, he discovered, to his intense regret, that he had lied to himself and his countrymen: by May 1932 it was evident that Hindenburg's mind was no longer clear all the time and that he was beginning to succumb to the influence of a friend of his son's, a retired cavalry officer in his early fifties, an arch-conservative, Baron Franz von Papen. Since he distrusted Hitler, the President was delighted to hear him denounce that "low class parvenu" in violent terms. This Baron believed himself to be the "genius" who would be able to curb the Nazis if he could induce Hindenburg to appoint him Chancellor.

With everybody in official circles busy spying on everybody else in the Berlin of 1932, the Nazis knew about the campaign Papen was waging against them and retaliated in kind. His friends in the White

House made sure that the President did not hear what the Nazis had to say about the shortcomings of his "protégé," which were numerous.

Von Papen had attracted public attention once in his lifetime. That had been in 1916, when he was deported from the United States for directing acts of sabotage while attached to the German Embassy in Washington. The highest political rank he achieved before courting Hindenburg, had been that of deputy in a local Diet, but that in no way diminished his exceptional arrogance and conceit, or his interest in spinning intrigues. The first victim of his intrigues in 1932 was the last able, honest, Chancellor of the German Republic, Dr. Heinrich Bruening. He managed to convince Hindenburg that he would do a much better job at fighting the Nazis than the careful, restrained Bruening. The latter was having difficulties with the Reichstag, whose members refused to pass reforms he deemed necessary. He asked Hindenburg to use the emergency provisions of the Constitution to help him. He refused to and Bruening resigned on May 30, 1932. The old man was delighted to name the greenhorn, Franz von Papen, Chancellor of Germany on June 1.

The baron had really won his heart when he talked about the importance of "restoring the power of the upper classes in Germany" and about his intention to form a "cabinet of barons." Hindenburg had been raised and had worked most of his adult life in a society in which even minor aristocrats were topdogs, and being one himself he liked the Baron's plan. In order to give the "cabinet of barons," which included only 4 of them, a few extra weeks in which to display their efficiency, he delayed the date for the election of a new Reichstag to July 31.

Aristocrats were still so important in the minds of the Germans that Hitler went after blue blood supporters. He managed to get hold of the upper echelon variety, with the Crown Prince himself calling upon his countrymen to vote for the Fuehrer! But the Nazi Party did not really need aristocratic help: the Papen cabinet managed to create such a havoc in the weeks before the election that the Nazis emerged from it with 230 deputies. This made Hitler the leader of the strongest Party in the country.

Tradition had it that this victory entitled him to the Chancellorship, but Hindenburg, backed by Papen and the Defense Minister General "Baron" von Schleicher, would grant him only the Vice-Chancellorship. He turned it down.

Papen was put in his place by the new Reichstag. Before he started to read his program a motion of non-confidence was filed by the Communists. It was accepted by 512 deputies from most parties, against 42 Nationalists and members of the People's Party. Before the counting was over, a livid Papen slapped a red folder, containing the order for the dissolution of the Reichstag, signed by Hindenburg, down on the lectern in front of Goering, the President of the Reichstag.

The next day Nazi deputies reported that they had never seen Hitler laugh as wholeheartedly as he had on the previous evening when they all got together to celebrate the defeat of von Papen. But a bit of anxiety was soon to creep into their ranks because it turned out that thanks to his very wealthy wife, the Baron had good friends among the industrialists who used to supply them with funds. They said that they would stand by Papen in the following crucial period. They were beginning to get annoyed at Roehm's S.A. and S.S. men and the unrest they continued to cause.

In mid-September Hindenburg summoned Papen and General von Schleicher to a conference at which, rumor had it, the President had chosen the General as his new Chancellor. Since Goering happened to be one of my dinner guests on the day the rumor started to circulate I asked him about it. He exploded: "Schleicher will pay a high price for what he did to the Fuehrer," and would say no more.

The meeting of the trio, Hindenburg, Papen, and Schleicher, was to have vitally important consequences. This is an oversimplified summary of information obtained from one of Goering's aides: when asked for his suggestions Papen said that he saw no reason for his resigning as Chancellor. The thing to do was to ban all the uniformed fighters, the Nazis and the non-Nazis and to have the Reichswehr help the police keep law and order.

Hindenburg was shocked. This would amount to a violation of the Constitution which he had sworn to defend. Schleicher asked how Papen expected 100,000 Reichswehrmen to control 400,000 to 450,000 S.A. and S.S. men, not to mention the Socialists, the Iron Guard and others? He knew that Gregor Strasser and a number of other Nazi leaders were against the idea of carrying on the near-civil-war in order to secure the all-Nazi cabinet Hitler wanted. Their inclusion in a new cabinet was bound to result in a split in the Nazi Party which would automatically weaken it and make it easier to deal with Hitler.

The idea enchanted the President. He gave the post of Chancellor to the General, telling him that he could include Gregor Strasser in his cabinet. He ordered the German people to go to the polls and elect a new Reichstag on November 6, 1932. He went out of his way to stress that von Papen continued to enjoy his absolute confidence. Little did he realize that his action was to drive his blue-blood protégé straight into the arms of Adolf Hitler, the man whom he had denounced as a menace to Germany the first time he met him.

Papen charged that Schleicher "had stolen the Chancellorship from him," by failing to reject it, when Hindenburg appointed him and he vowed deadly enmity against him. Hitler became an ardent enemy of the newly-named Chancellor when his spies informed him about the secret negotiations between Schleicher and Gregor Strasser. He kicked Strasser and his friends out of the Nazi Party. The grim threats Goering had mentioned to me in 1932 did not turn into blood-curdling reality immediately: General von Schleicher and his wife were spared yet many months.

Papen and Hitler had been intriguing against each other all summer long, basking in the belief that President von Hindenburg had no other candidate for the Chancellorship in mind and was choosing between the two of them. Hitler sensed that his chance of winning the post was dimming and that he had better look for reinforcements. President von Hindenburg was the only man in Germany who could appoint a new Chancellor if anything happened to Schleicher. Since the President continued to stress his devotion to Papen, the Fuehrer had go-betweens court the gentleman and lure him to his camp.

The ex-Chancellor was won over in no-time-flat. He even vowed solemnly to help Hitler become Chancellor and to be satisfied with the post of Vice-Chancellor. This sudden modesty surprised everybody. He admitted that it was inspired by the spectacular fiasco he had suffered in the Reichstag a few months earlier.

The new allies pooled their remarkable talents as conspirators to bring about the overthrow of the government of the General who had been a loyal friend to both of them for years! Some time later the statement of Goering that Hitler intended to make Schleicher "pay a high price" for what turned out to be his effort to weaken the Nazi Party, was to become reality: General von Schleicher and his wife were murdered by Nazi assassins, as were hundreds of others, including Gregor Strasser and Hitler's benefactor of Munich days, Captain Roehm, in the "Nazi Blood Purge" of June 30, 1934. Their lives were spared for almost two years thanks to the fact that the Nazi system did not hit its full murderous stride until Hitler had been in power for some time.

Back in the fall of 1932, after the Nazi Party suffered some minor losses in the November elections, members of a group of ardent anti-Nazi conservatives discovered that some of its leaders were in a state of near-panic. It was being harassed by creditors and the fear of bankruptcy, which would have meant the end of the Party, was spreading.

Hitler's new ally Papen came to the rescue. On January 4, 1933, he took the Fuehrer and two of his aides to Cologne, to the highly influential banker, Kurt von Schroeder. He fell for his oratory like millions of other Germans. He immediately sallied forth to seek help for the Nazi Party and the minute its creditors learned that this banker was supporting it, they agreed to delay bankruptcy proceedings for another month.

That Cologne meeting had additional, historical significance, because one of the aides Hitler brought along was the leader of his anti-Semitic groups, Heinrich Himmler, the man who was to direct the Nazi murder campaigns which cost the lives of millions of Jewish men, women and children, Germans and non-Germans—as well as the lives of millions of Poles, Russians and other nationals. The Nazis had shown restraint in their anti-Semitic propaganda in the early thirties while Hitler was fighting for the Chancellorship; the inclusion of Himmler in the Cologne meeting convinced anti-Semitic leaders that their movement was deemed important by the banker Kurt von Schroeder and the wealthy upper crust industrialists with whom he was associated.

In the meantime, General von Schleicher had presented remarkably efficient programs aimed at providing jobs for Germany's unemployed to the Reichstag, right after he became Chancellor. The Nazi deputies and their friends in other parties systematically prevented the passage of all-important bills.

Papen exploited the setbacks the new Chancellor was suffering, to urge his protector, Hindenburg, to oust Schleicher and to appoint him as Vice-Chancellor and Hitler as Chancellor of a new German cabinet. The old man insisted that Papen had to be the Chancellor of any new cabinet he might appoint and that Hitler would have to be satisfied with the post of Vice-Chancellor.

To show his loyalty to Hitler, Papen helped him organize a regular siege of President von Hindenburg. He saw to it that powerful industrialists the President had known in World War I descended on him in the Presidential Palace, or sent trusted aides to sow distrust of General von Schleicher in his mind and to urge him to forget his prejudices against Hitler. So did high-ranking officers who were secret members of the Nazi Party, and East-Prussian Junkers, neighbors of the President when he was on his estate in Neudeck, who were furious at Schleicher because he had ordered a thorough investigation of a big financial scandal in which they had been involved.

Hindenburg turned a deaf ear to their pleas. Hitler decided to try a trick of his own: on January 22, 1933 he had Papen invite the President's son, Colonel Oskar von Hindenburg, to a meeting of the members of the cabinet he was setting up for the day when Hindenburg senior would accept him as Chancellor. He took the colonel into a separate room and for more than an hour tried to scare him into believing that Schleicher was "Communist-minded" and that he planned to confiscate the estate of "Neudeck," which was precious in the minds of all members of the none-too-wealthy Hindenburg family, on the charge that the family's right to own the property was not clearly established. The colonel countered that there was no reason for him to be alarmed because the matter had come up years before and been straightened out.

Yet, Hitler must have felt that his lies had induced the young Hindenburg to help turn his father against Schleicker, because shortly after he became Chancellor he made the state increase the size of Neudeck by 5,000 tax-free acres and the none-too-bright colonel was promoted faster in the Reichswehr than was customary.

Six days after their talk, on January 28, Chancellor von Schleicher called on President von Hindenburg to seek his extra help in his struggle with the Reichstag. Hindenburg turned him down and Schleicher resigned.

The President turned to his protégé, von Papen, who rejected the Chancellorship offered to him. Papen presented the cabinet list Hitler and he had agreed on; only three of the ten men on the list were Nazis. Hindenburg rejected it, insisting that he would not grant the Chancellorship to Hitler. The battle went on until toward Sunday noon, January 29. The weary old soldier was won over by the promise of a kind of brother act. He was assured that Hitler considered Papen as his equal, not as a man who had to obey his orders, and that the two men would always report jointly to the President to show that they were sharing the power! Feeling that he had done all he could for his protégé, Hindenburg instructed his officials to prepare the swearing-in of the new cabinet.

Shortly before noon, on January 30, 1933, the former General Field Marshal of Kaiser Wilhelm II, named the ex-Corporal who had served in his Army in World War I, Chancellor of Germany after he had made him take the solemn oath of office. And right behind the new Chancellor of Germany, Adolf Hitler, stood the nine members of his cabinet ready to take the same oath.

To all of the foreign corerspondents on duty in Germany who had followed developments in that country closely for years, there was nothing surprising about the big news, but none of us old-timers had the slightest doubt about its extraordinary significance: we knew that in his secret conferences with influential militarists and barons of industry he had sworn to "arm the country to the teeth" and to conquer new lands for the German Reich.

That evening we watched some 70,000 khaki-clad S.A. men and steel-helmeters in field gray strut through the Wilhelmstrasse in the biggest torchlight parade ever staged in Berlin, singing war songs and their national anthem as they passed by the window of the Presidential Palace from which President von Hindenburg was watching them. They stopped shortly before the balcony of the Chancellory where Hitler stretched his arm up and down in unending Nazi salute, and the masses packed in the street cheered deliriously.

They were indeed ready to obey the orders of their Fuehrer blindly, whatever they be, as were masses in many other German cities.

Only in the districts where the poor people lived was there gloom and fear, since they knew a good deal about the ruthlessness of the Nazis even in the days when their Fuehrer was not Chancellor of Germany!

A quick look into the lobby and salons of the Hotel Adlon after the parade showed that a good number of members of "the Military-Industrial Complex" had come to town to celebrate Hitler's victory with their friends in the capital!

The only German who seemed to share my and my colleagues' sinister premonitions was the six-foot seven ex-grenadier standing guard at the entrance to the Hotel Adlon. He called a car for me and while we were waiting he said: "Those people we just watched sounded as full of confidence as our people did in 1914! Some of us old soldiers have a strange, alarming feeling in our bones . . ." Then, looking around nervously to make sure that nobody else had heard him, he raised himself to his fullest height and stood ramrod stiff as an old grenadier is expected to— but the worried look did not leave his face.

Sigrid Schultz was born in Chicago, Illinois, but spent most of her school years abroad. Her father was a portrait painter of royalty and his work took him all over Europe. Wherever they were Sigrid went to local schools, forcing her to learn languages which were to prove extremely valuable later on. She studied at the Sorbonne and Berlin University.

She began her newspaper career as "cub correspondent" and interpreter in the Berlin office of *The Chicago Tribune* in 1919 and her first scoop was getting the defeated German Navy command to tell their version of the Battle of Jutland. In 1926 she was named correspondent-in-chief for Central Europe, a post she held until early 1941. At the Munich Conference (1938) the job of broadcasting for the Mutual Broadcasting System was added to her other assignments.

Among other stories she reported the start of World War II from the German scene and served as a war correspondent for the *Tribune,* Mutual Broadcasting and *McCall's* magazine.

Her published works include *Germany Will Try Again* (Reynal & Hitchcock) and contributions to *The Reader's Digest, Collier's, McCalls, Red Book* and *Argosy.* She also was editor of *The Overseas Press Club Cookbook* (Doubleday, 1962).

She now lives in Westport, Connecticut.

Man Walks On Moon

As reported by JOHN NOBLE WILFORD

The banner headline that appeared on July 21, 1969 was the largest ever printed by the *New York Times*. For the first edition, which went to press at 9:30 P.M., the headline read "Men Land On Moon." Apollo 11 had landed at the Sea of Tranquility, but the two astronauts had not emerged from their landing craft. At 10:58, after Neil A. Armstrong had taken his "giant leap for mankind," the presses were halted for a new lead and a new headline: "Man Walks On Moon." For the final editions, after both Armstrong and Edwin E. Aldrin had planted their footprints in history, the headline ran: "Men Walk On Moon."

The headlines had been prepared well in advance. They had to be, because the *Times*'s largest headline type is 60 points and these lines, one-inch high and bigger than anything ever used for Pearl Harbor or Hiroshima or Presidential elections, were the equivalent of 96 points. The letters were set in the normal 60-point type, then photographed, enlarged to 8-column width, and converted into metal engravings.

As the astronauts moved about on the moon, and the *Times* editors in New York changed headlines from edition to edition, I was riveted to my typewriter, earphones, and closed-circuit television set at the news room close to Mission Control at Houston. I was working on the biggest single story of my career, one of the biggest stories of all time. Every time I recall that day and night in July of 1969 the thrill comes back with a rush.

I see the news room at Houston: the long rows of tables littered with flight plans, lunar maps, spacecraft manuals, mission trajectories, transcripts of the air-to-ground dialogue, typewriters, tape recorders, telephones, and coffee cups . . . the television sets flickering with the black-and-white images of men on the moon . . . newsmen waving copy in the air for the Western Union runners . . . the kleig lights of TV . . . rapt attention . . . throbbing disorder. . . .

I hear the news room: the voice of Apollo . . . the crackling sound of an open communications circuit with the moon . . . Armstrong's soft, halting words . . . the clatter of typewriters transcribing every one of those words . . . telephones ringing. . . .

I feel the news room: the racing heartbeat . . . the tingling nerve endings . . . the clammy hands at the typewriter keys . . . the tears of excitement and wonder . . . the weariness and wonder after the last deadline. . . .

For me, as for many of the reporters covering Apollo 11, it was the moment toward which I had been working and living for years. It was a glorious moment of fulfillment. For covering man's reach for the moon was more than a journalistic assignment, more than a job. It was a commitment.

I made the commitment in November 1965, when I joined the staff of the *New York Times*. As a contributing editor of *Time* magazine, writing cover stories on the subject, I had developed a feel for space exploration. Here was a story that had just about everything: romance and adventure, the drama of a race against time and an international rival, the politics and economics of mobilizing a team of 400,000 people, the challenge of human inventiveness, the reach for knowledge, and above all, the stuff of history. So when the *Times* editors offered me the assignment, assuring me that they shared my feeling that it might well be the story of the century, I quickly accepted.

Any journalist covering any story faces three challenges: the challenge of preparation, of perspective, and of performance. A story of Apollo's magnitude made the challenges all the more formidable.

How, for example, do you prepare to cover man's voyage to the moon?

The question, which I am often asked, reminds me of the story about the great sea captain who started out as a cabin boy and worked his way up until he was in charge of the world's largest ocean liner. The captain had one unvarying habit. Each morning he would go into his cabin, open his desk, and carefully read a slip of paper. He would then replace it and lock the desk. When the captain died at a ripe old age, the first act of his second-in-command was to open the desk and look for that slip of paper. It contained one sentence only: "The left side of the ship is port, and the right side is starboard."

The point is that I, like most reporters on the Apollo beat, had no particular technical training for the assignment, no engineering degrees or astronautical experience. We were journalists who had worked our way up, and to handle this assignment we had to do a lot of homework and had to refer daily to reference books that we kept on our desks. This is true of most journalists who cover science, technology, medicine, and other highly specialized fields.

My preparation consisted mostly of on-the-job training. Every story covered between 1965 and July 1969, in my case, added to my expertise. To report the Gemini earth-orbiting missions was to learn about celestial mechanics, the physical laws governing the movement of bodies in orbit, and to learn the fundamentals of rockets, communications, spacecraft construction. To report on the unmanned Lunar Orbiters was to get a feeling for the bleak, cratered lunar topography. To report the Surveyor missions, the five landings of three-legged robot vehicles on the moon's surface, was to learn the problems of landing on another world and to understand many of the questions scientists had about the chemistry and physics of the moon.

Between the coverage of these pathfinding missions, I logged thousands of miles to visit the plants where the Apollo spacecraft and rockets were built, in California, Louisiana, and on Long Island, and where they were assembled, at Cape Kennedy. I visited the National Aeronautics and Space Administration's centers in California, Texas, Mississippi, Alabama, Florida, and Maryland. I interviewed the administrators, the engineers and designers, the flight controllers, the scientists, and the astronauts. In nearly all cases, they were most helpful, taking time to explain over and over again the intricacies of spaceflight and lunar science. In all cases, I made it clear that I was a layman who wrote for laymen and that I, therefore, needed to go slow with the heavy jargon and difficult mathematics. I was never too embarrassed to stop an engineer and ask him to explain something once more. To do otherwise, to pretend to a non-existent understanding, is to waste his time and your own time.

Some of the most helpful backgrounding, I found, combined both the visual and the aural briefing. You begin to understand the Saturn 5 rocket, for example, after you have spent the better part of a day touring the mammoth Vehicle Assembly Building at the Kennedy Space Center in the company of an expert. You can thus see what it means when a rocket stands thirty-six stories tall. As you look at the five giant nozzles of the first-stage engines, you can ask questions and better appreciate the answers about the propulsion required to break away from earth gravity for a journey to the moon. It also gives you a feeling for the work that goes into preparing a rocket—the big work by cranes that move across the top of the building, the little work of men in white suits delving into a spacecraft's innards with surgical care, the mysterious work of machines examining other machines, computers activating and checking sensors, X-rays probing a rocket for any welding defects or hairline cracks.

I tried to include as many such visual-aural briefings as possible. I donned white smock, cap, and special slippers to inspect an Apollo spacecraft under construction at Downey, Calif. I saw the guidance and navigation electronics in production at Milwaukee. I sat in the firing room at Cape Kennedy and in Mission Control during simulations at Houston. I rode a centrifuge in Pennsylvania and took the controls of a Lunar Module simulator at Cambridge, Mass. I watched Armstrong and Aldrin practice in the simulators at Cape Kennedy and saw them run through their lunar surface experiment deployments at Houston. On these occasions, I was always accompanied by some knowledgeable person to answer the many questions that came to mind.

In line with the American policy of an "open" space program, NASA went to great lengths to provide reams of printed matter on Apollo. The major contractors published loose-leaf reference books on the spacecraft, lunar landing craft, important subsystems, and the rockets. NASA distributed a 250-page "press kit" on Apollo 11. About six weeks before the most crucial Apollo missions, NASA would hold several days of briefings at Houston, outlining mission rules (what you do if certain things go wrong), trajectories, flight control procedures, tracking arrangements, and the scientific objectives. You listened, took notes, and filed stories—and you filed it all away in notebooks for future reference. At such briefings, the crews for the next mission would present themselves for a news conference. These were usually unprofitable shows, producing little more than platitudes and bland expressions of self-confidence. (Few astronauts are good at expressing their thoughts and emotions before an audience.) Later, however, the astronauts would split up for a round of separate interviews of about forty-five minutes each with the major news services (AP and UPI), the television networks, national magazines, and major newspapers. These sessions, plus interviews with the astronauts' families and friends, were the source of quotations and insights into the personalities of the men.

During this time of preparation, it became essential to learn the new language of space. Strange words and acronyms were always cropping up in the briefings and interviews—words like interface . . . mode . . .

hypergolic . . . glitch . . . delta V . . . AOS and LOS . . . parking
orbit . . . staging . . . time hack . . . ullage . . . DPS (pronounced
"dips") . . . capcom . . . lox . . . perilune and apilune. . . .

We had to learn to use the jargon in speaking with the space men
and learn how not to use it in translating developments into common
English for our readers and listeners. Only rarely did the language prove
too arcane for the experienced reporters. One of the most frustrating
instances came during the Gemini Project when space engineers were
describing the various rendezvous maneuvers as M equals one, M equals
two, and so on. It meant a rendezvous between the Gemini spacecraft
and a target vehicle in one orbit, or two orbits, etc. At a news conference
Richard D. Lyons, then of the *New York News,* asked the mission director what the M stood for.

"Oh," said the mission director, "that stands for the number of orbits
it takes to make the rendezvous."

"I know that, but why M?" Lyons asked.

"Oh, that's arbitrary. We just picked M because it follows N in the
alphabet."

"You picked M because it follows N in the alphabet!" Lyons sput-
tered.

"Yeah," replied the engineer blandly. Whereupon Lyons and the rest
of the newsmen there at Cape Kennedy gave up in despair. Some questions are better left unpursued.

In time, through familiarity or for comic relief, the jargon crept into
our ordinary conversations, much to the puzzlement of outsiders, and
into our after-hour jokes. When someone got upset, we of the Apollo
press corps would say he "went critical." If he had too much to drink,
there was something wrong with his "inertial guidance system." If
something was right it was "nominal." If something went wrong it was
an "anomaly." It was all part of our initiation to Apollo—our "being
brought up to speed" on spaceflight.

A serious pitfall to avoid in covering any story is the loss of perspective. There is evidence that some reporters failed to meet this challenge
in covering Apollo. In an article in the winter 1967–68 issue of the
Columbia Journalism Review, James A. Skardon criticized the Apollo
press corps for lapses in perspective. He wrote:

> What seems a more plausible explanation of the lack of more
> analytical coverage of the Apollo program is that many of the journalists
> covering Apollo were so caught up with the rest of the country in the

challenge, drama, and excitement of the race to beat the Russians to the moon that they came to regard themselves as part of the space "team."

Two factors may have contributed to the drift that brought some members of the press too close to the Establishment. The first was the scientific-technical language the press and the space people used in common. This had the effect of drawing the press into the NASA "family."

The second factor involved the "hostile" outsiders, who came to be identified primarily as the Congressmen and their supporters who would cut the NASA budget. All hands, consciously or unconsciously, seem to have made a common bond that they would do nothing to endanger the cause; but once in a while they would even do something *for* it.

I confess that I believed wholeheartedly in the project and the goal. I believed in its thrust into the future—and I still do. A belief in the future was never more important than in that time of consuming despair over the present. Moreover, I subscribe to the view that Apollo, the reaching for the moon, represented an achievement of transcendental importance in human evolution. Centuries from now, historians will very likely remember the twentieth century primarily for two events— the harnessing of atomic energy and the beginning of travel to other worlds. But to believe in a project and its goals is not to accept its every manifestation, its every twist and turn.

Take, for example, the battle of the engineers versus the scientists within NASA, part of the larger war between the advocates of a strong manned space effort and those preferring a lower-cost unmanned effort. I reported some of these struggles as early as 1966, and alluded to NASA's internal split in several articles in 1967. But the split erupted more openly after the first moon landing, providing material for even more explicit articles. I wrote about this conflict not to take sides, but because it was a development that could shape NASA's future and because I felt it was important that the scientists and advocates of unmanned flight projects—a minority with little clout within NASA—got a fair hearing. At first such stories by myself and a few other reporters drew denials, then charges that we had exaggerated some minor internal differences. A reporter has to expect such reactions, whether it is from NASA, city hall, or the White House. What was more disturbing was the fact that so few other reporters bothered to write policy stories about NASA, largely ignoring NASA's activities between missions, acting more as conveyor belts for NASA-generated news, and thus proving that there was some validity to the *Columbia Journalism Review* criticism.

Most questions of reportorial perspective stemmed from the Apollo 1 fire of January 1967. Three astronauts died on the launching pad at Cape Kennedy when fire broke out in their spacecraft during a routine rehearsal. After the news broke, we all packed our bags and got on the next airplane for Florida, arriving early the next morning. What happened is revealing of the problems and pitfalls of covering Apollo.

On the morning after the fire, reporters assembled out at the Cape Kennedy press site and heard the bare details of the accident. There was a great deal of confusion about what had happened. Was the spacecraft on internal power, or was it drawing power from the launching tower? It might be important, or it might not be. We were left wondering because NASA was not forthcoming with any explanations. Was NASA hiding something? Or was the agency just confused itself? It was virtually impossible during the first few days to talk to anyone close to the investigation.

It was in this atmosphere, this vacuum of information, that space reporters reverted to basic reportorial instinct. There were no manuals to help us and previous little open information. I asked Douglas M. Dederer, the *Times* part-time correspondent at Cape Kennedy, to nose around and find out what he could. The result, within three days, was an exclusive story. We had talked with engineers who had heard the tape recordings of the astronauts' last words. Although grisly, the story showed that the astronauts did not die instantly, as NASA had said at first, and that with a different spacecraft hatch design and better emergency procedures at the pad, they might have been saved. A subsequent investigation by NASA and by Congress bore out both the facts and implications of the story. The spacecraft was substantially modified before it ever flew.

The episode won me no friends. In fact, I am told, some considered me an enemy of the program—and some of my accusers were even newsmen, which bears out my point that journalists can get so close to a story that they temporarily lose their critical powers. But to its credit, NASA became more open and prompt in its disclosure of information. And a number of industrious and experienced reporters redoubled their efforts to keep NASA honest.

It was nearly two years after the fire before men flew an Apollo spacecraft. When the time came, with Apollo 7 in October 1968, it was an important test run not just for NASA, but also for the Apollo press corps. We now faced the challenge of performance under increasing pressure.

In the eight most intense months of my career, I covered four Apollo missions leading up to Apollo 11. This meant going to Washington and Houston for briefings a few weeks before each mission, going to Cape Kennedy about a week before each launching. This meant writing the launching story at Cape Kennedy and, either late at night or early the next morning, catching a plane to Houston to be close to Mission Control for the duration of the flight. This meant writing at least a story a day for a month, getting up early for a briefing or a critical mission maneuver and staying up late to update the story for later editions. This meant writing a 1,500-word story for the first edition and writing possibly another 1,000 words in new leads, inserts, and "adds" until the astronauts went to sleep or the *Times* went "to bed," whichever came first. This meant eating dinner between editions, keeping a transistor radio plugged into your ear just in case an emergency developed. And when the mission ended and a few days after the astronauts returned to Houston, it meant closing your typewriter, disconnecting your telephone, packing your reference books, flight plans, notebooks, and old transcripts into an extra suitcase, and flying back to New York for a couple of weeks before resuming the harried cycle for the next mission.

All this was part of the preparations for the big one, Apollo 11. Let me try to set the scene.

More than three weeks before the launching, I went to Cape Kennedy to begin the coverage. I took an apartment in Cocoa Beach, one of the towns near the launching base, and turned it into a temporary "bureau," installing telephones, an AP printer, and the Voice of Apollo "squawk box," the telephone line that carries all announcements, situation reports, and news conferences from NASA. Since few other reporters had arrived so early, I was able to arrange a number of private briefings at the firing room and with the crew training people. I had interviews with some of the engineers who would be making the final checks on the spacecraft before lift-off. (After the countdown began, these people were too busy for such distractions.) In addition, I wrote a story a day on the preparations and the gathering excitement and put the finishing touches on a book about Apollo that was to be published after Apollo 11.

Within a week of the lift-off, the momentum picked up. The more than 3,000 registered newsmen began to arrive, swarming about the special NASA news center established near Cocoa Beach. This was twice the number of reporters who had covered Apollo 10. The principal Apollo contractors set up their own news centers, places where they dispensed press kits, coffee, and assorted tidbits of information. A number of the public relations men were conscientious about arranging requested interviews with company engineers, and scouting out information. A few were quite knowledgeable in their own right. Many of them, primarily the ones who came in acting like Hollywood press agents or who were there just to get out of the office, were useless and to be avoided.

Apollo 11 was, of course, more story than one person could handle. In New York, a special contingent of editors, copyreaders, and make-up experts worked in the "moon room" off the main news room of the *Times*. Nearly a dozen people were assigned to various reporting tasks—profiles of the crew, writing about the crowds and "color," descriptions of the technologies of spaceflight, historical accounts of the moon project, science objectives, and the preparations on the recovery ship in the Pacific. My apartment in Cocoa Beach became the clearinghouse for arriving correspondents, messages from New York, the coordination of assignments. Then on launching day, all reporting activities shifted twenty-five miles to the press site for Complex 39. There the *Times* had an old house trailer, which despite its rust and stuck refrigerator door, had served us well for many missions. It was equipped with telephones, television sets, an AP printer, and the Apollo "squawk box." This was where we waited.

As the countdown ticked away, you shivered with nervous anticipation. You listened to the squawk box, alert to any hint of trouble or delay. You wrote a few paragraphs. You went outside the trailer and with binoculars looked three miles across the sandy flats for reassurance that the rocket was really there, vapors venting into the hot Florida air, and that this meant that men really were going to the moon. You looked down the line at the other trailers and the grandstand, at the television crews and radio announcers standing in the sun and giving their breathless accounts to the world.

Someone was reminded of the radio newsman who once came to cover an early mission, an unmanned spacecraft test, with his lift-off script carefully written in advance, complete with all the dramatic adjectives. At ignition of the rocket, the reporter looked down at his copy and began the golden phrases—"And we have lift-off, and the giant rocket is rising into the beautiful blue Florida skies, streaking out over the Atlantic, a thunderous roar filling the area." Finally, looking up, he realized that he heard no roar, saw no rocket rising. The rocket still sat there. The engines had shut down automatically an instant after ignition. The radio man thought fast, then carried on—"And something has gone wrong, and four giant arms have reached out from the gantry and pulled the rocket back to the pad."

It was a true story, one that had been told and retold for years at the Cape, but this time the humor faded fast. There seemed to be little time for the camaraderie of missions past and future, the shared jokes, the cherished memories. We were too busy, too preoccupied, too caught up in the emotion of it all. I believe that most reporters wanted to experience this moment alone with their own emotional apparatus. It was a very public event, but a very private moment. As Victor K. McElheny, a Boston *Globe* reporter who has since joined the *Times,* said of that time, "Perhaps the greatest pressure was created by the difficulty that virtually everyone had in accepting the fact that a rocket really was taking off and carrying men to the moon's surface."

Armstrong, Aldrin, and Michael Collins, the third man in the crew, got off on time and without a hitch. We all wrote our stories, filed them, and left for Houston. Once the Saturn 5 cleared the tower, control of the mission transferred from the firing room at the Cape to Mission Control at Houston. And once the Saturn 5 arced out over the Atlantic and finally disappeared, a reporter's first-hand contact with the story, in one sense, came to an end. That was why it was important to shift to Houston where it was at least possible to have some first-hand contact with the men who bore the awesome responsibility for directing the flight.

At Houston, the routine went something like this. NASA assigned each news organization a desk or two in the large lobby off the auditorium, which became the news room for the mission. This was the area that normally served as a museum of old spacecraft and other memorabilia. To make way for the onslaught of newsmen, NASA moved the entire museum to a tent on the rubbery grass outside next to the actual Apollo capsule from a previous mission and next to a gleaming trailer like the one in which the Apollo 11 astronauts would be brought back from the aircraft carrier to Houston in a state of quarantine.

Virtually every seat at the tables in the news room was occupied. Most tables were filled to capacity with telephones, earphones, squawk boxes, typewriters, tape recorders, and copy-transmission equipment. The latter was a precaution taken against the possibility that Western Union's telex would be jammed with copy. It was also used, in my case at least, to transmit drawings and diagrams of spacecraft and maneuvers that could be used by *Times* artists to illustrate the story.

The floor in the news room was a wild criss-cross of wires connecting reporters' earphones to arrays of "jacks" provided by NASA so that reporters could hear the flow of talk between the astronauts and the ground. We stacked reference books wherever we could, sometimes on the top of the desk, often in old boxes and suitcases tucked beneath the desks. The polylingual shouting of reporters seeking to make themselves heard on every long distance telephone was much louder than any of the other Apollo flights. It was the United Nations in the loudest and most spontaneous decibels.

Across from the news room, in another building, NASA had a query desk to handle your specific questions, to arrange for interviews, and to otherwise direct traffic. Although the press kits were ample, NASA could not anticipate every question. A staff of NASA information officers fielded scores of questions, sometimes placing a call to Mission Control for the answer, sometimes going to engineers at the space center, or sometimes digging into their own file cabinets.

The most ingenious response to a query probably came from Julian Scheer, the assistant administrator of NASA for public affairs, the man who shaped NASA's policies of open relations with the public. A call came in shortly after the Apollo 8 astronauts had read portions of *Genesis* from lunar orbit on Christmas Eve. The Japanese correspondent thought the passages had a religious tone and wondered what they were. He asked if a text were available.

"Where are you?" asked Scheer.

"In motel room," came the reply.

"Well, look on your bureau. See if you can find a book marked Gideon. G-i-d-e-o-n."

"Have book," said the Japanese correspondent.

"Well," said Scheer, "NASA has provided each correspondent with his personal text. It's on page one, starting 'In the beginning. . . .'"

In the query room at the NASA news center, the major contractors also set up shop. They had seasoned public relations men and engineering experts on hand to answer detailed questions and help explain diagrams of the spacecraft systems. These were veterans, just as caught up in the excitement of the moment and most responsible in their attitude toward the "story." It was a far cry from the earlier Gemini and Apollo days when public relations men from some companies spent all their

time pressing for special-interest publicity and, when any of their companies' systems went haywire, fled for the airport and had nothing to say.

If there was any doubt that this was a big story, one had only to look
around the Houston space center and examine the special news-trans-
mission equipment and personnel. The major wire services had special
offices in a building nearby, and they were staffed with some of their
top by-line writers. The television networks had trailers anchored behind the auditorium, crammed with wire service tickers, telephones,
desks, and shelves of reference books. The *Washington Post* sent a team
of editors, including the man who is now managing editor of the newspaper, and special machines for providing copy direct to the *Washington
Post–Los Angeles Times* news syndicate. The *New York Times* had a
special editor, Douglas Kneeland, down to handle and expedite copy.

It is not surprising that in such a highly charged atmosphere that
conflicts could become explosive. On the evening of the landing, the
television cameras became so obtrusive in the news room that the "pencil
press" had trouble working and Julian Scheer felt called upon to shove
a cameraman who was not quick enough in heeding his order to withdraw. Scheer's action drew grateful applause from the writing press.

The reporter's normal flow of information came from the air-to-ground
conversations (which were "live" over the squawk box and were tran-
scribed and distributed after a lag of two or three hours) and from
briefings with flight controllers after each change of shift, or about three
times a day. The briefings were always followed by a question-and-
answer period lasting anywhere from five minutes to an hour, depending
on the number of outstanding problems.

If serious trouble developed, special briefings were arranged on short
notice. But usually you had to rely on your own experience and preparations and some hasty checks with engineers you knew or with con-
tractor experts if you were to be able to sort out the story in time for
your next deadline.

Since much of what you were reporting was happening some 250,000
miles away, the ability to empathize with the astronauts was important
in writing the Apollo story. This feeling for what was happening and
how it was happening came from long experience. The reporter had to
call on reserves of knowledge—the recollection of what it was like inside the spacecraft, of the astronauts' mannerisms, of the descriptions of
the moon from previous flights, and so forth. Empathy also came from
pausing ever so often during a mission and trying to imagine yourself
an astronaut in the spacecraft, a flight controller in Mission Control, or

a scientist hanging by every radioed description of the moon's surface. It was never really adequate. It will never be until you have made the trip yourself.

As the moment of the landing approached, I began to think of how I would begin that big story. I had been too busy before the mission to consider how I would actually write the stories. It was just as well, since pre-planned stories are often stilted and verbose. You should trust yourself to be able to attune yourself to the vibrations of the story and to reflect those vibrations in the tone, pace, and wording of the story. But the night before the day of the landing, words and phrases for the story crowded my thoughts so much that I could not fall asleep until I had scribbled a few lines on a piece of paper. Each trial beginning was shaped with a few rules in mind: keep the story simple, avoid gilding it with grand adjectives, do not allow minor technical problems of the flight to clutter the main thrust of the story. At last, I settled on the simplest and most direct sentence I could conceive, a sentence that said it all without detracting from the magnificence of the moment: "Men have landed and walked on the moon."

In a telephone conversation the next morning with editors in New York, I told them what I planned for my lead, assuming full success of the landing, and they told me what they had already thought of for the headline. Fortunately, our minds were on the same wavelength, and there was no conflict.

I honestly cannot recall many details of the day men landed on the moon for the first time. I recall running page after page through my typewriter. I recall trying to write the first edition story in such a way that it would be fairly easy to "top" it with new leads and inserts as events progressed through the evening. I recall straining to catch words coming out of the crackle of radio static. I recall other *Times* reporters crowding around me, helping me pick up a new quote from the moon, telling me New York wanted a new lead at such and such a time for the next edition, telephoning their own stories into the recording room in New York, shouting at some TV crew to get out of the way, handing me a cold but welcomed sandwich.

Just after Armstrong and Aldrin landed on the moon, in the late afternoon of July 20, I remember a man with a cardboard box coming around the newsroom and distributing small blue buttons, resembling a light in the lunar landing craft's control panel, which were inscribed with the white letters reading, "Lunar Contact."

Some reporters who were not so tied to the morning newspaper deadlines could watch the moon walk on a large screen in the auditorium. Journalists were joined by workers at the space center. Among these was a woman in black who sat in the front row, exclaiming over and over again, "Oh, dear Lord," at every word the astronauts said, and who, when the American flag was planted on the moon, leapt up to start singing, "Oh, beautiful for spacious skies, for amber waves of grain." She got through the whole verse before angry reporters, having suffered one amazement too many, could silence her.

And then it was over, sometime in the middle of the night. The last edition of the *Times* had gone to press in New York. The headline that would endure on posters, ashtrays, mugs, shopping bags, and umbrellas was on the streets and in the mail. Armstrong and Aldrin were back inside *Eagle* and ready to sleep. Then I recall standing outside in the clear, humid night of Houston and looking up at the shining moon and studying the dark smudge on the right side that was the Sea of Tranquility. I felt relief, I felt awe, I felt satisfaction. I also felt a vague disappointment. I wished I were up there with the astronauts, really "on" the story. And I wanted to go to bed and wake up the next morning to discover that the moon landing was yet to be. For I realized that I did not want to let go of the story that had become so much a part of my life.

No wonder journalists like to sit around at all hours and talk about all those great stories they covered, recalling, reliving, and savoring.

John Noble Wilford, Science Reporter, *New York Times.*

Born Oct. 4, 1933, Murray, Kentucky. Boyhood in Kentucky and Tennessee.

Education:
  University of Tennessee, B.S. in journalism, 1955
  Syracuse University, M.A. in political science, 1956
  Columbia University, International Reporting Fellow, 1961–62

U.S. Army Counter-Intelligence Corps, West Germany, 1957–58

Reporter, *The Commercial Appeal,* Memphis—summers of 1954 and 1955

Reporter, *The Wall Street Journal,* New York—1956 and 1959–61

Contributing Editor, *Time* Magazine, New York—1962–65

Science Reporter, *New York Times,* New York—1965–

Author, *We Reach the Moon* (1969); contributing author, *The Soviet Union: The Fifty Years,* edited by Harrison E. Salisbury (1967)

Winner, Book Award of Aviation-Space Writers Assn. 1970
Loeb Achievement Award, University of Connecticut, 1972 (for article on Energy Crisis for *New York Times*)

Covered all major missions of U.S. space program since 1965
First Western correspondent to visit and report from Star City, the Soviet Union's space center—1972
Listed in *Who's Who in the East* and *Who's Who in Aviation*
Member:
  Overseas Press Club (governor 1971–73)
  Sigma Delta Chi
  Aviation-Space Writers Association

Married, one daughter. Lives in Manhattan

In the Beginning—A Universal Language?

As reported by WILLIAM MORRIS

Publication today, September 15, 1969, of the American Heritage Dictionary puts before the average reader for the first time fruits of more than a century of linguistic research indicating that the many languages of the Western world may well have been originally a single tongue. Echoes of the biblical tale of the Tower of Babel inevitably suggest themselves in these words from the dictionary's introduction by Dr. Calvert Watkins, eminent Harvard linguist: "In the early part of the nineteenth century, scholars set about exploring systematically the similarities observable among the principal languages spoken now or formerly in the regions from Iceland and Ireland in the west to India in the east, and from Scandinavia in the north to Italy and Greece in the south. They were able to group these languages into a 'family' which they called Indo-European. . . . The similarities among the different Indo-European languages require us to assume that they are the continuation of a single prehistoric language (called Indo-European or Proto-Indo-European)."

Through a series of techniques never before used in a reference book designed for the layman, the American Heritage Dictionary indicates the path by which many thousands of words we use every day may be traced back to their origins in the hypothetical "single prehistoric language" called Indo-European.

Whether we decide to accept the biblical theory of the origin of the world's many languages as gospel truth or incline to the belief that a century and a half of diligent scholarship has revealed linguistic truth in the creation of a hypothetical Indo-European "corpus" of a tongue spoken by our ancestors long before written language existed, we all are aware that many hundreds of languages and thousands of dialects are spoken in the world today. Language expert Charles Berlitz puts it this way: "The world is inhabited by more than three billion human beings. The total number of languages they speak has escaped a precise determination due, among other factors, to countless dialects encompassed in every language. Linguistic research puts the number of live, spoken, present-day languages at more than 2,000 (more than 700 in Africa alone). Several hundred are spoken within the Soviet Union. There are so many languages in the Caucasus that the section is referred to as a 'mountain of languages.' The language having the greatest number of people who use it as a first tongue is Chinese—to be more specific, the Mandarin or Northern dialect of Chinese, with about 400 million speakers."

But English is the most widely used language in today's world, though the ever-widening activities of the Japanese in international trade may alter the balance in a decade or so. Still, as of this writing, English is the language of more than 300 million speakers to whom it is the native tongue and at least an equal number of non-native users of the tongue, for whom it is a vitally important second language.

And of all the varieties of English, American English must be counted the richest and most versatile. The Mother Tongue, as all English-speaking peoples call their language, began early in the Christian Era. Curiously enough, the occupation of Britain by Caesar's legions, though it left many relics in the form of roads, walls, and forts, had virtually no influence on the language spoken by the natives. A few traces can be found in place-names—notably those like Winchester, which clearly shows its descent from the Latin "castra," meaning camp, and London itself which the Roman invaders had called "Londinium," a name borrowed from the Celtish words meaning "the wild place."

However, the most important influences on what scholars now call "Old English" and which used to be known as "Anglo-Saxon" came from Germanic invaders. This was the language—mostly spoken, for few written records were made until much later in the period—from the sixth century A.D. to the time of the Norman Conquest, which as every schoolboy used to know, was A.D. 1066. The rude dialects of such invading Germanic tribes as the Angels, Jutes, and Saxons did much to shape the primitive language, as did occasional additions from the language of the Viking sea rovers who made many invasions from Scandinavia.

Among the contributions of these Vikings are many simple nouns we use every day—words like *leg, gate, freckle, seat, root, dirt, bull, birth,* and *trust.* They also contributed a lot of basic, earthy adjectives such as *awkward, ill, tattered, ugly, rotten,* and *odd.* These same Scandinavian invaders brought with them a number of the short, pithy verbs so beloved of headline writers: *gasp, guess, nag, scream, take, skulk, dazzle, call,* and *crawl.*

But the first truly great enrichment of the Mother Tongue came when William the Conqueror's Norman invaders brought with them many thousands of words of French and Latin origin. To the time of the Conquest and to the centuries during which the Normans consolidated their control of England, we can trace the arrival into English of words like *nativity, prayer, discipline, ministry, chancellor, parliament, penalty, attorney, poverty, traitor,* and *sacrifice.* These words, obviously, are longer and more ornate than the rude and simple words—mostly monosyllables —that the Angles, Saxons, and Jutes had made do with. Many of the new words clearly show their Latin origin—for example, *sacrifice* from Latin *sacer* plus *facio,* to make sacred.

Still others of the wealth of words brought by the Normans were concerned with matters of beauty and elegance which had been entirely foreign to the experience of the rude and relatively uncultured peoples who had originally occupied the land. Among these elegant contributions from the courtly world of Normandy were *palace, castle, ornament, tower, beauty,* and *mansion.* And the Normans, like their French descendants of today, were interested in food and drink. To them goes credit for introducing to England such words as *feast, pastry, sauce,* and *roast.*

During the next few centuries, which saw the growth of a great English literature from the pens of Chaucer, Spenser, Marlow, Jonson, Shakespeare, and Milton, the language was enriched still further by borrowings from across the Channel, notably from Spanish, Italian, Dutch, and ultimately, of course, from the literary works handed down through the ages from Latin and Greek, especially Vergil and Homer. Many of these classics had been known to scholars in British and Irish monasteries long before the Normans came. But it was not until they had been Englished by Shakespeare and his Elizabethan compatriots that they became part of the language of the common man.

Later, as British explorers and traders ranged throughout the world, they traded words as well as spices and piece goods with the natives of the lands they visited. From India, long the brightest jewel in England's colonial crown, came such homely words as *madras, bungalow, punch* (the drink, not the blow), *faker,* and *coolie.*

The Dutch, with whom the British conducted many wars, both military and trade, contributed their share of words to the English tongue. Among them: *freight, schooner, scum, scour,* and *landscape.* From the bitterness engendered by their long rivalry, the British also created a number of distinctly pejorative expressions to show their contempt for their rivals. Among them were *Dutch courage* (bravery based on the bottle), *do the Dutch* (commit suicide), *Dutch reckoning* (guesswork), *Dutch defense* (surrender) and, of course, *Dutch treat* (an entertainment at which the host expects his guests to pay their own way).

The next great stage in the expansion of English was undoubtedly the colonization of America. Henry L. Mencken points out in his monumental work, *The American Language* (Knopf, N.Y.) that the early settlers in the colonies had to invent a lot of Americanisms simply to create labels for objects and circumstances that they had never encountered in the Old World. From the Indians they borrowed names for animals never seen in England, such as *raccoon, opossum, moose,* and *skunk.* Other unfamiliar objects soon added their names to the language of the settlers: *hickory, squash, terrapin, persimmon,* and *pecan.* Not all of these words are precisely the way they appeared in the original Indian dialects, by the way. In an effort to make strange Indian sounds resemble familiar British words, the Pilgrims converted *otcheck* into *woodchuck* and *seganku,* into *skunk.* From other Indian dialects we have, over the centuries, made hundreds of other borrowings: *moccasin, powwow, toboggan, succotash,* to say nothing of such widely used expressions as *medicine man, pipe of peace,* and *bury the hatchet.*

The next enrichment of the language came from those Dutch colonists who settled in New Amsterdam and left there many words that are still a lively part of the language today—*cruller, cole slaw, spook, snoop, dope, waffle, boss* and, of course, *Santa Claus.* Interestingly enough, the very first Yankees were Dutchmen, for the word *Yankee* was derived from the words *Jan* (John) and *Kees* (cheese) and it was used by the English-speaking colonists as a derisive nickname for the Dutch.

Although the Spanish had occupied many of the islands of the West Indies, relations between them and the British were, to put it mildly, strained. As a result, there were remarkably few borrowings from Spanish into English at this time. Later on, the American cowboy was to take much of his lingo from his Mexican Spanish opposite number, the vaquero. These borrowings included *desperado, incommunicado, bronco, lasso, coyote, cinch, stampede,* and, of course, *rodeo.* Among the very few borrowings from Spanish during the colonial period, it should be noted, are two that remain very much in use, especially during the summertime, *barbecue* and *mosquito.*

At the end of the American Revolution our founding fathers were faced with a problem that created great controversy at the time but has now been long forgotten. Simply put it was: what language shall we choose as the official language of the United States?

Looking at the question from the vantage point of today, it seems ridiculous that anyone should ever have questioned that English would be the language chosen. But at the time of the founding of the nation many of its leaders debated very seriously whether or not English should be carried forward as the official language.

The bitterness of many colonists against the British was strong enough for many to feel that they should rid themselves of the British tongue, as well as of "the tyrant's rule." Some members of the Continental Congress solemnly proposed that English be banished and Hebrew made the official language. The twin facts that few colonists could read or speak Hebrew and that it had not been a living language for many centuries sufficed to kill that suggestion.

Then there was another proposal—that Greek be the official language. That idea lasted only long enough for one patriot to remark: "It would be a lot more convenient for us to keep the language as it is—and make the English speak Greek."

What finally happened, of course, was that we continued to speak our own brand of English which, after a century or so, became known as American English or, thanks in large part to Mencken, the American language. The differences between our version of English and that spoken in the British Isles remain great. Indeed, a fascinating book *British Self-Taught, with Comments in American* by Norman W. Schur (Macmillan, N.Y. 1973) treats extensively and wittily of the results of the circumstance that, as George Bernard Shaw put it, Britain and America remain "one people divided by a common language."

The period since the Revolution has been one of utterly prodigious growth of our language. During the nineteenth century some of the most colorful and characteristically American expressions were born. A case in point is *O.K.,* which also appears as *okay* and even, though rarely, as *okeh.* It's a word whose origin has puzzled scholars ever since its first appearance sometime during the first half of the nineteenth century. Called by Mencken "the most successful of Americanisms," O.K. was for a long time thought to be a Choctaw Indian word. President Woodrow Wilson supported this theory, but the only wide circulation the spelling *okeh* ever received was on the label of the long-defunct Okeh Record Corp., which lives in memory chiefly because, during the 1920's, it was the first firm to record such future stars of jazz as Louis Armstrong.

Then there was the notion that Andrew Jackson, while a county clerk, was so illiterate that he initialed documents O.K. as an abbreviation of "Orl Kerrect." This story seems clearly libelous on a number of grounds. First, Jackson's "illiteracy" was mostly a pose, not unlike that used by Southern senators today, to make their constituents feel that their elected representative is "just a good ol' boy." Long before Jackson reached the White House, he served in various elective offices, including the U.S. Senate, so it seems most unlikely that he was as untutored as this tale would have us believe. What's more, no shred of documentary evidence to support the theory exists.

And then there's the theory that O.K. comes from the initials of the Old Kinderhook Club, a political organization supporting Martin Van Buren (the Kinderhook Fox) in the presidential campaign of 1840. This theory, first put forward by Columbia Prof. Allen Walker Read, was widely accepted until a similarly distinguished scholar, W. A. Heflin, published evidence that O.K. had appeared in print a year or two earlier than Read's first example. This led to the sort of teapot tempest that delights onlookers and infuriates the participants. As for me, there's glory enough for both. The expression O.K. was certainly in the air before Van Buren began his campaign and, equally certainly, his campaign did a lot to popularize it.

But, though scholars may still argue about where O.K. came from, there's no question that it is just as American as the hot dog—and you might be interested to learn that the ordinary hot dog can cause serious arguments among scholars. One faction says that the first hot dogs were sold at New York's Coney Island amusement park about 1869, while another claims the name was first used about 1900 at the Polo Grounds baseball park. Both could be right, because the frankfurter certainly existed long before it came to be called the hot dog.

All this while, of course, the language has been steadily enriched by borrowings from all parts of the world. Among our everyday words are *denim,* from the phrase *serge de Nimes* (the city of Nimes in France); *slogan* from the Gaelic *slaugh* (army) and *gairm* (shout)—adding up to *battle cry; dungaree* from the Hindustani *dungri,* a fabric first used for tents, later for sails, and finally for sailors' work clothes; *jeans* from Genoa, where the fabric was first woven; and *galoshes* from a special sandal (*galoche*) worn on rainy days by courtiers of Louis XIV.

The most extraordinary expansion of the language, however, is seen during the years since World War II. Scientists use the term *quantum jump* (itself a postwar coinage) to describe the altogether incredible growth of language in this period. Scientific *breakthroughs* (another recent term) have brought with them entirely new vocabularies. Most of the technical terms will remain in the jargon of the scientists themselves, but hundreds have already come into the common tongue. It's hard to believe that *radar* was a military secret until 1945, that *transistors* were unknown outside laboratories until 1955, and that *laser* and *quasar* both first saw print in the 1960's.

But the physical sciences are not the only sources of the thousands of new words which have entered our American language during recent years. Many words have come as a result of vastly increased trade with other nations in all parts of the world—trade which has today made our language indisputably the world's most important medium of communication among the world's businessmen and its scholars.

But, important though English may be in helping all the peoples of the world to communicate with each other, it is not the single universal tongue that our prehistoric forbears knew—the tongue that either disappeared with the destruction of the Tower of Babel or the tongue that has been reconstructed by linguistic researchers. The story of a new completely universal tongue remains to be written—and its dateline appears still to be far off.

William Morris, editor in chief of the recently published *American Heritage Dictionary of the English Language* is a typecaster's dream. Behind his clipped beard and Ben Franklin glasses, William Morris is the very essence of his lexicographical ancestor, Dr. Samuel Johnson.

Beneath the scholarly appearance, Morris is possessed with a delightful sense of humor and an enviable vitality. He has an inexhaustible supply of fascinating anecdotes about words and their fast-changing usage in America today. He completely enjoys his role for what has been labelled "the first entirely new dictionary of the 20th century." In strictly personal terms, Morris regards the American Heritage dictionary as the culmination of his thirty years' labor in the "lexicographical vineyards."

Morris started his dictionary career in sales (1937), as a college traveler for the G. & C. Merriam Co., publisher of the Merriam-Webster dictionaries. He quickly moved up the ladder to the position of managing editor and later, editor in chief of *Words: The New Dictionary,* for his post-war employer, Grosset & Dunlap, Inc. The work received praise from such legendary wordsmiths as H. L. Mencken and S. I. Hayakawa.

From 1947 to 1960, Morris served successively as executive editor and editor in chief of Grosset & Dunlap's trade book department, creating—among other lines—the Universal Library, one of the first of the "quality" paperback series. During this period he also served as advisory editor for the Funk & Wagnalls dictionaries with special responsibility for the F & W International Edition. He started writing a daily newspaper column for the Bell-McClure syndicate, "Words, Wit and Wisdom," which now—under the joint byline of William and Mary Morris —is distributed internationally by the *Los Angeles Times* syndicate. The husband and wife team has also written several books for Harper & Row, including *Dictionary of Word and Phrase Origins,* a 3-volume set chosen as a selection by the Book-of-the-Month Club in 1967. Their *Your Heritage and Words: How to Increase Your Vocabulary Instantly* was published by Dell.

In 1960 Morris joined Grolier, Inc., as executive editor of *Encyclopedia International,* later becoming editor in chief of *Grolier Universal Encyclopedia,* a post he relinquished in 1964 to join the American Heritage firm. He was editor in chief for the *Xerox Intermediate Dictionary* (1973) and *Weekly Reader Beginning Dictionary* (1974).

A native of Boston, Morris graduated from Harvard University in 1934. He resides in Old Greenwich, Connecticut.